Helen Chadwick

HELEN CHADWICK

CONSTRUCTING IDENTITIES
BETWEEN ART AND ARCHITECTURE

Stephen Walker

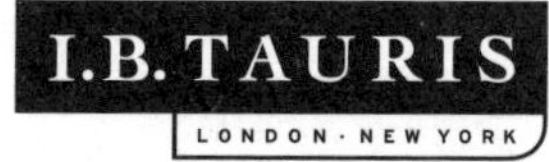

Published in 2013 by I.B.Tauris & Co. Ltd
6 Salem Road, London W2 4BU
175 Fifth Avenue, New York NY 10010
www.ibtauris.com

Distributed in the United States and Canada exclusively by Palgrave Macmillan
175 Fifth Avenue, New York NY 10010

International Library of Modern and Contemporary Art: 14

ISBN 978 1 78076 007 0

A full CIP record for this book is available from the British Library
A full CIP record for this book is available from the Library of Congress

Library of Congress Catolog Card Number: available

Printed and bound in Great Britain by Page Bros Ltd, Norwich

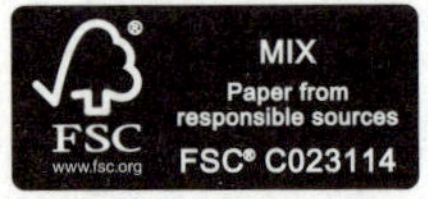

to Julia, Felix and Benjamin

Contents

Illustrations

All works by Helen Chadwick.
All images © Leeds Museums & Galleries (Henry Moore Institute Archive)
and The Helen Chadwick Estate

Acknowledgements

I would like to acknowledge the support of the Henry Moore Institute in Leeds, the staff there including Penelope Curtis, Martina Droth, Ellen Tait and Jon Wood, and in particular to thank the archivists Victoria Worsley, Ian Kaye and Claire Mayoh. Jeremy Till and Andrew Ballantyne gave their advice and support during the formative stages of this research, and Louisa Buck and Ashley Givens provided their help with particular details on the way through.

I am very grateful to Andrew Benjamin, Mark Haworth-Booth, and in particular Philip Stanley and Marina Warner, all of whom generously gave time to discuss their personal recollections of Helen Chadwick.

At I.B.Tauris, I would like to thank Philippa Brewster, Liza Thompson and Alex Higson for their enduring support throughout the process of publication. Annie Jackson was once again a patient and sympathetic proofreader.

I would also like to thank Florance and David Notarius from the Estate of Helen Chadwick for generously granting image rights, and the editors of AMBIT magazine for their permission to reproduce Chadwick's articles.

Finally, I am grateful to the Henry Moore Institute for their financial support during my initial archival research, and to the Arts and Humanities Research Council for a Research Leave Grant that was invaluable for the writing of this book.

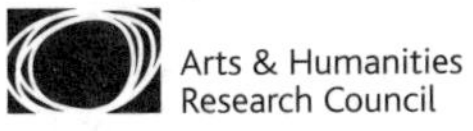

Preface

The artist Helen Chadwick (1953–96) produced such a diverse range of work it is not possible to name a 'typical' piece or say for what she is best know. Perhaps her *Piss Flowers* or her chocolate fountain *Cacao*, or her photographic works *Viral Landscapes* or *Meat Abstracts* or *Wreaths to Pleasure*, or her operatic installations *Ego Geometria Sum* or *Of Mutability*. Her impact in the art world remains similarly hard to pin down; the first woman nominee for the Turner Prize, some-time broadcaster, curator, teacher and mentor, her contemporaries and younger generations of artists frequently acknowledge her influence.

Yet despite such acknowledgements, or perhaps because of such diversity, her realised work has never really established a place for itself in the public eye. It might be said that she was an artist slightly out of her time. Work that was controversial and experimental when it was produced now seems too easily accepted; her work was far too prescient for its own good.

While most art-historical reception of Chadwick's work has understandably concentrated on her realised projects (and within these, the later projects such as those just mentioned), her notebooks reveal the extent to which these were informed by expansive research work and theoretical developments that were as creative as the realised pieces. Considered through this lens, her apparently diverse œuvre becomes far more coherent: life-long preoccupations were tirelessly explored, interrogated and developed in concert with her artistic making.

Nevertheless, it is not my intention to demonstrate such consistency in this book, although it might emerge as something of a by-product. My primary concern is to enjoy the range, depth and continuing currency of Chadwick's research and theoretical positioning. Chasing one of her enduring preoccupations—the construction and maintenance of personal identity—Chadwick's work can offer insights into a number of major, enduring questions: the relationship between body, space, self and world;

between art and science; between artifice and nature; between theory and practice, creative self and creative process.

Chadwick was as witheringly critical of the damage done to people by monotonous physical surroundings as she was of the impact of limiting political, philosophical and scientific constructions. Never backing away from a fight, she was determined to find ways of renegotiating our relationship with and understanding of the world, even if this meant taking on the whole of the Western tradition:

> New negotiations. It may be a little grand to claim to try to dismantle and outmanoeuvre the western inheritance from Plato to Descartes to Freud
>
> of difference set against difference[1]

This book operates across her œuvre at the level of these manoeuvres, steering close to her theoretical workings while remaining effectively at one remove from her realised projects. It combines a close reading of her notebooks with some far broader speculation regarding their ongoing relevance, dismantling and reassembling her thoughts in order to undertake some new negotiations of its own. Even for Chadwick, this layer of work was discontinuous; to pull certain aspects out and re-establish them within new conversations is inevitably selective and partial. While this does make her research available to a new audience and raise its status within the reception of her œuvre, I cannot claim any fidelity to the overall composition of her research interests, or to follow the relative importance she attached to these.

This should not be taken to suggest that her research activity was sporadic or disorganised: quite the contrary. Within the Helen Chadwick Collection at the Henry Moore Institute Archive in Leeds, her notebooks, preparatory notes and drafts for lectures and essays, as well as the marginal notes she made in her books, reveal her to have been a rigorous and systematic researcher. Some of this research was clearly undertaken to support particular projects, while much seems to have been done for broader interest or pleasure. The issues she explored were numerous and wide-ranging, stretching from the highly practical to the theoretical and philosophical, forming part of an ongoing conversation with her realised projects and her broader interests.

As Marina Warner has observed, Chadwick was like 'a latter-day Neoplatonist', gathering up disparate fragments of knowledge, ingesting and metamorphosing them, bringing them up to date in ways that reinvigorate their relevance for contemporary issues. Chadwick's gatherings tended towards the more messy issues that usually remain unacknowledged by the discrete disciplines that police knowledge formation and availability. She explored the unpredictable aspects of nature, decay, dirt and death, gender, desire, the monstrous, the under-valued senses of touch, taste and smell; she explored uncertainty and the formless, the role of myth, of personal and collective memory. Informing this process of dismantling, gathering and outmanœuvring, she was influenced as much as anything by highly rational sources: a number of her key methodological moves were informed by writers on the philosophical implications of modern science such as Italo Calvino, Fritjof Capra, Stephen Jay Gould, Arthur Koestler, and Erwin Schrödinger.

Despite this breadth and rigour, her research does not suggest she was trying to 'do' theory, either on its own terms or to work up some overarching artistic theory. Chadwick provided a caveat that should hang over this whole book, reminding us that her primary concerns lay with making and experiencing artworks, and with the somatic more broadly. Making notes regarding the preparation of a written piece for one of her catalogues, she wrote:

> let the essay use theory but only as an OXO cube to the dinner, let stronger meats carry the appetites.[2]

Integration of sources

Throughout the text I have drawn extensively, and almost exclusively, on Chadwick's own writing and reading, using this as raw material for the discussions at hand. References to this source material have been maintained within the main text, and follow a simple set of abbreviations that are given below. All the works listed here are kept in the Helen Chadwick Collection at the Henry Moore Institute (HMI) Archive in Leeds, England.[1]

Chadwick's writing

Frequent reference is made to the expansive notebooks that Chadwick kept. I also make use of notes in her *Filofax* (*c*.1987–96), as well as loose-leaf preparatory work, draft essays and lectures. Such citations use a sans-serif font and approximate the layout of the handwritten notes. The *Filofax* is in the HMI collection but is currently uncatalogued and unpaginated: when making reference to *Filofax* notes, I use the rare instances of dated pages to provide some basic orientation. References to loose-leaf sources such as lecture notes are made to the relevant archival box in the HMI collection.

References to the notebooks follow the HMI accession numbering, such as 2003.19/E/1. There is a degree of overlap between the notebooks that Chadwick kept, and she seems to have had several on the go at any one time. As with her *Filofax*, notebook entries are rarely dated: the following list of the notebooks is by HMI accession number, and gives rough dates of their periods of coverage. Where they clearly coincide with the development of a particular piece of work this is indicated. At the time of writing, eight of Chadwick's notebooks are available online as virtual books on the HMI website (www.henry-moore-fdn.co.uk).

2003.19/E/1   *c*.May 1972–1975
2003.19/E/2   March 1975–*c*.1978

2003.19/E/3	*c.*1980 (includes *Model Institution*)
2003.19/E/4	1981 (on *Fine Art/Fine Ale*)
2003.19/E/5	*c.*1981–1983 (on *Ego Geometria Sum*)
2003.19/E/6	*c.*1983–1986 (on *Of Mutability*)
2003.19/E/7	*c.*1984–1992
2003.19/E/8	July 1987–1996
2003.19/E/9	1988–1989 (on *Viral Landscapes*)
2003.19/E/10	*c.*1990–1992
2003.19/E/11	*c.*1991–1996
2003.19/E/12	*c.*1994–1996
2003.19/E/13	*c.*1995

Chadwick's reading

The following works are drawn from Chadwick's library, held at the HMI.
Chadwick annotated the books she read extensively, underlining,
commenting, arguing and adding often lengthy notes into their margins and
covers. References in the main text are given according to the following
simple abbreviations.

AEA   Etienne-Louis Boullée, *Architecture, Essay on Art* (*c.*1780–1799),
edited and annotated by Helen Rosenau, tr. Sheila de Vallée, in
Helen Rosenau (ed.), *Boullée and Visionary Architecture*, Academy
Editions, London, 1976.
(Although this wasn't in Chadwick's library, it is certain that the
notes she made refer to this edition, as she repeats oblique
observations from Rosenau's introductory essay.)

AHP   Joseph Rykwert, *On Adam's House in Paradise: The Idea of the
Primitive Hut in Architectural History* (1972), MIT Press, Cambridge,
MA, second edition 1981. (Unusually, Chadwick dates this inside
the front cover: July 1984.)

AM   *The Allegory of Misrule*, exhibition catalogue, Birmingham City
Museum and Art Gallery, 13 August–9 September 1987.
Includes short texts by Chadwick (*Underwriting History*) and by
Tessa Sidey (*The Continuity of Allegory*).

AV   A. S. Koch and T. Tarnai, 'The Aesthetics of Viruses', in
Leonardo, 21.2 (1988), pp. 161–6.

BI   Arthur and Marilouise Kroker (eds), *Body Invaders: Sexuality and the
Postmodern Condition*, Macmillan Education, Basingstoke, 1988.

BS   Julia Kristeva, *Black Sun: Depression and Melancholia* (1987), tr. Leon
S. Roudiez, Columbia University Press, New York, 1989.

BT   Fred Gettings, *The Book of Tarot*, Hamlyn, London and New
York, 1973.

CC   Italo Calvino, *'Cosmi-Comics'* (1965), tr. William Weaver (1968), Abacus, London, 1982.

EF   Helen Chadwick, *Enfleshings*, Secker & Warburg Ltd, London, 1989.

FP   Jane Gallop, *The Daughter's Seduction: Feminism and Psychoanalysis*, Macmillan, London, 1982.

FS   Stephen Jay Gould, *The Flamingo's Smile: Reflections in Natural History*, Penguin Books, London, 1984. (A volume of essays from monthly columns in *Natural History Magazine*.)

G   James E. Lovelock, *Gaia: A New Look at Life on Earth*, Oxford University Press, 1979.

GD   Marina Warner, 'In the Garden of Delights', (1986) in *Enfleshings*, Martin Secker & Warburg Ltd, London, 1989, pp. 39–63.

GM   Arthur Koestler, *The Ghost in the Machine*, Pan Piper (Hutchinson Publishing Group), London, 1967.

HB   *Herculine Barbin: Being the Recently Discovered Memoirs of a Nineteenth-Century French Hermaphrodite*, introduced by Michel Foucault, tr. Richard McDougall, The Harvester Press, Brighton, 1980.

HC   Naomi Miller, *Heavenly Caves: Reflections on the Garden Grotto*, George Allen & Unwin, Boston, London & Sydney, 1982.

JPVA   *Architecture. Space. Painting: Journal of Philosophy and the Visual Arts*, Academy Group, 1992.

NSL   Rupert Sheldrake, *A New Science of Life: The Hypothesis of Formative Causation* (1981, 1985), Paladin/Grafton Books, London, Chadwick's edition 1987.

OM   Helen Chadwick, *Of Mutability* (exhibition catalogue), Institute of Contemporary Arts, London, 1986.

PCSV   Andrew Scott, *Pirates of the Cell: The Story of Viruses from Molecule to Microbe*, Basil Blackwell, Oxford, revised edition 1987.

PM   Pierre Teilhard de Chardin. *The Phenomenon of Man* [*Le Phénomène Humain*, 1955], tr. Bernard Wall, 1959, Fount, London, 1986.

PS   Gaston Bachelard, *The Poetics of Space* (1958), tr. Maria Jolas, Beacon Press, Boston, 1964.

RO   *Rococo Ornament. A History In Pictures*, Victoria & Albert Museum, London, 1984.

SF   Helen Chadwick, 'Soliloquy to Flesh', in *Enfleshings*, Martin Secker & Warburg Ltd, London, 1989, p. 109.

SW   Arthur Koestler, *The Sleepwalkers: A History of Man's Changing Vision of the Universe* [1959], Penguin, London, 1982.

TH   Italo Calvino, *Time and the Hunter* (1967), tr. William Weaver (1969), Abacus, London, 1987.

TP   Fritjof Capra, *The Tao of Physics: An Exploration of the Parallels between Modern Physics and Eastern Mysticism*, Fontana/Collins, London, 1975.

TPB   Francis Barker, *The Tremulous Private Body: Essays on Subjection*, Methuen, London and New York, 1984.

VP   Thomas A. and Mary Markus, *Visions of Perfection: the Influence of Utopian Thought upon Architecture from the Middle Ages to the Present Day*, Third Eye Centre, Glasgow, 1985. (Published on the occasion of the Architecture & Utopia exhibition, Third Eye Centre, Glasgow, 9 February–16 March 1985.

VST   Alberto Veca, *Vanitas: Il simbolismo del tempo*, Galleria Lorenzelli, Bergamo, 1981. (Contains an English translation 'Vanitas: The Symbolism of Time', pp. 161–221.)

WD   Helen Chadwick, 'Withdrawal: Object, Sign, Commodity', *Architecture. Space. Painting: Journal of Philosophy and the Visual Arts*, Academy Group, London, 1992, pp. 68–73.

WIL   Erwin Schrödinger, *What Is Life? Mind and Matter* (1944, 1958 respectively), Cambridge University Press, 1967.

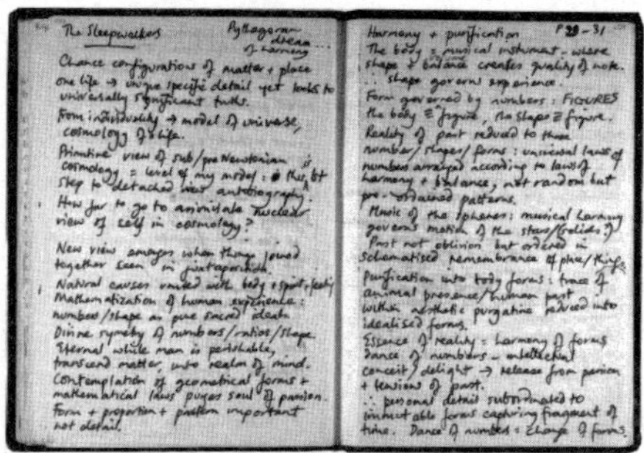

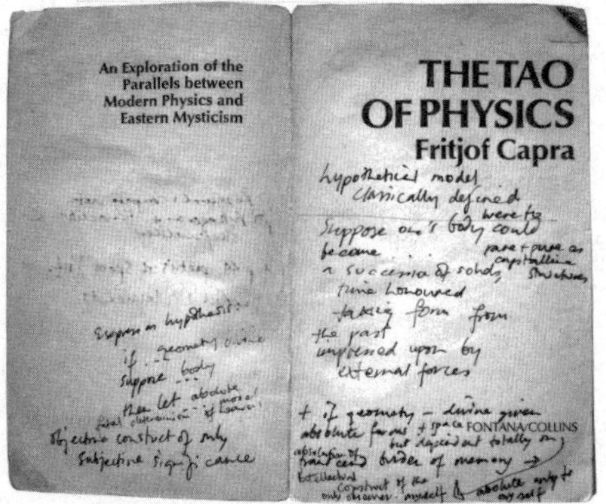

1 Examples of Chadwick's notebooks and books from her library.

Above, pages 100–1 from notebook 2003.19/E/5 (*c*.1981–83) which she kept during the preparation of *Ego Geometria Sum*. Here, notes concerning Koestler's *The Sleepwalkers*.

Below, notes that she added to the inside cover of Capra's *The Tao of Physics*. This is typical of the extent to which she added notes and comments all through most of the books in her library, which in turn were picked up in her notebooks.

Introduction: New negotiations

If we are supposedly constructed and maintained by a tissue of received information, why is there a range of experience, undeniably vivid and potent, that resists definition and closure? There must therefore be boundaries and limits to knowledge and meaning. Can we cross these boundaries and explore the territories beyond? [...] If I have an intent, it is to open up a crease in language and look at what cannot be articulated—the phenomena of consciousness, the enigmas and riddles of selfhood, the momenta of emotionality and sexuality [...] [If I have an intent, it is to open up] a possibility for beginning to look at identity and the conditions where it destabilises and threatens to collapse.

Helen Chadwick (*WD* 69)[1]

Helen Chadwick did not shy away from big questions. Although she did not seek controversy, neither was she content to accept received wisdom where this manifestly failed to account for the world as she encountered it. She believed that human experience far exceeded the limits given by philosophical, religious, scientific or psychological definitions and policed by the great patriarchs of the 'western inheritance from Plato to Descartes to Freud'. Following experience beyond these limits, she put herself, her artwork, into situations that exceeded ready explanation. For Chadwick, to move beyond the limits of accepted meaning was not to ignore them; her new negotiations challenged by trying 'to dismantle and outmanoeuvre' the status quo. Like an explorer bringing finds back from unknown lands, she would then set these up in new relationships with the very structures they threatened, precipitating conditions where the whole had to be reconsidered.

In particular, Chadwick was concerned to encourage new negotiations with the ingredients that structure identity. As the passage cited in the epigraph indicates, she frequently set out these negotiations in spatial terms, a spatiality at once lived and physical, scientific, mathematical and metaphorical. Happily mixing metaphors, she transgressed the accepted limits of spatial, linguistic, epistemological and ontological good practice: she was comfortable in this tangle, actively seeking the points of collapse in those structures that constrained identity and experience.

Architecture has of course frequently been enlisted literally and metaphorically to account for and govern the behaviour and identity of people and knowledge. Chadwick's interest in architecture was enduring and multi-faceted; her work enjoyed a two-way relationship with it, although the phasing and modality of this relationship is complex, reflecting her more fluid or transgressive approach to negotiations more generally. Although her early work was overtly concerned with identity, this was explored through the spatial, architectural conditions where it was stabilised or petrified. Partly motivating such work was her clear belief that while the impact an environment had on identity ought to involve a two-way process,[2] architecture's traditional approach, product and judgement system all too frequently imposed on its occupants. She quickly came to believe that this imposition had been able to continue more or less unchecked not only because of its traditional liaisons with political power, but also because of the extent to which architectural assumptions were commensurate and complicit with a broader world-view based on empirical, Newtonian physics. While she would go on to develop ways to critique this theoretically, she was concerned that the everyday was adequately explicable by Newtonian physics, to the extent that the other approaches, or new negotiations, would fail to gain any real purchase there. This reflects the extent to which architecture appears to be common sense, something that we just take for granted.

Chadwick's early pieces, such as *Menstrual Toilet* (1975–6: figure 2), *In the Kitchen* (1977: figure 3), *Train of Thought* (1978–9: figure 5) and *Model Institution* (1981–4: figure 4), reflected her close observations of the impact an environment had on people. They combined institutional critique with explorations of gender and power relations, took the form of installations with sound or performance, and announced concerns that she continued to examine throughout her career. *Model Institution*, for example, was an installation with a soundtrack, or as Chadwick describes it, 'An architectural sculpture for 5 voices' (2003.19/E/3.23), and while it might have been a response to the contemporary unemployment crisis, the closely observed physical, technical, acoustic and normative environmental characteristics that informed its stark architectural interface can stand more generally for the intimidation felt by the vulnerable within any institutionalised environment. In Chadwick's words, it was a 'model of control + pressure' (2003.19/E/3.24). *Train of Thought* similarly developed around Chadwick's

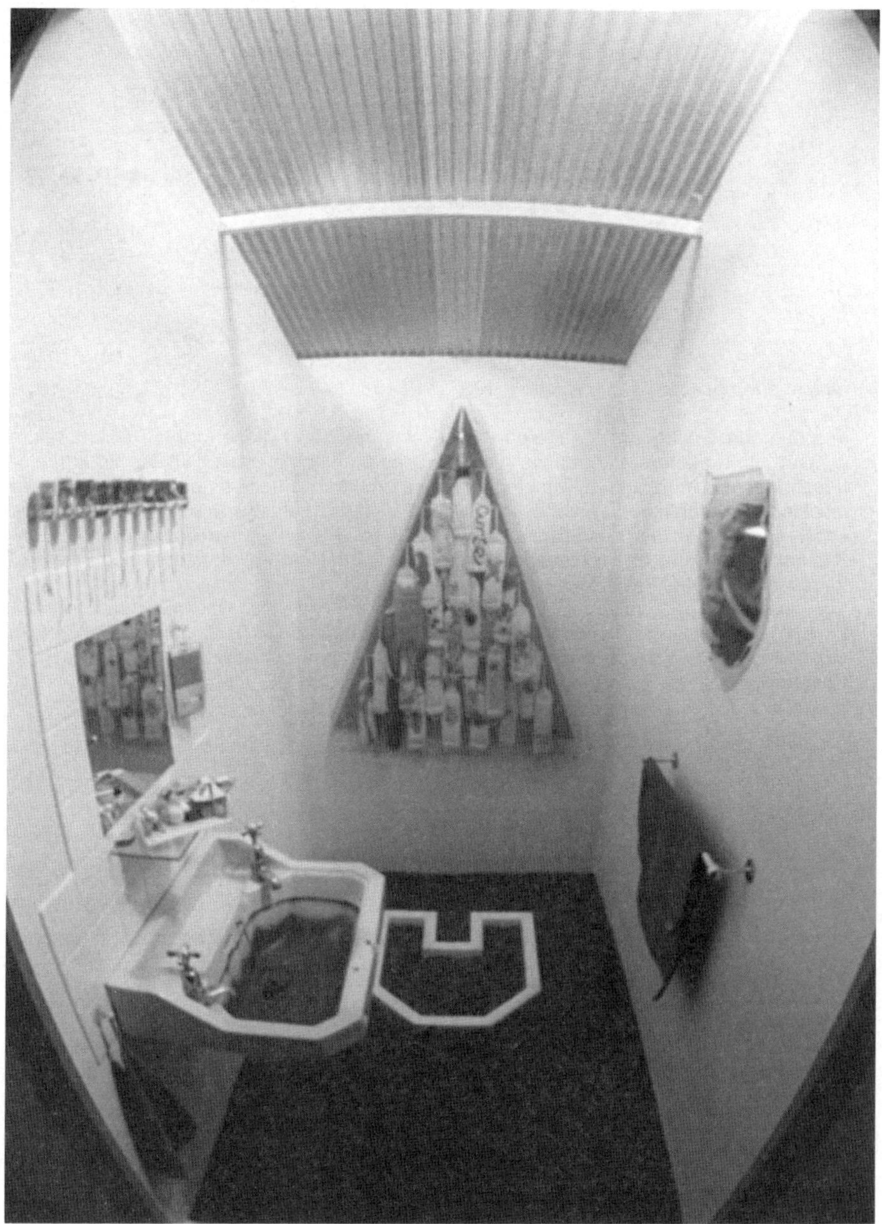

2 *Menstrual Toilet*, 1975–6.

An early example of work she referred to as 'Architectural Sculpture', here from Chadwick's Undergraduate Degree, Brighton Polytechnic, Sussex.

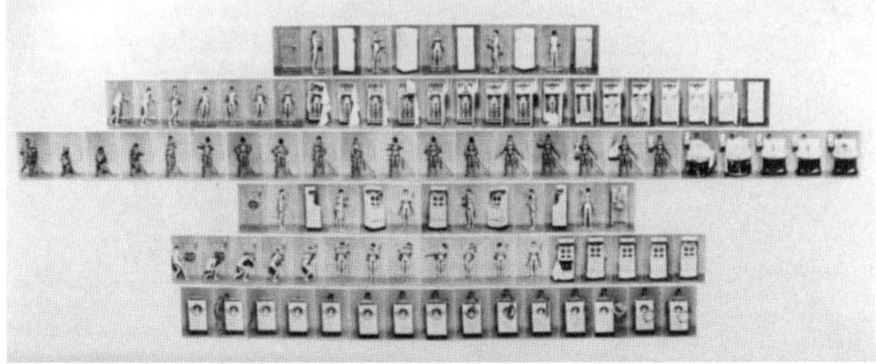

3 (above and opposite) *In the Kitchen*, 1977.

In a humoured critique of gendered power relations, Chadwick and three collaborators dressed up in elaborate costumes (Chadwick as an electric cooker; others as a fridge-freezer, a sink unit and a washing machine) conflating female body and domestic machine as a comment on the power relationships that she observed in domestic space, in who designed and made these machines and who actually used them. *In the Kitchen* played out, at a domestic scale, some of the central issues of both *Train of Thought* and *Model Institution*.

This work was undertaken as part of her Master's Degree at Chelsea School of Art, London, and shown at Art Net, 10–11 Percy Street, London, 6 to 17 June 1977. As with most of her performance/installation work, this show combined 'Machines and Photographs'.

carefully observed impact of an environment (here, an underground train carriage) on people, though it articulated various issues that were to become increasingly important. What was clear in this piece was the importance she attached to the non-physical aspects of this interface between self and environment; the physical environment might appear innocent enough, but there are other institutional and individual factors that bear strongly on both individual experience and social interaction (here manifest in the soundtrack to the piece, where internal monologues of the two characters demonstrated the total misunderstanding of one of them).

The threat to identity that Chadwick re-staged in these early projects was effectively that sanctioned, constructed and maintained by the status quo, and must be distinguished from the kind of destabilisation of identity that Chadwick herself actively sought as a process of empowerment. Her attitude towards such anonymous institutions found voice in a passage from Arthur Koestler's *The Ghost in the Machine*, one of a number of related works she read during the early 1980s and which had a significant impact upon the development of her thinking. At the beginning of Chapter XIII 'The Glory of Man' (which Chadwick annotated heavily in her own copy) Koestler argues:

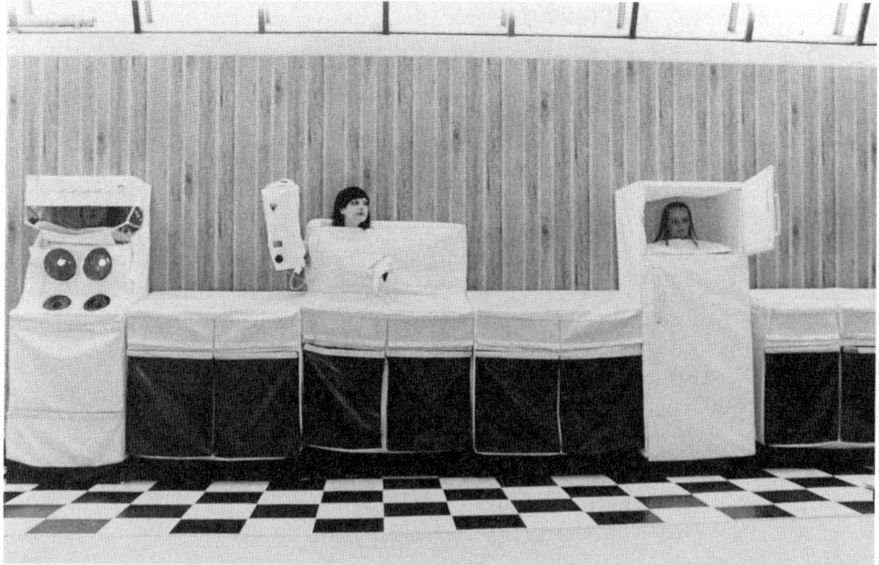

> The activities of animal and man vary from machine-like automatisms
> to ingenious improvisations, according to the challenge they face.
> Other things being equal, a monotonous environment leads to the
> mechanisation of habits, to stereotyped routines which, repeated
> under the same unvarying conditions, follow the same rigid, unvarying
> course. The pedant who has become a slave of his habits thinks and
> acts like an automaton running on fixed tracks; his biological
> equivalent is the over-specialised animal—the koala bear clinging to
> his eucalyptus tree.
>
> On the other hand, a changing, variable environment presents
> challenges which can only be met by flexible behaviour, variable
> strategies, alertness for exploiting favourable opportunities. (*GM* 201)

There are several important issues that can be pulled out of this passage,
the most direct of which is the relationship between the stimulus provided
by an environment and the well-being of those using it. Considering her
early projects such as *Model Institution* with Koestler's passage echoing in our
ears, Chadwick's installation can clearly be read as one of the monotonous
environments that Koestler links to the mechanisation of habits and
stereotyped routines. As Chadwick's entry in her notebook reminds us, she
considered this 'An architectural sculpture for 5 voices', although the range
of issues she considered indicate the complexity of factors that make up
such environments (and can move them from monotony to menace). The

architectural sculpture faithfully repeated the kind of institutional architecture Chadwick had researched, though this far exceeded the simple reproduction of the architectural object or cubicle.

The Institution
Heating—fanheaters   Light
Atmosphere
Unit cubicles
Surveillance cameras: phasing
Control
Work
Health: throat   Tapes
Food   Files
Beauty   Forms
Fun
Scale: distortions lengths heights

Research government papers
Optimum light + temp levels
    Surfaces

muffled sound
frequency of light- flickering tubes

Cubicles: a sculpture for five

bureaucratic menace
2003.19/E/3.2–3

The soundtrack was every bit as carefully researched and developed, and more nuanced than the architectural cubicles themselves; it played out both the audible aspect of the monotonous institutional environment—*Tinnitus | Ringing in ears | Sound accompaniment*—while also relaying encounters with and resistance to the kind of mechanised, routine behaviour that Koestler suggests will result from monotonous environments, giving voice to those subjected to this kind of monotony. Chadwick's development of the cast ran together with the dialogue, and included '5 arguments with 5 different personalities/roles'. The soundtrack inclusion of the five voices staged a short moment of resistance and primed the audience to relate to the piece rather than leaving it uninhabited and somewhat abstract. Nevertheless, Chadwick's admission that these characters were 'burdened down by intolerable positions, crying out impotent unable to change anything', (2003.19/E/3.31) acknowledges that the soundtrack, like the architectural

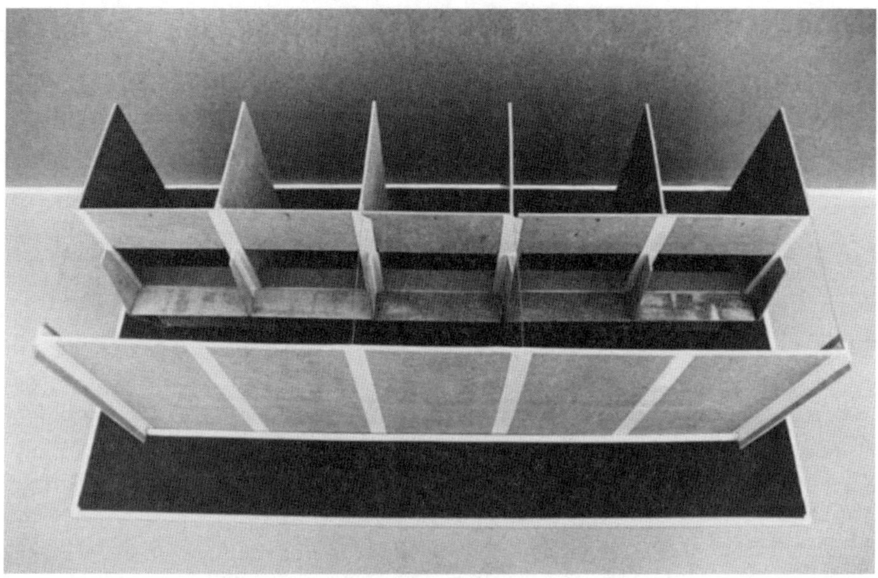

4 *Model Institution*, 1981–4 (above, and following pages).

Here above, a preparatory scale model for the final piece, shows how Chadwick designed a line of five booths, mimicking the physical interface that she observed between members of the public and national Institutions such as the Post Office, the DHSS (Department of Health and Social Security), British Telecom, polling booths and the Home Office. In each booth of her installation an audio recording played out fictional monologues, dialogues and confrontations that might take place across such an interface. Pictures overleaf show the installation itself from inside one of the booths, and behind the bureaucratic glass screen.
Model Institution was shown at Newcastle Polytechnic Gallery; Sheffield Polytechnic Gallery; The Architectural Association; Chalmers Art Gallery, London; Cockpit Gallery, London; Oval House, London; Battersea Arts Centre, London; Brighton Polytechnic; and Orchard Gallery, Derry.

environment of this piece, ultimately repeats the overall monotony that Koestler suggests will lead to the mechanisation of behaviour and the steady conversion of these people into automatisms.

Now while Chadwick appears quickly to abandon the outward, faithful reproduction of architectural environments after *Model Institution*, the issues she raised there continued to occupy her, although they developed a good deal over the decade that followed. Her research around the time of this change had begun to investigate more nuanced uses of space. Her notebook from this period includes sections that address John Berger's *Ways of Seeing*, Edward T. Hall's *The Hidden Dimension: Man's Private and Public Use of Space*, Bernard Rudofsky's *The Unfashionable Human Body* (1872), and Rudolf Broby-Johansen's *Body and Clothes: An Illustrated History of*

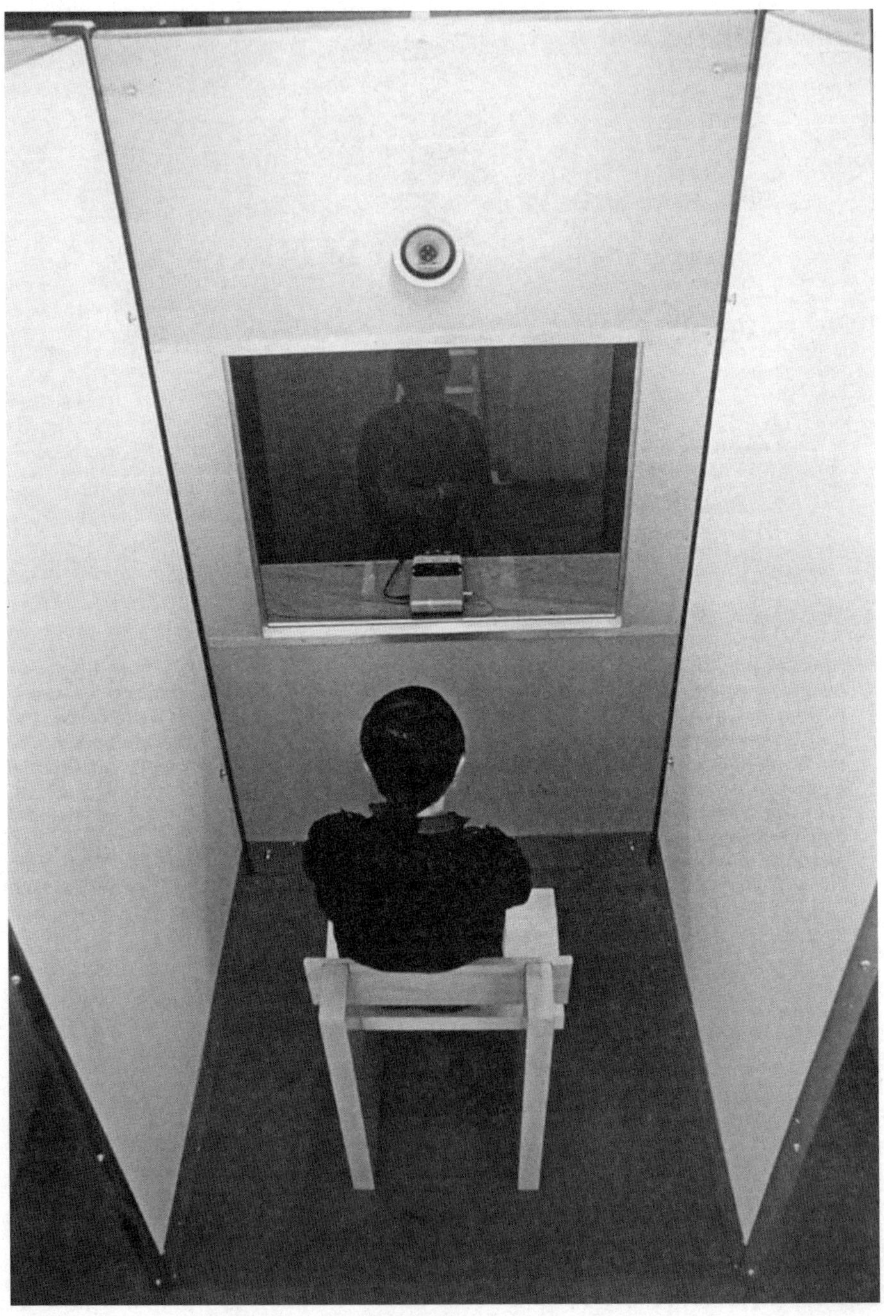

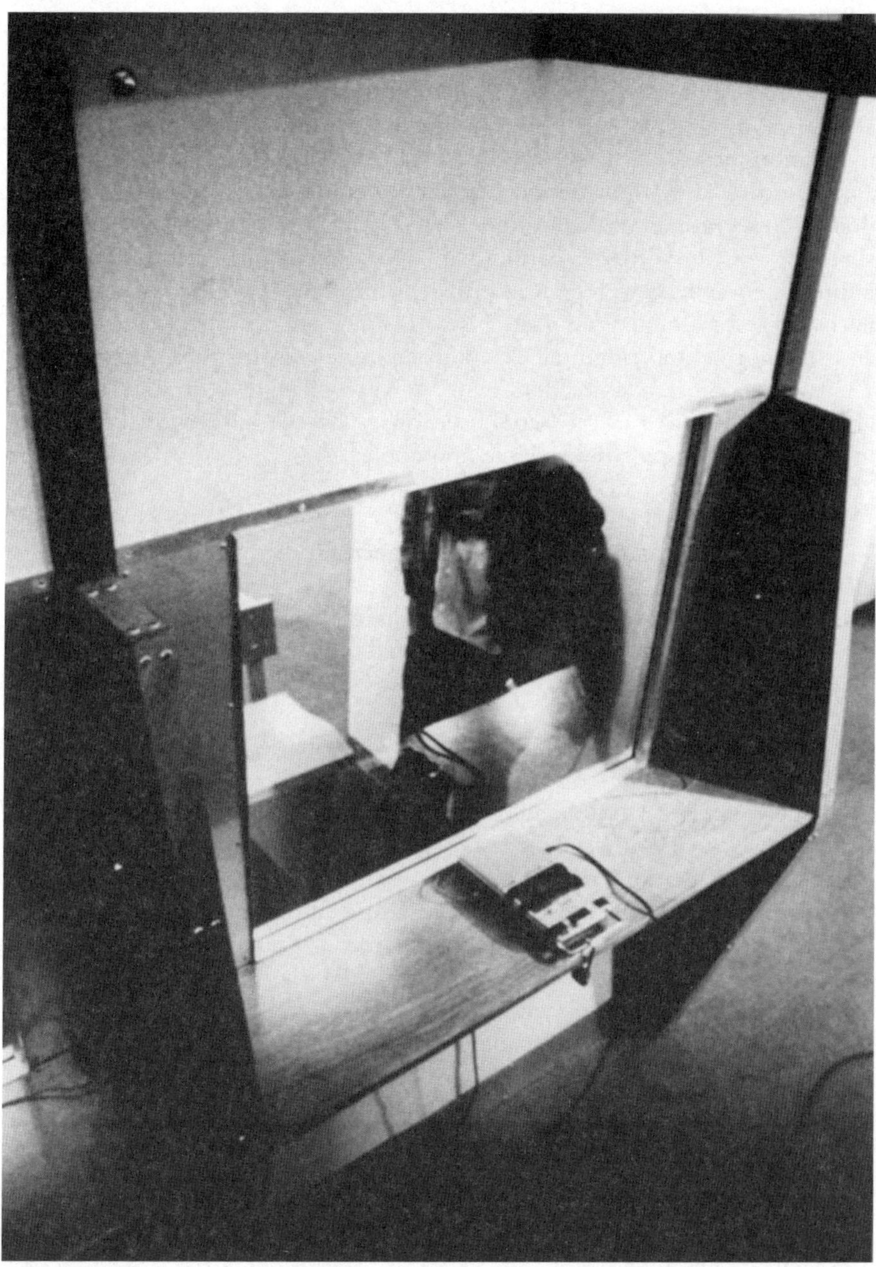

Costume. These books informed her growing interest in and awareness of the politics of viewing, overt and covert uses of space, and the complex roles played by clothing in allowing simultaneous (social) conformity and contestation, all of which were already manifest in her architectural installation pieces.

The notes from this period also indicate her changing conception of both architecture as an institution (and this in both the sense of buildings standing for the broad institutional values they purportedly upheld or imposed, and which were played out so strongly in *Model Institution*, and also in the sense of architecture itself as professional and disciplinary institution) and of the role and potential of art to address such institutionalisation. In 1982, more or less coincident with a clear change in attitude towards architecture in her realised work, she observed the almost overwhelming impact buildings appeared to have on people:

> alienation v. loss if identity
> bricks and mortar remain, physically concrete yet memory + past life gone, evaporated
> buildings stronger than people,—more enduring, more real than lives led.
> [...] Buildings as lost souls.
> 2003.19/E/5.1

While this can be read as a lament, and contextualised within her œuvre as the point she gives up on architecture, I want to argue that it marks a moment when she stops banging her head against the wall of architecture by trying to tackle it head-on, and instead begins a more vigorous and complex investigation into how this apparent and problematic 'strength' could be negotiated. However nuanced and well observed installations like *Model Institution* were, Chadwick had come to realise that institutional critique was for her a cul-de-sac, and that a direct attack on the monotonous environment would be fruitless.[3] Nevertheless, she stressed her desire to ameliorate the problems she observed, rather than turn her back on them: she wanted to 'resolve reality not [take] flight from it [...] Change relationship with reality – affect it' (2003.19/E/7.55). Her interest in this relationship between people and their environment remained every bit as strong, though this desire to 'change' and 'resolve' reality sought more oblique and nuanced approaches that she came to believe would provide more successful ways to negotiate with and counter the 'strength' of buildings. While the detail of these investigations will form the basis for the rest of this book, it is worth saying here that by the end of the decade, Chadwick had become far more up-beat about architecture, which suggests that her work in this area had made progress. Her considerations had moved from architecture-as-object to architecture as creative and experiential process where, in her own terms, the self becomes a building site around which these renovated architectural readings could take place: 'architecture grows corporeal and I am enfleshed' (*SF* 109).

This broad reconsideration regarding how best to approach architecture is echoed around the same time by questions she posed concerning the role and method of her own work. Towards the end of the notes she kept during the development of *Model Institution*, she includes the first of what would become frequent reflections regarding both her own creative process, and the broader relationship between art and life:

> remove art from its own institutions + legitimised manner of viewing/seeing—put it in unrelated institutions so functions under varying set [of] parameters
> 2003.19/E/3.32

Just as she had begun to express dissatisfaction with her work's response to architecture, so here she appears restless with artwork that operates within the status quo of the art institution. Her reaction to both these situations was to try to vary or broaden the parameters against which the work might operate, to try to get beyond established rules governing people's relationship with art or architecture. It could be said that both these aspects of her work move away from direct contestation towards more involved and creative engagement, towards new negotiations. The changes she sought in her own work reflected her broad belief, following a suggestion she developed from another of Koestler's books, that art (and architecture) were 'ripe for change'. Writing in *The Sleepwalkers*, Koestler argues:

> The symptom that a particular branch of science or art is ripe for change is a feeling of frustration and malaise [...] This is the situation which provides genius with the opportunity for his creative plunge under the broken surface. (*SW* 530)

Chadwick underlines this section of her copy, and adds in the margin, 'contemporary modern art?' Just as her lament about the strength of buildings gave way to a more celebratory assertion of *enfleshing*, so in this more or less contemporary remark alongside Koestler she saw an opportunity for a plunge under the broken surface of contemporary modern art that links to her consideration, a decade later, of her work as 'a leap across'. Writing in 1992, Chadwick demanded 'Take these works as clues to the value of ambivalence, of doubling, of a leap across, of the helix of pleasure around language. Pleasure is the field, the reward when the singularity of want is transformed into simultaneities that cannot be divided or closed' (*WD* 73). Just as her later realised works combined monstrous and beautiful, taboo and accepted, entrails and flowers and so on, her written advocacy of pleasure here must not be taken simply to replace the gritty social realism of her early, more militant politics. Indeed, the value she placed on ambivalence, simultaneity and openness had by this time become central to her position regarding politics, art and architecture.

Chadwick developed an attitude towards these values and their potential overlap; they were located across several layers that she believed affected the experience of space and its impact upon identity, and that were mediated across an interface between person and environment. In a notebook she kept between March 1975 and 1978, during the time she developed *Train of Thought*, she labelled the dynamics that occurred across this interface as the 'Triplet', and the piece itself, in both performance and publication, showed her interest in the availability of various overlapping readings of the same place. Although the *Triplet* is mentioned only once, among notes referring to the preparation of images of *Train of Thought* that Chadwick developed for publication in the magazine *AMBIT*, it can help to articulate several of the key negotiations that Chadwick consistently pursued in her considerations of identity.

> Series same image
> Furniture area
> Arch. drawing ergonomics of figure
> Narrative
> "Spaces of sensations
> Spaces of desire
> Spaces of negation"
> <u>Triplet</u> object/action | architectural area plan | diagram paths to destiny
> Façade/cross section/ (sex) action
> Annotated markings in real space
> Manifesto: plot/fantasy desiring a space to exist.
> HERE→space desiring a plot
> 2003.19/E/2.26.

The ambiguity or tension within the *Triplet* between the architectural arrangement of objects in space and the potential animation of that space by people marks not only a temporal scale (a discontinuous scale to be sure, set out between the prior architectural plan of the area, the actual action that takes place there at any point in time, and a notional future point projected by the users and marked by Chadwick as destiny or fantasy) but also the superimposition of aspects from various points along that scale and the complex power relations in play between them. While the

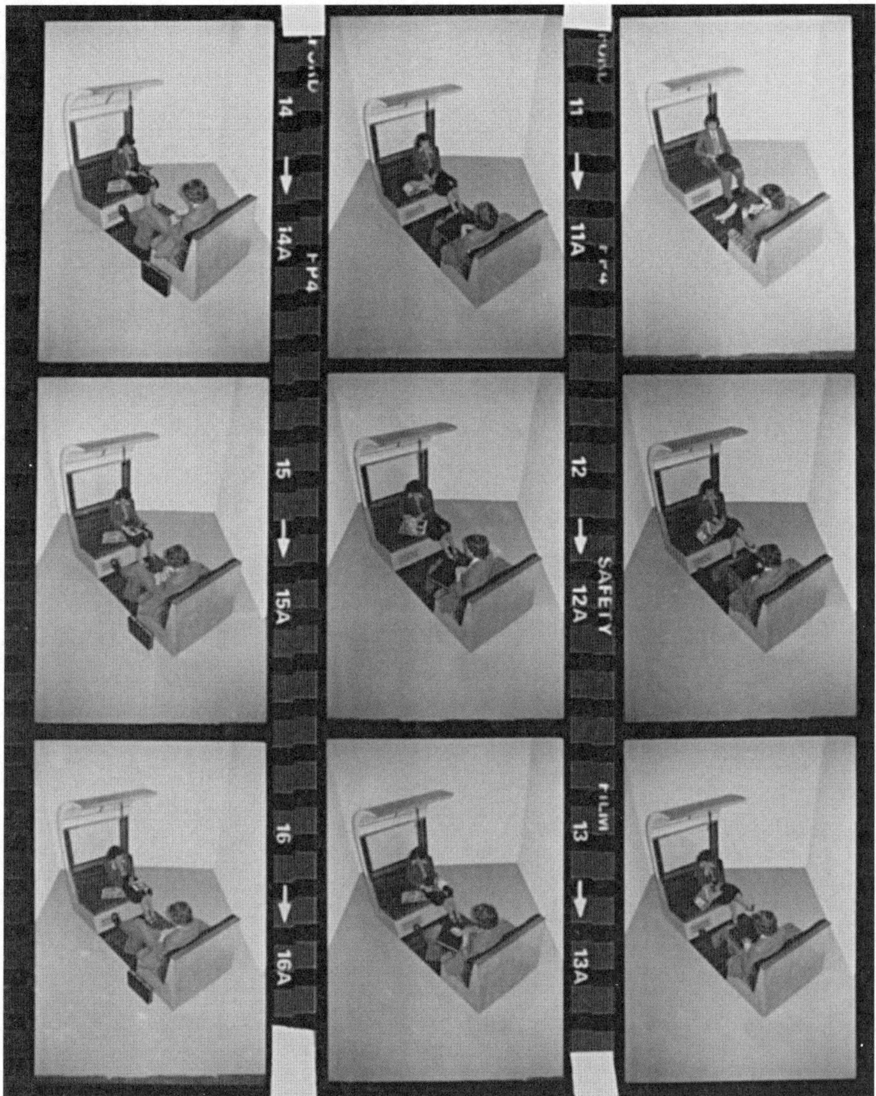

5 *Train of Thought*, 1978–9 (above and following pages).

Just as *Model Institution* addressed many non-physical factors reinforcing the monotony of its architectural cubicles, so Chadwick's earlier project *Train of Thought* similarly operated with an institutional architectural setting—here, a bay of seating from a *London Underground* carriage—over which several other ingredients affecting the experience of that environment were layered. A recorded soundtrack relayed the internal monologues of two passengers; the woman became increasingly worried that the man might attack her, when he was in fact just worried about his work.

The piece itself was performed by Silvia Ziranek and Brook Hoadley at the Acme Gallery, London, and by Chadwick herself and Philip Stanley at the Spectro Gallery, Newcastle, and the Ikon Gallery, Birmingham.

22

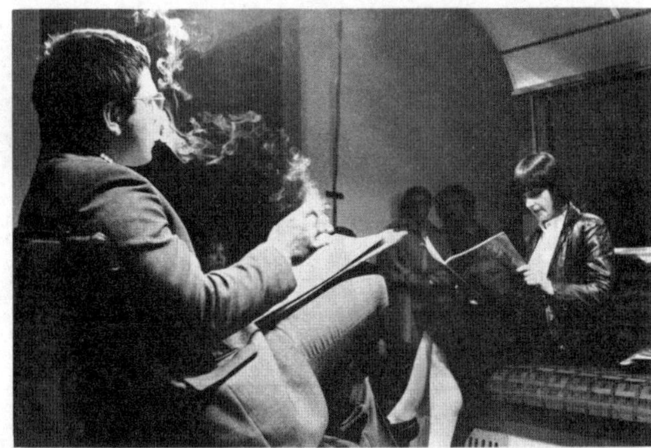

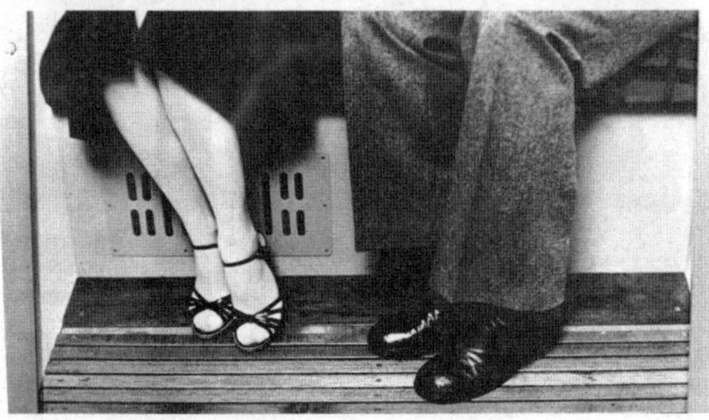

He developed a weakness for ladies shoes with high heels and actually went about trying to catch sight of ladies wearing pretty shoes. Sight alone was sufficient in the case of elegant shoes — of black leather and having very high heels.

Nothing else in the opposite sex aroused his sensual feeling. The shoes without the wearer were sufficient. At the height of sexual excitement, cruel thoughts about the shoe arose. He was forced to think with delight of the death agonies of the animal from which the leather came.

. . .'The sight of an elegant boot, on the foot of a girl at all pretty, intoxicated me; I inhaled the odour of leather with avidity.

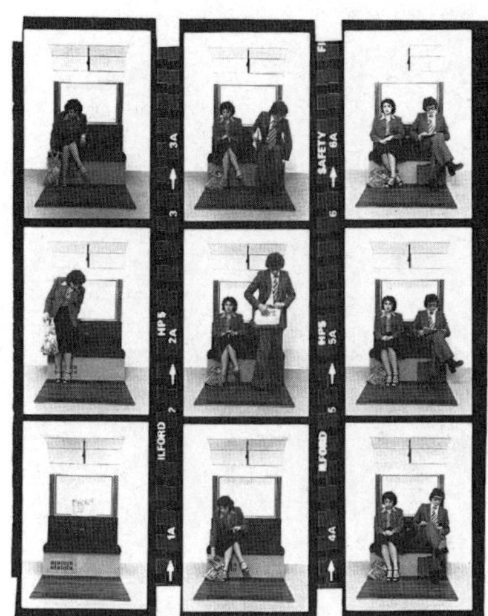

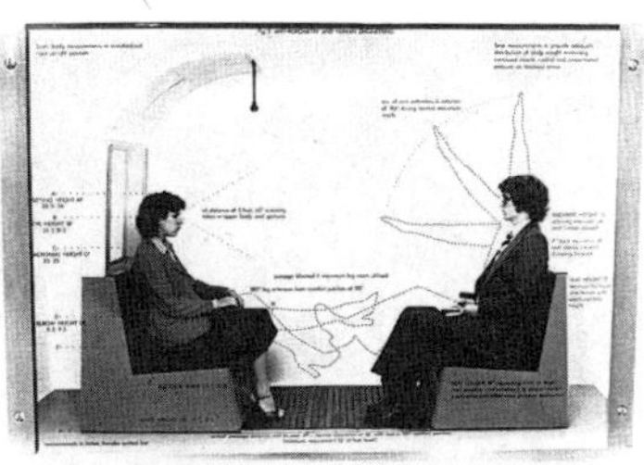

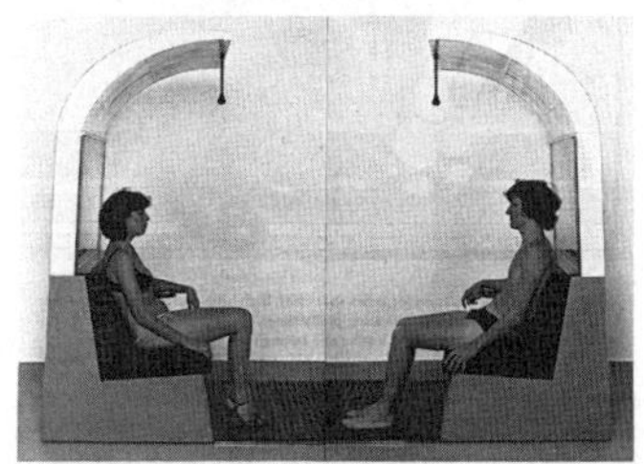

(above and opposite) *Train of Thought* as it was published in *AMBIT* ('A quarterly of poems, short stories, drawings & criticism') No.81, 1979, pp. 17–22. In addition to photographs of the performance itself, this article included annotated photographs of the architectural environment. The graphic style of these photos mimics orthographic architectural drawing (here, the cross-section) and also the presentation of anthropometric and ergonomic data in design guides used by architects and designers such as the *Metric Handbook* or Ernst Neufert's well-known *Architectural Data*.

In that article's 'Figure 5: Anthropometry and Human Engineering', for example, (top right) the typical highly rationalised presentation of 'average' human data is applied to a photograph of the two protagonists in the piece (here, Silvia Ziranek and Brook Hoadley). In addition to the conventional data such as 'Eye Height', 'Elbow Height', 'Buttock–Knee', and so on, Chadwick continues within this graphic style to replay some of the central themes of the performance: 'Passage blocked if maximum leg room utilised' indicates the potential zone of contact between the two overlapping, dotted anthropometric figures.

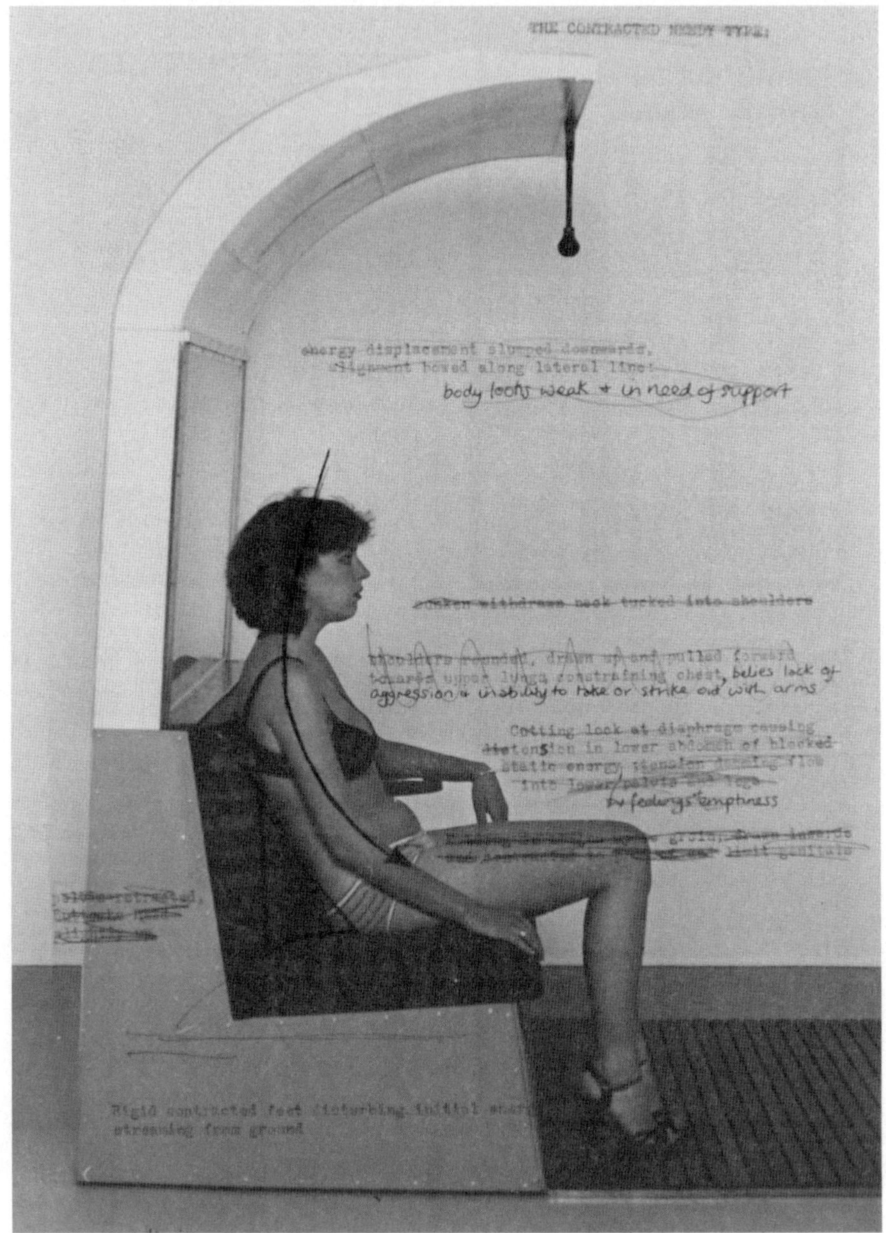

THE CONTRACTED NEEDY TYPE:
energy displacement slumped downwards,
alignment bowed along lateral line:
body looks weak + in need of support
...ken withdrawn neck tucked into shoulders
shoulders rounded, drawn up and pulled forward
towards upper lungs constraining chest, belies lack of
aggression + inability to take or strike out with arms
Cutting lock at diaphragm causing
distension in lower abdomen of blocked
static energy stagnation leading flow
into lower/pelvis and legs
by feelings emptiness
Rigid contracted feet disturbing initial energy
streaming from ground

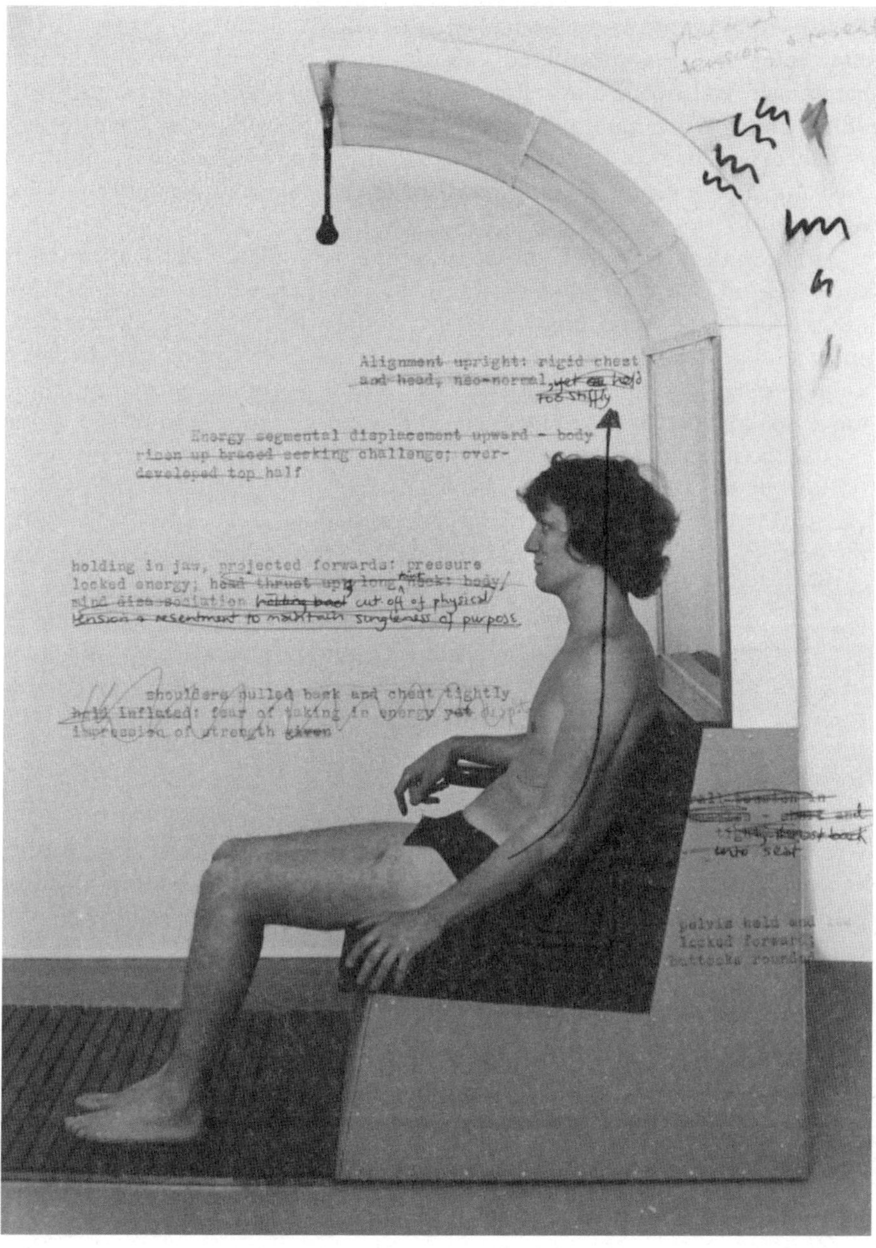
Alignment upright: rigid chest
and head, neo-normal, yet still held
too stiffly
Energy segmental displacement upward — body
risen up braced seeking challenge; over-
developed top half
holding in jaw, projected forwards: pressure
locked energy; head thrust up, long neck: body/
mind dissociation cut off of physical
tension + resentment to maintain singleness of purpose
shoulders pulled back and chest tightly
held inflated: fear of taking in energy
impression of strength given
pelvis held and
locked forwards:
buttocks round

'annotated markings in real space' become legible on the images in *AMBIT* and refer to the unrealised, unwelcome potential for interaction, harassment and conflict, this also marks Chadwick's more general criticisms of the impact that rationalised approaches to planning can have on the actual experience of a space (monotony), and indeed her enduring preoccupation with the relationship between science and our understanding of the world.

The significance for Chadwick of geometry's relationship to the body and space in particular, and of the relationship between science and our experience of the world more generally, cannot be overstated. Her research and theoretical work explored the ambiguity and potential conflict between a rationalised 'average' person portrayed in the anthropometric figure and the actual identity of the individuals who used the space (and played out in greater complexity in the soundtrack of *Model Institution*, for example). Although her early projects clearly had as their target the impact of excessively deterministic approaches to producing architectural space, and the concomitant reduction of individuals to a lowest common denominator anthropometric diagram, the various dimensions of the interface brought together in the *Triplet* sustain Chadwick's considerations of what was to become one of her most enduring concerns: how to reconcile or negotiate between a Newtonian-Cartesian world-view and those offered by more recent work in psychoanalysis, identity politics and modern science, in ways that can acknowledge the *range of experience that resists definition and closure [...] the enigmas and riddles of selfhood*.

To assist his own negotiations, Arthur Koestler insisted on using the term 'Philosophy of Nature' rather than 'science' because the former carried so many more overtones (*SW* 9). Chadwick worked from a similar position, and emphasised the importance she placed on redressing this balance between science, philosophy and nature:

> Science not only way of gaining access to truth of universe. Access nature of reality thro' non scientific means.
>
> What left out – to heal divide of art science—might be consciousness/ subjectivity/ lived time IDENTITY
> 2003.19/E/8.143

Chadwick's suggestion that identity might be sought in the (growing) gap between art and science not only stands as a neat summary of her position, but also provides a framework for the present book. The two central parts of the main text explore the divide, along with Chadwick's attempts at healing, from different positions. While the separate chapters across these two parts work around issues of the separation of science and humanities in the various ways, Parts One and Four respectively take up Chadwick's interest in the consequences of this separation on the creative process itself, and on the links between theory and practice.

Another of Koestler's proposals that Chadwick explicitly embraced as part of this healing process concerns the re-use of existing rules. The implications that this can have for a creative process or creative persona will be addressed in Chapter 1, which will expand on Chadwick's interest in the complex figure of The Juggler or *Le Bateleur*. Chadwick identified herself with this figure, and although the complexity of this association can only unfold gradually, its relevance as a metaphor for her own creative process can be readily grasped. This includes the wide range of objects that were brought together and combined through *Le Bateleur*'s juggling skill, while also extending to address the particular ambiguities regarding *Le Bateleur*'s unstable (and possibly multiple) identity, and their (disputed) ability to see beyond exoteric form, beyond the surface appearance of things. *Le Bateleur*'s access to knowledge, identity and process also provides a useful motif for issues that run through the whole book, as well as for the structure of the discussion itself. It prompts reflection on the new kinds of knowledge or epistemology that Chadwick's œuvre offers, both in terms of what might be juggled and by whom, and on the impact this knowledge has on the creative process more broadly. Around this motif, though, *Le Bateleur* also provides a lingering warning, a nagging doubt; however skilful the juggling, the entertainment provided was fleeting and possibly deceptive.

Part One: The creative process and the creative persona

1 The creative self

the Juggler, *le Bateleur*

Chadwick's thoughts on the figure of the artist developed through the analogy of a particular Tarot card, *The Juggler*, also known in English as *The Magician* and *The Conjurer*, or more traditionally according to the 'Marseille pack' that Chadwick researched, *Le Bateleur*. *Le Bateleur* is a deeply ambivalent card that epitomises the Tarot's layered symbolism in many ways, and provides a number of significant avenues along which analysis and speculation can develop. In an attempt at clarity, I will refer to Chadwick's own development of this figure as The Juggler, in contrast to the general discussion of the Tarot card *Le Bateleur*.

Chadwick's development of this figure was personal, and the particular projects that developed from it were explicitly autobiographical: her considerations of *Le Bateleur* can help to shed light on her development as an artist and the apparent changes in her realised output. However, the wide range of issues this analogy touches upon give it a far wider relevance: the breadth and complexity of concerns that Chadwick associated with The Juggler can be understood in relation to her broader ambitions to renegotiate the framework through which we understand the world and our place within it.

Chadwick's first reference to this figure of *Le Bateleur* comes midway through a notebook she kept between 1981 and 1983 (during which time she was preparing what is conventionally received as her first 'mature' project, *Ego Geometria Sum*).

The Juggler's Table

Theoretical model of the universe.
Pulling together of ordinary life + analysed as a passage of symbolic shapes/baubles imbued with significance of personal life.

I represent juggler
2003.19/E/5.85

The sheer range of reference that *Le Bateleur* was conventionally taken to harness would clearly appeal to Chadwick, and her readiness to adopt this persona signals something of the ambition she had for her own art. But in addition to the breadth of this ambition, the desire to combine a universal understanding with the ordinary, personal and everyday epitomises a characteristic of her working that became manifest in a number of ways through her œuvre, and that will be discussed throughout the chapters that follow. Indeed it could be said that her attraction to the figure of *Le Bateleur* was due in no small part to its ability to hold, or at least juggle with, apparently contradictory issues simultaneously.

Nevertheless, and as with many other interests she held, Chadwick's adoption of this figure did not simply follow received wisdom. Although *Le Bateleur* provided a rich allegory through which she considered the relationships between theory, practice and understanding, between 'looking' and the acquisition and application of knowledge in the creative process, she did not extend her interest to other Tarot figures, nor did she pursue the interrelationships offered within the Tarot as a system itself. While the appeal of conventional approaches to reading the Tarot lay for Chadwick in its complex, multi-faceted connotations, and encouragement to combine both 'upright' and 'reversed' meanings, her adoption of *Le Bateleur* was not unqualified and can be understood implicitly to turn convention on its head.

double connotations and identity

To develop an understanding of the range of issues packed into the allegory of *Le Bateleur*, and to open up Chadwick's willingness to associate so closely with this figure—*I represent juggler*—the detailed allegories at work around the card can be introduced with reference to what Fred Gettings describes as its 'double connotation'. Chadwick had a copy of Gettings' *The Book of Tarot*, which significantly influenced her own position on the Tarot in general and on the figure of The Juggler in particular. Amongst pages where she took notes from Gettings there is a photocopy of B. P. Grimaud's *Le Bateleur* card from his 1969 pack of the *Tarot of Marseille* (figure 6): this rendering of the card supports Chadwick's allegorical readings discussed here.

Although interpretations of the Tarot are too numerous to follow at a nuanced level, both Gettings' and Grimaud's accounts are consistent with the generally agreed principles of *Le Bateleur* and its role in the broader system. The card itself is numbered 1 of the *Major Arcana*, a term used to

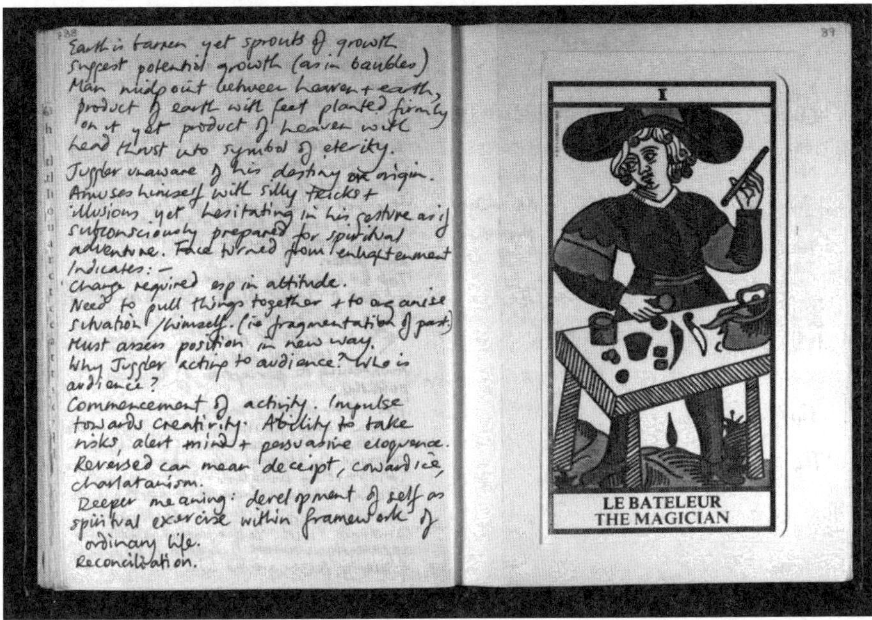

6 *Notebook* 2003.19/E/5.88–9.

Amongst pages where she took notes from Gettings there is a photocopy of B. P. Grimaud's *Le Bateleur* card from his 1969 pack of the *Tarot of Marseille.*

describe the first 22 cards of the Tarot deck. When considered within the divinatory role for which the Tarot is best known in the English-speaking world, these cards work to represent the challenges within a particular stage of life, or the cycle of life itself. Although divination can operate exclusive through the *Major Arcana*, it is far more common to combine these with the other cards in the Tarot deck known as the *Minor Arcana*, which follows the setup of a traditional set of playing cards, with four suits of fourteen cards each. In addition to the various connotations the *Minor Arcana* can give to the major, each card in the deck enjoys both 'upright' and 'reversed' meanings according to its orientation when dealt.

Chadwick's interest was clearly not in the Tarot as a divinatory system, although the interrelationships and reversed meanings just described, which generally operate across the deck as a whole, are important because of the way they are folded into the particular symbolism of *Le Bateleur* itself and the implications this has beyond the Tarot. One of the principal readings of *Le Bateleur* is as 'everyman', who fails to read the broader layers of meaning available in the world around him.

The Tarot: Card 1   <u>The Juggler</u>

  Le Bateleur
Juggler: 'everyman' : 'MAN AS HE IS'
("doesn't see spiritual potential for development + vision in these objects
[...] examining their exoteric form but cannot understand their
significance.")
2003.19/E/5.86.[1]

Chadwick highlights this 'everyman' characteristic and summarises the standard reading of this situation from her reading of Gettings. Indeed, Gettings addresses the 'everyman' when he singles out *Le Bateleur* as one where 'we find a rarefication [*sic*] of meaning in certain of the isolated details', and elaborates on this 'double connotation' as follows:

> if we examine the various items on the table before the Juggler in Arcanum 1, we see that what is intended is a double connotation, for on one level they represent the ordinary juggling paraphernalia, such as peas, dice and thimbles; at the same time they represent the embryonic form of the four symbols of the Minor Arcana. We see that the thimble is an embryonic Chalice; the knife, the Sword; the peas and dice, the Pentacle; and the rod, which the Juggler is holding in his left hand, is the Sceptre or Wand. The implication in this double connotation is obvious, then, for it suggests that the Juggler, who is everyman, has before him all the potential of these rich symbols—in other words, everyman has the possibility of spiritual vision and spiritual development—but he does not see their real potential or significance. (*BT* 17–18)

In his later chapter devoted to close readings of this card, Gettings goes on to emphasise that 'The Juggler [*Le Bateleur*] is meant to represent man as he is [...] This image is an incredibly rich statement of man's state of being in his normal level of consciousness.' At face value, the 'incredibly rich statement' might be assumed to reflect the incredible richness of everyday life; however, as Gettings continues it becomes apparent that normal levels of consciousness are less valued, and that the rarefaction of meaning associated with *Le Bateleur*'s 'double connotation', while available, is never taken up, indeed cannot be taken up, because in that state he (or 'we') pay attention to the wrong things, are 'distracted from distraction by distraction'.

So in light of the pejorative nature of these conventional readings, Chadwick's likening of her own position to that of *Le Bateleur* is more remarkable and clearly political. While she does take up the potential of these rich symbols, for her their 'real potential and significance' lie in the impact they can have on the everyday. Chadwick knowingly took up this position as something to celebrate, and approached the relationship between the 'everyman' and the systems of 'greater' understanding as one to be renegotiated. While this direct contestation of received hierarchies echoes something of her early architectural-sculptural work, it is a more nuanced position that repeats and develops something of the 'double connotation' so as to allow for the coexistence of these two modes of human being rather than simply demanding the switch (or 'progress') from one to the other.

Chadwick's growing interest in these issues of artistic and personal identity, and her awareness of the potential of the figure of The Juggler to anchor her explorations of these issues, is apparent in her 'economical' statement for a small project called *The Juggler's Table*:

Dear Andrew [Nairne] OK?

My text/statement for "Hand Signals" as follows:

Economical n'est ce pas?
Hope you approve,
best wishes

The Juggler's Table Helen X

Poised in the act of entertaining an invisible audience, the Juggler stands before a table laid with the paraphernalia of time.

2004.19/1[2]

The equivocal tone of Chadwick's statement draws attention not only to the materials with which The Juggler (or artist) has to work, but also the relationship they have with the audience of their work. While the presence of the (invisible) audience is implied in the traditional Tarot card rendering of The Juggler, Chadwick's *The Juggler's Table* (figure 7) appears to further this invisibility by removing the presence of The Juggler or artist herself (on closer inspection, her presence has become inscribed onto the objects themselves). The awkwardness, and in particular the *instability*, of the relationships that bear on The Juggler's identity warrant further comment, as Chadwick's statement and project draw attention to other aspects of *Le Bateleur* that reflect both individual and social dimensions of this awkwardness, as well as an awkwardness with the natural world.

Le Bateleur enjoyed an awkward relationship with the social and natural worlds. Interestingly, when this figure emerged in the fifteenth century it was as part of a system of astrologically based social analysis and commentary, where he held an itinerant or nomadic role, travelling from fair to fair for his living. In literally a peripheral and unstable position with

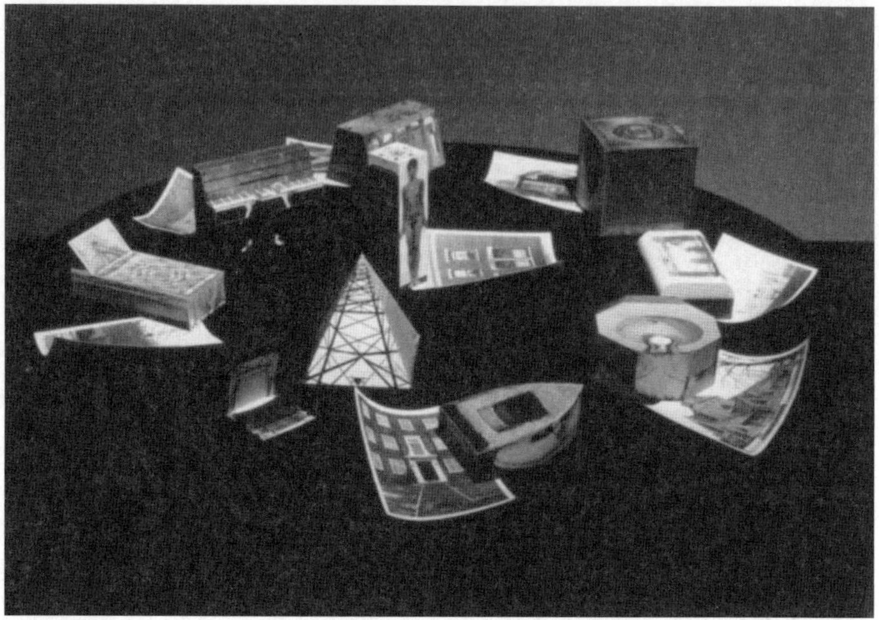

7 *The Juggler's Table*, 1983.

> Developed as one of three parts of *Ego Geometria Sum* and containing all the ingredients of that work, *The Juggler's Table* comprised ten cardboard maquettes for the *Ego Geometria Sum* sculptures, placed on top of photographs of the buildings that relate to each of the ten stages of her life referenced in the main piece (such as the hospital where she was born, childhood home, schools and so on).

respect to 'stable' society, his marginal status brought with it both a certain kudos or mystique, and resentment.[3] (The name itself was somewhat double edged: while the *Bagatella* or *Bateleur* of the earlier Italian and French Tarot figures is usually referred to as the *Juggler* or *Conjurer* in English, the words can also translate as 'buffoon'.) Within this early system, *Le Bateleur* formed part of a societal group that was represented in *Children of Luna* images, which brought together professions that were believed to display fickle, capricious, unstable and independent behaviour and nature that manifested the fluidity and speedy movement of the moon. As such, this reading of the card was essentially a commentary on man as an actor of different roles, with little or no identity of his own. Charles Zika's analysis suggests that while some of the *Children of Luna* were accorded benign, 'natural' identity flaws (the child-like in the *Children*), *Le Bateleur*'s situation was deliberate. Zika stresses that *Le Bateleur*'s 'living, and by virtue of that his *identity*, is premised on the manipulation of reality by the use of trickery, illusion and falsehood'.[4]

The socially peripheral position of *Le Bateleur*, based in large part on this ability to manipulate reality, is reinforced and nuanced by the conventional links made between this card and card zero, *The Fool* or *Le Mat*, around their involvement with what Chadwick terms 'the paraphernalia of time'. As Gettings suggests,

> we may presume from the symbolic reference that the things contained in the [Fool's] sack are the very baubles with which the Juggler is playing. The Juggler is at least examining the exoteric form of the baubles and cannot see their significance, cannot see through the *maya* of the world, but the Fool is merely weighed down by them—he does not even examine them, for they are locked away in the darkness of his bag, and he does not know why he carries the weight. The Fool card, within this symbolic structure, represents ordinary man caught up in the eternal round of material illusion: the Juggler card represents man who is both showing off, and yet interested in the questions raised by the baubles. (*BT* 17–18)

While the accounts given by Zika and Gettings of *Le Bateleur*'s identity and social status develop around the way the latter engages with reality, attempts to read them together meet with difficulties; either *Le Bateleur* knowingly manipulates reality or he cannot see its significance. Chadwick's work offers a way out of this paradox. One of the important aspects of this allegory is the extent to which *Le Bateleur*'s identity is 'unstable', and the fact that this is based on the conscious, skilful manipulation of reality: *Le Bateleur* is a creative figure, conjointly producing 'reality' and self identity. Chadwick's various notes explicitly put herself in both positions: as creative figure and within the objects of reality. Gettings goes on to make similar observations regarding *Le Bateleur*'s creative identity, although this remains couched within a certain idea of 'self-development'. He suggests that the card indicates 'the commencement of activity' and the mercurial impulse towards speech, acting or the written word, and that it also indicates the ability to take risks, as well as alert intelligence and persuasive eloquence.

This extension of the creative persona recalls and reinforces the earlier observation that Chadwick's contestation of received hierarchies develops Gettings' 'double connotation', inasmuch as the traditional criticisms of *Le Bateleur*'s identity and social status clearly relied on a framework that valorised the celestial over the mundane, that expected human 'betterment' away from 'The Fool', and aspired to associate the objects of the world with stasis rather than change. Against this, Chadwick's adoption of The

Juggler as some kind of creative persona has echoes of a much earlier understanding of The Juggler figured as *The Magician*, as a link between the higher spheres of understanding and the sub-lunary world, a figure whose role remained clearly within society where only they were entrusted to tamper with reality.

Chadwick's extension not only returns higher understanding to everyman and the everyday, it also places The Juggler or creative persona in different positions, different modes of existence. While in any one of these, Chadwick's work would contest the pejorative, traditional readings of *Le Bateleur*'s unstable identity, the broader point is how they can be understood to operate together while retaining their different modalities; this assertion marks the point at which Gettings' notion of double connotation, however revised, no longer provides an adequate model to account for Chadwick's theoretical work; instead, to account for The Juggler requires a framework that is able to hold together various overlapping and potentially contradictory claims: the artist is juggler, and positioned both within and beyond the objects that comprise reality, but also the juggler is everyman.

If this understanding of the creative persona is taken seriously, a very different appreciation of the creative process could be developed. This move can have a number of further connections, which raise interesting questions that apply not only to the figure of the artist, but also for the architect and for architectural practice. In contrast to the conventional expectations of the architect regarding their stability, reliability and so on (i.e. their identity), as well as the status of their skill and knowledge, to consider the architect as The Juggler raises the question what would happen if this were not the case, if the identity of the architect could be acceptably quixotic. While this would at a stroke acknowledge the collaborative reality of most architectural practice, rather than the charade of individual genius, the greater impact would be found by examining the consequences of accepting unstable relationships between audience (or users) and creative persona, as could undoing artistic and architectural preoccupation with static objects, and more searchingly with the epistemological systems upon which this presupposition is based.

the manipulation of reality: artifice and nature

Chadwick's extension of the figure of *Le Bateleur* also raises a number of serious questions regarding his relationship with the stuff he juggles with. To push Chadwick's extension of this allegory further onto the artistic and architectural process, these questions draw on several other 'double connotations' that the traditional Tarot symbolism offers. Frequently referred to as 'worthless objects', 'baubles', and so on, the peas, dice, coins and cups that are traditionally portrayed on *Le Bateleur*'s table have an allegorical role that relates them, for those able to see beyond everyday appearances, to the very make up of the universe. On Chadwick's *The Juggler's Table* these become the 'paraphernalia of time' (a phrase that itself enjoys a double connotation given the particular stages of her own life that these objects refer to).

Putting aside discussions of the position assumed by the artist or architect and the audience in terms of the impact this has on their identity, suffice it to say that as an allegory the table in Chadwick's project positions both of these in detached, quasi-divine positions, and within the worthless objects themselves: this raises questions about the status of this stuff, about how and how much 'we' can know of anything. These objects represent the stuff of reality that *Le Bateleur* manipulates, or the stuff that *Le Bateleur* uses to manipulate reality, or the everyday stuff of reality that prevents *Le Bateleur* ascending to a higher plane of understanding.

The Juggler's Table points to some of Chadwick's most enduring concerns regarding the stuff of reality, and to substantial considerations of the relationship between artifice and nature. In this context, The Juggler opens onto questions of epistemology, and posits that all of reality is always already manipulated. 'Our' relationship—as both the creative persona of the missing juggler and as the audience—to the baubles on *The Juggler's Table* plays out various ambiguities and conflicts: those raised by an insight into the 'inner qualities' of the baubles and the differences between a divinely sanctioned or contingent understanding, between ideal and empirical positions on the world. Beyond these, Chadwick's work considered the possibility of their chances of connection (or not), it underlined problems of holding any clear-cut distinction between nature and artefact, and implicitly examined and operated within an epistemology that caters not only for the knowable but also for the unknowable.

> Vital familiars from the cradle, they are bright with origin. Their undeniable presence confounds the tyrannies of Plato's cave—the play of shadows gives the illusion of fresh movement, a springing into life. Yet these marks exist outside of knowing
> 2003.19/E/8.1

The questions of autonomy, interrelationship, and particularly the connection of opposites can be understood to be at work in *The Juggler's Table*, in its capacity to provide an allegory for a 'Theoretical model of the universe'.

theoretical models

One of the most fruitful allegorical associations of *Le Bateleur* lies in the accounts it provides of the theoretical model of the universe. As with many other associations, the 'double connotations' of the card in this respect are frequently contradictory. Inscribed at the core of this particular contradiction are the conflicting theoretical models offered by ancient (classical) and Newtonian-Cartesian science. These disputes were an enduring interest for Chadwick, but they can also be understood to have had a central influence on the shape of architectural education and practice, in terms of both the baubles that were on the table and the system of knowledge into which these were placed.

Gettings introduces the allegory of classical science while he reiterates assertions regarding The Juggler's inability to see beyond everyday appearances: 'the worthless objects on the table before him, with which he is entertaining his audience, or merely passing away his own time, are actually the primitive forms of the four great symbols of the Minor pack.' To repeat a passage already quoted, Gettings gives more detail around these four great symbols when he suggests that:

> if we examine the various items on the table before the Juggler in Arcanum 1, we see that what is intended is a double connotation, for on one level they represent the ordinary juggling paraphernalia, such as peas, dice and thimbles; at the same time they represent the embryonic form of the four symbols of the Minor Arcana. We see that the thimble is an embryonic Chalice; the knife, the Sword; the peas and dice, the Pentacle; and the rod, which the Juggler is holding in his left hand, is the Sceptre or Wand. (*BT* 17–18)

The four symbols of the *Minor Arcana* represent the four basic elements in classical accounts of physical nature: the chalice or cup represents *Water*; the knife or sword, *Air*; the pentacle represents *Earth*; and the wand represents *Fire*.

Now in addition to these classical accounts, *Le Bateleur* adds a layer to the allegory that refers to the emergence of modern science; in his detailed analysis of *Le Bateleur*, Gettings argues 'The image as a whole is the visual equivalent of the Paracelsian idea of man as the midpoint between heaven and earth […] but of course the Juggler is unaware of his greatness, his origin or his destiny'. Although this Paracelsian motif figures for Chadwick's self-representation as The Juggler, where she can mediate 'between ordinary life and symbolic shapes', the impact of this analogy is not straightforward. Nevertheless, this Paracelsian motif can offer an important and useful way to consolidate into the creative persona or process much of Chadwick's later theoretical work, her experimental approach, the balance and reconciliation she sought between art and science, and also her work around particular (overly) geometrical approaches to life. It is appropriate here to emphasise that this is just a motif, and that although many of the references taken through *Le Bateleur* appear to back-pedal into issues that are so arcane as to be irrelevant for contemporary practice, her own work was forward-looking, combining the big questions that *Le Bateleur* could raise regarding the making and understanding of our world with contemporary developments in science such as cellular biology and virology, quantum physics, and so on.

To a limited extent, the classical and modern views rendered through *Le Bateleur* share a belief in the interrelationship between micro and macro, between the body and the world, although the basis of such interrelationship differed greatly and signalled a fundamentally different approach to the understanding of the cosmos and our place within it. Allen G. Debus has argued that a particular 'object of the Paracelsians' attack was the ancient system of elements: Earth, Air, Water and Fire with their attendant qualities and humours. This was a complex system, but a potentially fragile one, since a rejection of even one might result in a collapse of the whole.'[5] Instead of this classical, overarching elemental approach, epitomised at the microcosmic scale by Galenic theory of bodily humours, Paracelsian 'views were that sickness and health in the body relied on the harmony of man, the microcosm, and Nature, the macrocosm'.[6]

The role played by the body in this Paracelsian schema is echoed in the importance Chadwick gives it in her own work, but it can also act as a motif that has strong resonance more broadly regarding her appetite for *pulling together of ordinary life + analysed as a passage of symbolic shapes/baubles imbued with significance of personal life*, and her determination to balance an understanding of the everyday with the cosmological. The appeal for Chadwick would lie in the ability of a Paracelsian harmony to balance difference rather than be generated by one unified system. Even at one pole of this Paracelsian motif, the lemniscate form of *Le Bateleur*'s hat both figures for eternity, and represents the reconciliation of opposites in the 'yoking together the female (moon) and male (sun)'. (*BT* 26) This balance, brought into play with the everyday issues represented at the other pole, is one of the best-known characteristics of Chadwick's realised work (and the theoretical consequences of this are something to which I will return). Moreover, any Paracelsian inclination she may have displayed can be understood as a desire to start in the middle, with experimentation and observation, rather than with an elemental system provided by, and tied back to, a transcendental (even quintessential) authority.

Around *Le Bateleur*'s ability to balance such understanding a number of further questions arise concerning this role of authority, again linked to allegorical connotations of the card. The broader impact of Paracelcus' conception of the body was commensurate with other contemporary developments that affected the balance of the physical sciences, as Debus suggests: 'the significance of [Paracelcus'] opening of medical thought to this new approach can be compared with that of the influence of Copernicus on astronomy and physics during the same period'.[7] Whatever its impact on these and other scientific observations, the Copernican revolution's real challenge and lasting impact was upon divine authority, which human enquiry effectively replaced or at least rebalanced.

Considering *Le Bateleur*'s posture in more detail, this has traditionally been read as reinforcing the position as mid-point between earth and sky: it is argued that his upper body form represents the Hebrew letter aleph (א) itself referring to a divine-creative unifying principle. Side-stepping the many disputed readings of the aleph (for *Le Bateleur* in particular and the Tarot in general), Gettings suggests that its general role as mid-point is reinforced by *Le Bateleur*'s hand gestures: 'In the two basic symbols [in *Le Bateleur*'s hands, the coin, the equivalent of the Pentacle or Host, but which The Juggler holds down towards earth, and the rod, equivalent to the material world, here being held aloft] we have an intimation that everyman is reversing the natural order of things, to judge from the look on his distracted face, *because he does not know any better*!' (BT 26) Although Gettings' reading of posture and gesture reiterates *Le Bateleur*'s traditional situation as mid-point between earth and sky, Chadwick's development of The Juggler calls these traditional readings into question by suggesting that there is no 'natural order', and that The Juggler's (re-)adjustment of their relationship is not mistaken, that in fact he, or she, does know the consequences of their actions.

theory and practice, position and posture

Following Chadwick's various considerations of The Juggler, these issues of *Le Bateleur*'s posture and gesture reinforce what might be referred to as the viewing positions and directions adopted by the creative self. For the artist (or the architect) to take seriously the analogy between the creative self and *Le Bateleur*, this is not only to juggle with wide-ranging issues already introduced, but to challenge what is perceived to be the 'natural order of things', including a social hierarchy of knowledge. Chadwick recognised early on that this challenge must be more than the simple reversal that Gettings reads into *Le Bateleur*, who foolishly looks the wrong way. Instead, her expanded Juggler invites the creative persona to combine idealism and empirical observation (viewing from the heavens *and* from the earth) but also to balance both of these with a further position symbolised by *Le Bateleur*'s close relationship with card zero, *The Fool* or *Le Mat*, and inscribed into his very centre through the aleph of his posture. Re-reading this relationship against Gettings, *Le Mat* is not not-knowing through the lazy ignorance of the fool, but the symbol of that which is beyond thought, beyond knowing.[8]

This more complex balance of different kinds of knowledge (and non-knowledge) is important in Chadwick's theoretical position. It is worth reiterating her enduring interest in geometry, and the awkwardness of its theoretical and practical role in her thought. Returning to the Paracelsian motif, Allen Debus observes the shift in the status of geometry in Paracelsian thought:

> In his summary of Paracelsian medicine, Peter Severinus argued that Aristotle's work as well as Galen's was flawed by its overemphasis on mathematical logic (1571). The use of weights and measures was acceptable for the physician—and even the mystical use of numbers as one might find in the hermetic texts—but not the logical-geometrical use of mathematics. Far more acceptable was the analogy of the great world and man which might be used as a guide to truth. Paracelsus had written that 'everything which astronomical theory has searched deeply and gravely by aspects, astronomical tables and so forth—this self-same knowledge should be a lesson and teaching to you concerning the bodily firmament'.[9]

This suggestion that geometry and mathematics should be a *guide to truth* rather than the truth itself is relevant for Chadwick's thought. It also echoes the quiet balance struck between empirical observation, the 'logical-geometrical use of mathematics', and a philosophical agenda that was part of the development of 'modern' science and that links Paracelsus with the Copernican Revolution. (Copernicus' system didn't quite stack up, and relied more on such interplay than is usually made out.) Chadwick's own corruption of pure geometric forms on *The Juggler's Table* indicates something of this balancing, where they respond to the contingent and personal while acknowledging the universal: *Pulling together of ordinary life + analysed as a passage of symbolic shapes/baubles imbued with significance of personal life.*

In notes taken shortly after those on *Le Bateleur*, Chadwick developed some of the issues that pass through the Paracelsian 'mid-point'; important here was the ambivalent role of geometry, such that Chadwick can be understood to be caught between logico-geometric rules and the softer, Paracelsian analogical guide to understanding.

Geometry draws away from corruption of age
adulthood to eternal. Purification + liberation. Science helps
contemplation of eternal. Ecstasy of discovery [...]
Individual ⇔ universal, micro ⇔ macro etc.
2003.19/E/5.102

Geometry: frame of reference as to Kepler + Pythagoras.
Unable to wrench it forward, my work left behind in geometry: static
model of pre-Newtonian Universe. No depiction of dynamic changes:
concept of momentum/ impetus denied [...]
2003.19/E/5.105[10]

The frustration she voiced here around her work's attraction to (static) geometry motivated her ongoing attempts to escape the pre-Newtonian universe. Her desire to escape was offset by a recognition of the impact that Newtonian physics, and Newtonian-Cartesian science more broadly, has had on 'our' experience and understanding of the world. Although the theoretical considerations that develop from this position will be explored throughout the remaining chapters of this book, it should be noted here that for Chadwick they remained ultimately inconclusive. Nevertheless, the consequences of her explorations move into increasingly recognisable architectural territory, and raise a number of questions that architecture can continue to consider. These concern the role and limitation of mathematical logic for architectural practice and experience, as well as broader questions regarding the balance between theory, practice and understanding, or what could be considered 'looking' as the posture and position of the creative figure—architect, artist or *Le Bateleur*—as they go beyond an examination or production of exoteric form.

However rich the analogy of *Le Bateleur*, it remains something of a static model of the creative persona. To develop the issues just raised, it is necessary to examine Chadwick's considerations of the creative process more broadly. The associations she related to in *Le Bateleur* concern not only the baubles on the table, the materials the artist has at her fingertips, but also the various and possibly conflicting understandings of these materials and their relationship to the world provided by *Le Bateleur*'s various viewing positions and directions. How the creative persona responds to these, to the capacity, responsibility even, to combine different modes of understanding in their creative process, was an issue that Chadwick considered throughout her œuvre. Although her theoretical position develops significantly, particularly to address *dynamic changes*, *momentum* and *impetus*, the armature of issues legible in *Le Bateleur* remained constant.

2 The creative process and *total pattern*

Chadwick addressed her worries that her work was stuck in a 'static model of pre Newtonian universe' in several ways. Of particular significance here is how her interest in science, and the philosophy of science, led her to reconsider not only the operations involved in the creative process, but the limits of this process itself. There is a strategic similarity between this response and that which she made to an earlier impasse, namely her recognition that *buildings stronger than people*. Although some specific insights of modern science did directly inform certain aspects of her work, its relevance for her desire to see the creative process address *dynamic changes, momentum* and *impetus* raised at the end of the last chapter was more analogical.

Indeed, this analogical address can be considered as an important characteristic of the creative process as she develops it: Chadwick considered this characteristic through a phrase she borrowed from Arthur Koestler, *reculer pour mieux sauter*, step back the better to jump forward. Although her considerations of *Le Bateleur* clearly provided significant insights regarding the creative persona, the broader relevance of the stuff at The Juggler's fingertips, this chapter looks elsewhere, exploring the consequences of stepping back from this immediate engagement with and around *The Juggler's Table*. To continue juggling, albeit in a slightly different way, nevertheless remained within, repeated and reinforced the static model of understanding Chadwick criticised. By stepping back from the table, she attained a theoretical position from which the creative process could jump forward, could make the 'leap across'.

The prospect of this jump forward has a significant impact on the relationship between the creative persona and the audience. Developing traditional criticisms that *Le Bateleur* had little identity of his own, Chadwick's creative process can be understood to revolve around the possibilities this offers for much more positive ambiguity concerning the identity of the creative persona; rather than this being identified with one person, it might become a role that involves multiple selves, and that as a process is not simply constrained to the recognisable 'juggling' performed by *Le Bateleur* or the artist more broadly, but is considered as something to be picked up and sustained by the (invisible) audience around the table, something that continues long after *Le Bateleur* has packed up and gone.

from objects to rules, rules to guides

To return to the difference between the rules and the guides that pass through the Paracelsian mid-point of *Le Bateleur*, Chadwick's marginal notes to her copy of Arthur Koestler's *The Sleepwalkers: A History of Man's Changing Vision of the Universe* [1959] anticipate almost verbatim the entry in her notebooks cited in the previous chapter.

> here my work departs: left behind in geometry:—static model of pre Newtonian universe, no depiction of dynamic of change. (*SW* 341)

Rather than repeating her frustration with the static, the relevance of this to the current discussion lies in the importance that Koestler and other related writers on the history and philosophy of science held for Chadwick's ability to manœuvre around this impasse. Several of the issues raised in *The Sleepwalkers* (and another of Koestler's books *The Ghost in the Machine* [1967] that Chadwick read closely) can be understood to relate to *Le Bateleur* and to Chadwick's theoretical development of artistic process, less in terms of the specific science or scientists that either Koestler or Chadwick addressed, and more in the frameworks within which the scientific or creative processes were understood.[1]

While Koestler's writing clearly struck a chord with Chadwick in several areas, it was perhaps in his overarching criticism of the increasing separation of the scientific from the creative processes that his influence on her thinking can be detected most strongly. Koestler advocated if not a re-combination of arts and sciences, at least a rapprochement. While the various issues that passed through the allegory of *Le Bateleur* chart the breadth of potential for this figure, Chadwick's contestation of traditional readings of the allegory highlights the important issues for the creative process. In contrast to traditional readings, which advocated the acquisition of 'higher' knowledge as way of separating oneself from the ordinary world of events, both Chadwick and Koestler were interested in the ablity to hold these together, to relay the relevance of such understanding to the everyday, to the 'everyman'. Their principal motivation was the amelioration of current, everyday conditions.

It is important to stress that *Le Bateleur*, Koestler and Chadwick, while addressing a range of historical issues, did not figure or agitate for any kind of regression to a mythical golden age prior to the split between art and science (and the dominance of science over art). Their aim was forwards not backwards, and in this, Koestler's considerations of 'evolution' relate to Chadwick's developing understanding of artistic process. In her copy of *The Ghost in the Machine*, she highlighted the following passage:

> the decisive breakthroughs in science, art or philosophy are successful escapes from blind alleys, from the bondage of mental habits, from orthodoxy and over-specialisation. The method of escape follows the same undoing-and-re-doing pattern as in biological evolution: and the zig-zag course of advance in science or art repeats th[is] pattern. (*GM* 207)

A few pages later she double underlines *reculer pour mieux sauter*:

> the creative act in mental evolution again reflects the pattern of <u>*reculer pour mieux sauter*</u>, of a temporary regression, followed by a forward leap. We can carry the analogy further and interpret the Eureka cry as the signal of a happy escape from a blind alley—an act of mental self-repair. (*GM* 211)

This characterisation of the creative act, stepping back to jump forward, is legible at both individual and broader socio-cultural levels, where it is brought about when an impasse is reached: Koestler refers to this as a challenge which 'may exceed a critical limit' (*GM* 201). It is important to emphasise that for Koestler and for Chadwick, such an impasse, and the creative response it precipitates, can occur within the ordinary run of anyone's day, and range through to the most significant biological evolutionary change or scientific breakthrough. The nature of the response to a critical limit is also important, as it distinguishes their respective understanding of the creative act from the slavish pursuit of disciplinary rules.

association and bisociation

Koestler develops his considerations of the impasse by introducing a process he refers to as *bisociation*, which he contrasts with unimpeded or 'orderly' thinking. While he recognises that orderly thinking can draw on a wide range of references and connections, ultimately this is a normative, rule-driven process. He stresses the difference between creative bisociation and normative association: 'the term "association" simply indicates the process by which one idea leads to another'. This difference was seized upon by Chadwick, and it is worth quoting Koestler's distinction at length to suggest why:

> [A]n idea has associative connections with many other ideas established by past experiences; and which of these connections will be activated in a given situation depends on the *type* of thinking we are engaged in at the moment. Orderly thinking is always rule-governed, and even dreaming, or daydreaming, has its own rules [...] Let me repeat: all routine thinking is comparable to playing a game to fixed rules and more or less flexible strategies. The game of chess allows for more varied strategies than draughts, a vaster number of choices among moves permitted by the rules. But there is a limit to them; and there are hopeless situations in chess when the most subtle strategies won't save you—short of offering your opponent a jumbo-sized Martini. Now, in fact, there is no rule in chess preventing you from doing that. But making a person drunk while remaining sober oneself is a different sort of game with a different context. Combining the two games is bisociation. In other words, associative routine means thinking according to a given set of rules on a single place, as it were. The bisociative act means combining two different sets of rules, to live on several planes at once. (*GM* 211, 213)

Chadwick highlights this last sentence, and it can be clearly understood to resonate both with her realised works and working process, where it animates the figure of The Juggler. As a process, Koestler's notion of bisociation provided her with a relevant and robust framework within which she could consider her work, although Koestler's own account of the creative process of the artist paradoxically serves as a kind of impasse that Chadwick in turn had to leap across. One aspect that Koestler emphasises over and again, and which Chadwick highlights, is its experimental quality, its essential capacity to work with existing stuff:

> The creative act does not create something out of nothing, like the God of the Old Testament; it combines, reshuffles and relates already existing but hitherto separate ideas, facts, frames of perception, associative contexts. This act of cross-fertilization—or self-fertilization within a single brain—seems to be the essence of creativity, and to justify the term 'bisociation'. (*GM* 214)

The creative process, the creative response to an impasse, involves a 'shaking together', a cross-fertilisation whose consequences stretch beyond the creative act or particular problem, by instigating a new frame of understanding that can bear on broader issues. Koestler emphasises this impact on our 'cognitive matrices': '*Bisociation means combining two hitherto unrelated cognitive matrices in such a way that a new level is added to the hierarchy, which contains the previously separate structures as its members*' (GM 213, original emphasis). In another of his books that Chadwick read around this time, Koestler emphasised these broader implications of the creative process:

> This operation of removing a problem from its traditional context and placing it in a new one, looking at it through glasses of a different colour as it were, has always seemed to me the very essence of the creative process. It leads not only to a revaluation of the problem itself, but often to a synthesis of much wider consequences, brought about by a fusion of the two previously unrelated frames of reference. (*SW* 341)

Alongside this paragraph Chadwick adds: 'i.e. my life + past:—with geometry and objects combined'. Although Chadwick's response to possible re-evaluative aspects of the bisociative act appears to be autobiographical (that these notes were taken during the preparation of *Ego Geometrica Sum* only reinforces this), her ambition to (re-)combine personal and collective memory, the abstract thought epitomised by Platonic geometry and the messiness of the everyday world of objects, pushes her own take on the creative artistic process beyond that understood by Koestler.

In a later marginal note to her copy of *The Sleepwalkers*, Chadwick considered her response to the creative combination of bisociation as 'combining apparently unassoc[iated] images'.[2] Although at face value this combination of images could appear tame, if we bear in mind her appreciation of the possibilities of bisociation and her broader ambition to 'resolve reality not [take] flight from it [...] Change relationship with reality – affect it' (2003.19/E/7.55) the potential for this combination should be taken seriously. Moreover, the combining of *apparently unassociated images* marks a divergence from Koestler, whose own account of the specifically artistic bisociative act frames it within a very traditional, medium-specific struggle for artistic expression: 'All creative activity is a kind of do-it-yourself therapy [...] In the artist's case, challenge and response are manifested in his [*sic*] tantalizing struggle to express the inexpressible, to conquer the resistance of his medium, to escape from the distortions and constraints imposed by the conventional styles and techniques of his time.' (*GM* 207)

Faced with this rather reductive account of the artist's role, Chadwick's own response can be understood to echo *reculer pour mieux sauter*, to draw back and acknowledge the fuller potential of bisociation before reformulating an account of the artistic process. The *combination of apparently unassociated images* emerges here as a significant issue; Chadwick's considerations of 'the image' permeate her œuvre, where they take on a central and complex role in her developing conception of the creative process. The demands placed on her conception of the image are many and various, and it is an issue that will come up on several occasions through later chapters of this book. At this point, it is important to stress that this charged understanding of 'the image' retained something of its mediating role, although the general equation where this mediation occurred between artist and audience, and occurred within a received framework of artistic meaning, was radically reformulated. To make the same point through the allegory of *Le Bateleur*, Chadwick's reconsideration of this creative figure no longer has a single person separated from an audience by a table, juggling baubles (making 'images'), but instead the image itself is taken as a composite, a combination where apparently unassociated images or issues are brought together—*bisociated*—and encountered in this uncombined, unsynthesised arrangement by an active, engaged audience. Rather than the 'tantalizing struggle to express the inexpressible', Chadwick approached the creative act as one that could pass on questions to those who encountered it. The possible revelation of presuppositions, the exposure of rules and paradoxes that such a creative process might involve, has significant consequences for both art and architecture.

In Chadwick's complex reformulation of the creative process, the image itself can be understood to carry, support and sustain the process. This is an issue she consistently wrestled with without ever resolving: the ingredients of her reconsiderations can be indicated in this extract from a notebook:

> Having fixed the body as object/subject of feeling
> →chance combinations around it that lend interpretation become <u>active</u> field around it. Not still + arrested at moment but sequences leaving path/traces behind. From single to multiple Static to Dynamic. Symbol→event.
> Energy not matter
> Away from static physicality/sensuality to dynamic.
> How? Light Caught.
> Image/object→Energy Field Actions
> Photocopies as electrons!
> Take chance as in photocopies

'arrested moment' of automatic / mechanical image
→action
'image' changed—series of actions/traces.
Self as <u>event</u> not <u>matter</u>
[...] Dissolution of boundaries of self→the dynamic potential probability
pattern
Self as particle
2003.19/E/7.52–1

While this indicates the increasing importance of considering the artistic
process alongside her reconsiderations of body, self, identity and audience,
the active, dynamic demands that Chadwick makes on the image are also
apparent. In what she refers to elsewhere as 'composite images', the interest
she invests in these is motivated by their potential to overcome the
limitations of the 'Newtonian/Platonic view of reality' that underlay a
general view that *buildings stronger than people.*

Veiling of image over form as in EGS [*Ego Geometria Sum*] freed from
'terrestrial' prison—liberates as a series of composite images (not even a
single instance as in a moment at which photograph is fixed...) →
Newtonian/Platonic view of reality as matter/mechanical model opened
into quantum mechanics—open dynamic, inter-related fixing of
occurrences as an 'image'
i.e. FICTIONS
2003.19/E/6.147

Her attention to composite, unassociated or bisociative images focused on
the dynamic potential that could open once 'static physicality' and 'matter'
were considered to be contingent rather than absolute. While such an image
is ambiguous and multivalent, the image's role within the creative process is
charged with passing on traces that link self, others and the world as an
event, combining *hitherto unrelated cognitive matrices in such a way that a new level
is added,* but added not to *the hierarchy* as Koestler had it, but as a straight
overplus that sustains questioning after the creative figure has passed it on.
The creative process where such an image plays a role can be grasped as
being more concerned to juggle with processes and rules than with (static)
objects per se. Indeed in many instances, it seems that Chadwick
considered rules *as objects*, and argued that they have as much or more
impact than tangible objects.

Chadwick's deliberations over the overlaps and interrelationships
between objects–rules–images bears witness to an awkwardness regarding
their easy definition; that this will have an impact for our grasp of process,
product and audience is clear, even if the actual consequences are not. To

reconsider *Le Bateleur* around this point can be taken to reiterate some of the principal assertions of the previous chapter regarding his deliberate juggling not only with the baubles on the table but with the systems and politics of understanding within which such objects were positioned. This situation can clearly have a significant impact on the ways in which an understanding of the architectural design process might be refocused away from the static object building and onto the broader relationship between creative persona and process. Moreover, to accept this role of the image has significant consequences, not only for the understanding of the creative process (event) but also for the creative figure: no longer are there clearly bounded individuals productive of and witness to the creative process, no longer are there clear ingredients on the table, and no longer is there a clear direction or institutional framework that such a process is obliged to follow. Chadwick was well aware of the implications of removing such commonly accepted certainties: although she sought an amelioration of conditions, she acknowledged that this could best occur through greater understanding of existing conditions and rules rather than starting *ex nihilo*.

Several difficulties related to this acknowledgement have been raised in a different context by the architectural historian and theorist Manfredo Tafuri (1935–94). These concern the relationship between creative and critical process, and their individual or combined relationship to institutional values; the status of an artistic object; the dynamics of the interrelationship between such an object and audience; and the role of history. Sidestepping and reformulating some of the difficulties Tafuri had to address, Chadwick's active creative process, and the composite image charged with mediating it, altered the relationship between work and audience, such that it might include both critical and creative aspects. The 'object' of art was absorbed neither into the institutional processes of modernity, nor into the audience; instead, she posited that these two might become more mutually self-installing, reciprocally presupposing. Here, the role of bisociation and composite image attempts to manoeuvre around some of the difficulties involved. Recall the following:

> →action
> 'image' changed—series of actions/traces.
> Self as <u>event</u> not <u>matter</u>

While this elliptical statement is short on detail, it successfully carries Chadwick's advocacy of an active process, one that enjoys (several) different viewing distances and directions. Of the many issues this *changed image* might mediate, of the many possible matrices, one that was particularly significant for Chadwick (as for Tafuri) was history. Chadwick's œuvre, more than those of many of her peers, opened onto a wide understanding of history, and enjoyed a creative rather than reverential or dismissive attitude towards it, such that its creative, bisociative combination with other ingredients was charged with posing questions rather than producing static form. As with many other issues on *The Juggler's Table*, 'History is only an *ingredient* to be manipulated'.[3] The Juggler's view is forwards not backwards, however much they might acknowledge historical materials.

While the manipulations of various ingredients are smeared across *actions/traces*, where they are intent on precipitating a multiple and dynamic concept of object-image and self-as-'event' where the distinction between creative figure and audience becomes blurred, these two roles are not conflated. As Tafuri notes around this same issue, the artistic process aims to 'plan' events, to combine critical understanding of past and present situations for immediate consumption. The process leading to events of immediate consumption anticipates Chadwick's interest in bisociation, a guiding framework for which was offered by Koestler's *total pattern*.

creative process and *total pattern*

Chadwick was mindful of the need not to conflate the creative figure with the spectator (or with the scientist), and acknowledged the demands this placed on her work. She borrowed one response from Koestler's *The Sleepwalkers*, where she indicates his notion of *total pattern* provides a reasonable account of her installations.

> A whole is defined by the pattern of relations between its parts, not by the sum of its parts; and a civilisation is not defined by the sum of its science, technology, art, and social organisation, but by the total pattern which they form, and the degree of harmonious integration in that pattern. (*SW* 527)[4]

The importance for Chadwick was that the various ingredients just discussed were not synthesised or sublimated into a unified whole, but rather that they remained legible on their own terms while contributing to an equally legible *total pattern*. As a description of her installations, the motivation in passing on this *total pattern* rather than a sum total was to provide the spectator with a variable, invigorating environment. Chadwick's hope, clearly relevant for architectural environments and their impact upon human identity more broadly, was that the experience of *total pattern* would instigate or encourage a wider variety of responses than those possible in environments represented by her early work such as *Model Institution* and *Train of Thought*. As she wrote in a later essay: 'Take these works as clues to the value of ambivalence, of doubling, of a leap across' (*WD* 73). Such a leap reflects her hopes for the creative process, where this includes the actions of both the artist (or architect) and the spectator or user: it reflects her perception of a need to plunge under the broken surface of contemporary practice, and links this to the particular direction of her own plunge, where spectators were encouraged, empowered, to leap across from prescribed responses in order to regain something of the 'strength' previously claimed by static objects and buildings. The leap across draws together both the creative figure and the user, it draws together the need for and potential of bisociative acts with the potential of *total pattern*.

The governing characteristic of *total pattern* as Chadwick adopts this from Koestler is its ability to accommodate differences, to maintain the gaps and interstices that sustain any person's engagement and response. The desire for 'harmonious integration' that inscribes difference, for gaps that encourage and accommodate subjective qualities into the experience of the world, was characteristic of both Koestler and Chadwick and a key part of their *total patterns*, however much their interpretations diverge. Any desire for harmony can be understood more clearly by asking what it was not: namely, a narrowly scientific world-view, where value is mediated through a quantitative understanding of nature.

Koestler's hero in this respect is Kepler, his villain is Galileo: the latter is charged with 'reducing all nature to "size, figure, number, and slow or rapid motion," and by relegating into the limbo or "subjective" or "secondary" qualities everything that cannot be reduced to these elements—including, by implication, ethical values, and the phenomena of the mind' (*SW* 535). In contrast, Kepler's *Harmony of the World* (1618) was the last attempt at an 'all-embracing synthesis of geometry, music, astrology, and epistemology' (*SW* 394–5).

Although Chadwick's adoption of harmony within *total pattern* would look forwards rather than backwards, it would share this role as a counter to any fragmentation of experience and instrumentalisation of response, a counter to any attempt to divide the world into 'primary' and 'secondary' qualities. It is important to stress, in contrast to conventional overtones of 'harmony' as something nice or agreeable, anodyne and inoffensive, Kepler–Koestler's harmony involves 'the most astonishing […] mixture of cleanness and uncleanness' (*SW* 339–40). The operative potential and quality of *total pattern* in fact depends on this mixture, reiterating and extending the demands put upon the bisociative act, and it is in this mix that the detail and breadth of Chadwick's conception can be approached. In preparatory notes for a conference address in Japan, she explores issues that relate to this mixture and which can clarify their fit into a broader understanding of *total pattern*: in particular here, the complex role of *the in-*

between reinforces the close association in her thought between issues raised above regarding the creative process and those relating to identity and experience.

> ④ About <u>the in-between</u>: exchange, contact between 2, between difference, which is an erotic condition. Both 2+1—embraces difference of gender, motion inside/outside. Skin as frame, image as innards
> ⑤ Technique also "between" Object/image: i.e. body—status of being Objects—a kind of libidinal materialism
> 2003.19/E/8.55

This *in-between*, understood in the present context as in-between within *total pattern*, is set up to contest any approach that could perpetuate binary opposites, and can stand as a manifesto both for her own creative process and for her expectations of spectatorial experience. The *in-between* complements an earlier note she made, where she summarised her working process as a *creative + manipulative theft*.

> A creative + manipulative theft [...]
> *figures both object + subject.
> exist as feeling itself+ remainder of feeling
> seen both from within and without.
> 2003.19/E/6.124

Around these notes, the figure of The Juggler can be recombined with the considerations of the creative process opened up here. In particular, the complex identity of The Juggler—recall this was traditionally a character flaw of *Le Bateleur*—is in part a consequence of a genuine multiple, schizoid make up. While the creative persona might initiate or plan an 'event' (and while this creative persona might already be multiple, literally a collaborative group rather than a single individual, particularly relevant for architectural production), the *in-between* that is sought in the *total pattern* of whatever it is that is produced (again, this is complex, an ambiguous object-image or installation) contributes to the extension of The Juggler's identity by continuing the creative process through the various kinds of exchange that it aims to set up. The identity of the creative persona is never complete and always potentially multiple, *both 2+1*.

Successful juggling demands the harmonious mixture of clean and dirty, the production of a *total pattern* that not only includes a variety of everyday baubles traditionally used by *Le Bateleur*, but also inscribes the wider connotations of these baubles raised in the previous chapter, combined as different and potentially competing systems of understanding, knowledge and power, *seen both from within and without*. While The Juggler knowingly steals from the past, this creative, manipulative recombination moves the variety of stolen goods beyond autonomous object status, and instead attempts to revitalise their relevance for the present. The ability to see from a variety of situations simultaneously is a demand on The Juggler, but this is also passed on as an opportunity to those encountering such work.

While Chadwick was confident that her installation work might realise *total pattern* and the various significant issues it involved, the possibility that this might in turn provide a way to reconsider architectural practice must be approached more carefully. As has already been suggested, the figure of *Le Bateleur* can provide an allegory for the architect. The issues that can be unpacked across *Le Bateleur* cover more or less the whole Vitruvian shopping list of what an architect should be able to do (including micro-macro considerations, theoretical and practical understanding of geometry, astronomy, medicine, the law, society and so on). Whatever the promise of *total pattern*, it bears a strong similarity to very traditional accounts of the discipline. To return to Tafuri's considerations of the difficulties involved in renegotiating the relationships between the object of the creative process, the audience, history and the role of the institution, he warns that 'what is specific to architecture is the way of relating the various structures [functional, technological, symbolic, geometrical and so on] that converge in it. And this constitutes, not by chance, the problem of architectural theories, from Vitruvius's to the treatises of the nineteenth century.'[5]

The most important issue to arise through the explorations undertaken in Part One is the need for the subjects of both chapters to be taken together. If this doesn't happen, if *total pattern* is not taken simultaneously as a motif for the persona of the architect *and* the process of architecture, then its promise will reduce back into a quasi-Vitruvian conception. *Total pattern* needs to be considered by architects as part of a broader epistemological shift, within which buildings continue to figure but with an altered status; the planning of architecture, akin to Chadwick's operations regarding planning events, needs to extend beyond the built object to not only include but pass on the *creative and manipulative theft*, so that the user of the environment becomes part of the creative process. The architectural 'whole' can be reconsidered through this new notion of 'whole' as *total pattern*, informed by Chadwick's reconsideration of self as event.

Chadwick's own interest in architectural rules developed through her reading of Boullée's *Architecture: Essay on Art*; her advocacy of a *clean+dirty* mixture within the harmony of *total pattern* was in part informed by Boullée's own attack on Vitruvius. Boullée's dispute with Vitruvius centred on the latter's overbearingly reductive, practical approach to the discipline. As the title of his *Essay* indicates, Boullée advocated a wider approach to architecture as art, not as a simply practical subject. Chadwick's reading of

Boullée follows her own advice, and as a *creative + manipulative theft* its impact on the *total pattern* of her thinking produces several unexpected results. While some of these, particularly their relevance for her lengthy considerations of geometry, will not be addressed until later, Boullée's epistemological assumptions regarding both nature and geometry play an important role in Chadwick's theoretical understanding of the politics of viewing, which will be discussed, along with her work on the body and identity politics, in Part Two.

Part Two: Experience, architecture and identity

3   Body and self

One of Chadwick's principal complaints against architecture concerned the ways in which this had come to control relationships between body and space, played out crudely in her early projects such as *Model Institution*. As these concerns developed, they became clearly associated with one of her most significant and best-known strands of realised work, which explored the heuristic possibilities of art in the context of identity politics. Her radical reappraisals of both Cartesian dualism and autonomy, undertaken with reference to the insights of modern science as much as to psychoanalysis and philosophy, can have significant consequences for our understanding of the relationship between users and architecture.

Chadwick's dissatisfaction with prevailing conceptions of the relationship between body and world gathered up a number of significant and complex factors, but a fairly clear motif for her dissatisfaction can be provided by the illustrations of *Train of Thought* she published in the journal *AMBIT*. Across this range of factors, these illustrations demonstrate the broad tendency towards the simplification and instrumentalisation of this relationship. The body was reduced to a formal set of mathematical descriptions, its interaction with the environment was mechanised, and the role of individuality, memory, gender, sexuality, and nature in identity formation was denied. Faced with this situation, which she felt was particularly acute within the built environment, Chadwick's response can again be described as *reculer pour mieux sauter*. In this case, her leap forward was informed by a range of work from disparate areas: although identity politics was clearly a common cause amongst several fairly established disciplines by the time Chadwick was working, her own theoretical position cannot be simply aligned with any one of the various schools of thought then on offer.

A fairly clear idea of Chadwick's concerns and hopes for the role of the body in personal and collective identity, experience and epistemology comes through in some notes she made in her copy of Francis Barker's *The*

Tremulous Private Body: Essays on Subjection [1984]. Barker's book provided Chadwick with an opportunity to step back and consider the role played by the body in seventeenth-century society, through which she could reformulate its potential for a contemporary situation. As Chadwick noted inside the back cover:

> body from secret half-life of contemp. social order to spectacular materiality—stage—place of danger/aspiration.
>
> the body as <u>site</u> not object
> between subject and object
> yearns to the ideal—not
> ideological ie. concerned with
> values/moralities
> process discovery –invention
> not analysis.
>
> Marina – in "Nature" section
>   =look at in terms <u>Materiality</u>
>   Corporeal reality

Chadwick's allusion to a 'secret half-life' refers to a key distinction that Barker makes between the Cartesian and the earlier body; the latter lay 'athwart that divide between subject and object, discourse and world' (*TPB* 24). Barker's text maps the significant redefinition of the body that occurred during the course of the seventeenth century, such that its role changed profoundly from that of spectacular, public corporeality towards the 'privatised' and 'sexually embarrassing body' of modernity, where it was 'pushed away from discourse into a furtive half-life beyond the text'. Arguably, Barker's point that this mode of corporeality not only provided an index of social order, but also reflected prevailing epistemological values and authority, has a certain currency today.[1] As Chadwick's notes suggest, her ambition to reinvigorate the role of the body, to shift it out of its 'furtive, private half-life' into 'spectacular materiality', engages with a similar range of issues. Moreover, her approach to the body as *site not object* can be linked with another passage from Barker's text in order to introduce in more detail the particular issues she would go on to consider, and that will be addressed in this chapter and the next. Barker writes, and Chadwick highlights:

> However necessary it may be to isolate the body for analytic purposes, the body in question is not a hypostatized object, still less a simple biological mechanism of given desires and needs acted on externally

by controls and enticements, but a relation in a system of liaisons which are material, discursive, psychic, sexual, but without stop or centre. (*TPB* 12)

Chadwick's conception of the body shares much with Barker's account here, such that the body as *site not object* can be understood to be the site of Barker's relations, a site no longer defined primarily by the physical boundary of the body but as an a-centric, boundless field, although the particular development of Chadwick's understanding and her attempts to grant this field coherence was unique. Chadwick did share Barker's interest in earlier conceptions of the body—indeed, Chadwick's interest was in many ways more wide-ranging and eclectic—and was motivated to reflect on earlier understanding, which situated the body 'athwart that divide' just noted. Although this situation was of interest to both, this interest was academic; neither was advocating a return to this early conception, but both were concerned instead with considering how the role of the body is caught up in any world-view, and how in particular the various 'relations' that contributed to the contemporary view might be altered to improve relations between selves and worlds.

While mindful of and interested in conceptions of the body prior to its 'isolation' during modernity, Chadwick's considerations of the body were undertaken as part of her broader concerns with how to articulate the world in its post-mechanistic world-view. Where Barker's historical analysis untangles the consequences of a seventeenth-century paradigm shift, Chadwick's approach was to question what the body might be, given more recent shifts. Indeed, the reduction of body to object belonged to an earlier, mechanistic-modern paradigm; Chadwick instead asked of the implications of the modern sciences. At its most concise and enigmatic, the interface between self and world involved:

> Unification + dissolution not separation
> No subject/object   viewer/viewed
> both encapsulated in itself
> 2003.19/E/7.54

In a passage from the same notebook, she spells out her interest in extending the consideration of the body 'from Xian curse to new physics: theories relativity/probability'. Chadwick's œuvre demonstrates an ongoing and ultimately unresolved preoccupation with 'new physics': whereas much reception of her work highlights its potential for psychoanalytic and feminist reading (although the latter divided opinion at the time of the work), I want to argue that these were important ingredients within what was actually a broader attempt to address the potential impact of modern science on epistemology, on the way in which this might have an impact on our everyday involvement with the world. Chadwick's attention was clearly on the dynamic potential that opens once 'static physicality' and 'matter' are considered to be contingent rather than absolute:

> Having fixed the body as object/subject of feeling
> →chance combinations around it that lend interpretation become <u>active</u>
> field around it. Not still + arrested at moment but sequences leaving
> path/traces behind. From single to multiple   Static   to   Dynamic.
>   Symbol→event.
> Energy not matter
> Away from static physicality/sensuality to dynamic.
>
> How? Light Caught.
> Image/object→Energy Field Actions
>
> Photocopies as electrons!
> Take chance as in photocopies
> 'arrested moment' of automatic / mechanical image
>
> →action
> 'image' changed—series of actions/traces.
> Self as <u>event</u> not <u>matter</u>
> [...] Dissolution of boundaries of self→the dynamic potential probability
> pattern
>
> Self as particle
> 2003.19/E/7.52–1

While this passage was discussed earlier in terms of Chadwick's conception of the creative process, the terminology she uses echoes both Barker's notion of body as a 'relation in a system of liaisons without stop or centre', and draws more broadly on quantum mechanics as a metaphor for the body and as a framework within which creative process and interpretation occur. Replacing body as object, so long the principal metaphor for architecture, with a quantum conception that holds body as active field offers a chance to consider the metaphoric, theoretical and praxis-based impact on architecture both as a metaphor for epistemology, and as a practice.

Given this background to her approach to the body as site, Chadwick's specific theorisation of the body can be explored in terms of three 'challenges' she hoped to pose through her work. She identified these challenges in some lecture notes prepared towards the end of her career:

> body
> →challenge notions identity + selfhood
> body as site of sovereign singular experience
> integrity bodily boundaries
> gender as a single true sex
> Transgress boundaries + hierarchies static singular self + static singular sex
>> pose new possibilities [...]
>> →vagrancy: [...] (vagrant self)
>> →ambivalence + doubling: [...] (ambivalent + doubled self)
>> →bi-sexual indifference: *Piss flowers*
>> →liquid viscous conscious dynamics of *Cacao*. Identity as a
> "chemochanical" organic gel
> VL [*Viral Landscapes*]: simultaneously of inside /outside; self/ other
> HMI Box 19 (Chadwick, lecture notes) 'Coventry 9.5.94'

boundaries and mixing, indeterminacy

Although Chadwick's first (and foremost) challenge was to the *body as site of sovereign singular experience*, it is difficult to approach this directly. Instead, her second and third challenges will be examined together here, as they help to clarify the complaint Chadwick raised against structures that maintained conceptions of body as object. While such structures had developed from a variety of historical periods and issues, Chadwick's broad complaint was against the impact they had on self and identity, reducing these, through the role that bodies play here, towards states of homogeneity. Her interest in situations that could not be made to conform to such simplified states influenced her conception of body as site, and her understanding of the body's role within and relationship to much broader epistemological systems. In particular, she held an enduring interest in hermaphrodites and Siamese twins, both situations that had a long history of raising difficult questions for systems that desired easy classification: 'The between: inside/out; hermaphrodite; Siamese twin' (2003.19/E/8.57). As Chadwick highlighted in her copy of Stephen Jay Gould's *The Flamingo's Smile*, these situations could not conform because the questions that were asked of them were wrong:

> We inhabit a complex world. Some boundaries are sharp and permit clean and definite distinctions. But nature also includes continua that cannot be neatly parcelled into two piles of unambiguous yeses and

noes [...] Ritta and Christina lay in the middle of another unbreakable continuum. They are in part two and in part one. And this, I am sorry to say, is the biological nonanswer to the question of the centuries. If this argument leaves you with an empty feeling after so much verbiage, I can only reply with the paradoxical phrase that is, so often, the most liberating response to an old mystery: The question has no answer because you asked the wrong question. The old question of individuality in Siamese twinning rests upon the assumption that objects can be pigeonholed into discrete categories. If we recognise that our world is full of irreducible continua, we will not be troubled by the intermediate status of Ritta and Christina. (*FS* 76–7)[2]

For Chadwick, the relevance of such examples commonly referred to as 'freaks' or 'monsters' was that while their usual exclusion from categories of bodily 'normality' allowed the questions they raised to be sidelined, to recognise the 'irreducible continua' that they demand would have a fundamental impact on self-identity. This emphasised the problem of reducing conceptions of the body to that of object, with the associated tendencies that attempted to define a 'perfect' form or common measure. As Georges Bataille noted in this context, 'each individual form escapes [the] common measure and is, to a certain degree, a monster'.[3] Even at the level of body-object, we all raise the questions of Ritta and Christina. Although Bataille's analysis stems from systems that operated only with physiognomic form, Chadwick's reading of Bataille pushes this towards more general aspects of *personal incongruity*:

> Bataille
> <u>Monsters</u> 'a source of malaise' Personal incongruity – elements of monstrous.
> Dialectical opposites of geometric regularity in an irreducible way.
> 2003.19/E/8.98

To acknowledge *personal incongruity* demands the acceptance of the irreducible continua as part of our own make up, as part of our 'self-definition'. Gould's essay just cited goes on to reiterate this consequence and emphasise its impact: 'The old paradox addresses an issue that could not be more fundamental—<u>the definition of an organism and the general question of boundaries in nature</u>' (*FS* 79). In the margin at this point, Chadwick adds VL [*Viral Landscape*], a reference to a project that exemplified the extent of the irreducible continua as Chadwick saw this. Associated notes on the conceptual position so legible in this project include other examples of continua; examining the cathartic potential of creative acts on an everyday, individual level, she related Koestler's account of moments when there might be a shared desire:

> to transcend the island boundary of the individual, to enter into a symbiotic communion with a human being, living or dead, or some higher entity, real or imaginary, of which the self is felt to be a part [...] The very young child [...] is aware of events, but not of itself as a separate entity. It lives in a state of mental symbiosis with the outer world [...] The universe is focused on the self, and the self *is* the universe—a condition which Piaget called 'protoplasmic' or 'symbiotic' consciousness. It may be likened to a fluid universe, traversed by the tidal rise and fall of psychological needs, and by minor storms which come and go without leaving traces. (*GM* 222)[4]

A parallel to Chadwick's interest in Siamese twins was her frequent return to examples of hermaphrodites. Her marginal notes to Michel Foucault's introduction to a book on the famous case of the hermaphrodite Herculine Barbin, while clearly reiterating some of the issues raised by Ritta and Christina, do more to position the impact of this example as part of a wider question of authority and the control of knowledge, rather than remaining as 'simply' biological issues. Foucault writes: 'Biological theories of sexuality, juridical conceptions of the individual, forms of administrative control in modern nations, led little by little to rejecting the idea of a mixture of the two sexes in a single body, and consequently to limiting the free choice of indeterminate individuals. Henceforth, everybody was to have one and only one sex' (*HB* viii). Chadwick highlights this paragraph, and writes in the margin 'to crush the value of indeterminacy'. While this term arises within Foucault's discourse, it is also one that Chadwick highlighted in texts on quantum mechanics. In both situations, its attraction for her lay in the particular impact on epistemology that was brought about by modern science, one that could be associated with her emerging conception of body as site. Regarding this particular example of hermaphrodites, as with the other 'monstrous' category of Siamese twins, Chadwick believed that hermaphroditic characteristics are shared to a greater or lesser extent by everyone. The push and pull of the two sexes across the site of the body situate that body within what Chadwick later referred to as 'patterns of potentiality', where the notion of sovereign identity based on the certainty of accepted truths is replaced with a contingent identity established across a complex vector of forces. While this contingent, ambiguous notion of identity and selfhood was one that Chadwick became increasingly confident about, her œuvre wrestled with some of the difficulties of gaining acceptance for this notion in everyday situations and across a wide audience. Within these considerations, the traditionally accepted stability and certainty of bodily form was called into question, a move that in turn can be understood to have an impact on considerations of architectural form and identity.

> Gender as a leaky, dissipative + viscous sensibility.
> form as a temporary stability in patterns of potentiality + flow, not fixed + given [...]
> Body as trophy has become the body as a libidinous garden.
> HMI Box 19 (Chadwick Lecture Notes)—Handwritten notes for a lecture 'Trophies to Ambivalence: to the value of a doubtful status' Glarus—1.7.95.[5]

To accept bodily form as temporary stability rather than as *fixed + given* would have a significant impact on conceptions of selfhood. As Chadwick suggests elsewhere, the dynamic understanding she sought would be brought about in part by providing a number of points of view that could be occupied simultaneously by the same self, bringing about the liberating dissolution of object boundaries and the bonds that these have traditionally placed on notions of identity:

> seen from within, without
> felt from inside
> not image of object of gaze
> self looking + feeling at self feeling towards dissolution of self not to capture another's gaze but <u>dissolve boundaries</u> – not subject the self to be object for another's consumption but mirror of own nature/desires
> 2003.19/E/7.54

The impact not only on our conception of the body but also on prior certainties of knowledge cannot be overstated. The most familiar thing we have, our own body, becomes an excessive site, 'a libidinous garden', that will always evade our grasp. The feminist theorist Elizabeth Grosz writes of a closely related point in terms that, like Chadwick, try to reassure us that this evasion is empowering:

> we don't know what a body is because a body is always in excess of our knowing it. It is always in excess of any representation, and indeed, of all representations. This is part of Deleuze's point: that we don't know what a body can do, for the body is the outside of thought, which doesn't mean that it is unthinkable but that we approach it in thought without fully grasping it [...] This ignorance is pervasive.[6]

Chadwick emphasised that it is precisely across this field that identity must be sought, while recognising that it will henceforth be haunted by the imminent threat of collapse: 'a possibility for beginning to look at identity and the conditions where it destabilises and threatens to collapse' (*WD* 69). Grosz again is clear on the implications this concept of identity has on notions of agency, and issues a warning against those who take this notion of self as site as a kind of laissez-faire invitation to be whatever 'you want to be'.

> Your identity is changing all the time, but it's you who is being changed rather than you who is the agent of that change. We are effects more than causes [...] It would be nice to be able to choose an identity, but in fact it is chosen for us. Our agency comes from how we accept that designated position, and the degree to which we refuse it, the way we live it out.[7]

It is important to consider Grosz's warning here; our agency is exercised most fully around the knowing balance—we might say juggling—between the acceptance and refusal of the forces that contribute to identity. Throughout her œuvre, Chadwick considered a number of different aspects to such agency, all of which related to or could be understood around the framework of body as site. Her expressed interest in conditions when identity destabilises can be brought together with Grosz's notion of agency, in particular the opportunities that might arise for both accepting and refusing *body-as-site* as a potential counter to the strength of buildings. Indeed, Chadwick's general attitude toward the potential of agency became more upbeat, due in large part to this ongoing reconfiguration of her conception of identity politics. This suggested ways to counter the Newtonian strength of buildings by providing a clearer understanding of how and where architecture might operate, identifying more effective tactics and strategies for contesting architecture's traditional role in policing identity formation. Although her projects themselves clearly differ as much as the way she theorised the interface between the self and environment, she was consistently seeking ways in which to encourage and expand the potential for fuller interaction and exchange to occur around this locus (the body, however defined) and across the interface, the *Triplet*.

construct 'thing'

In the margin of her copy of Julia Kristeva's *Black Sun: Depression and Melancholia*, Chadwick leaves a note to herself; *construct 'Thing'*. This raises further questions regarding the relationships that might pertain between the self and objects in the world. Kristeva's distinction between object and

'*Thing*' drew Chadwick's attention, and she held this up as something that would inform the production of her work.

The particular bit of Kristeva's text that precipitates this discussion is as follows: 'The depressed narcissist mourns not an Object but the Thing. Let me posit the "Thing" as the real that does not lend itself to signification, the centre of attraction and repulsion, seat of the sexuality from which the object of desire will become separated' (*BS* 13).[8]

Although Chadwick's interest in Kristeva's work is perhaps unsurprising, given her interest in notions of self and the role of boundaries therein (or thereon), there remain some significant difficulties in her attempt to take this on so directly. What is it to *construct* '*Thing*'? Could architecture as object simply be replaced by architecture as '*Thing*', and for whom would this bring a benefit? Although *Black Sun* gathers several essays that explore the relationship between melancholia and the creative process, it is important to draw out the potential impact upon the reception of such work as much as on the creative figure, and the extent to which it is either desirable or possible for architecture to *mean*. As questions, some of these may sound counterintuitive, reductive even, but they mark a moment when the ability of Chadwick's work to step back, then jump forward towards architecture's involvement in the construction of identity, must be examined.

In a way that echoes Chadwick's interest in 'freaks' and 'monsters', one of the important qualities of melancholy that Kristeva notes near the beginning of her book is, following Aristotle, that it is natural, and not a sign of disease or illness as it has come to be understood. Their interest in this concept lies, broadly put, in its ability to 'assume [...] a "properly balanced diversity" [...] The melancholia he [Aristotle] evokes is not a philosopher's disease but his very nature, his *ethos*' (*BS* 7). Although neither wants to restore this classical version, they do share an interest in regarding it as something within everyone's make up, as one of the forces that contribute to and are balanced across the *body-as-site*. Chadwick emphasises in the margin at this point: 'melancholy as philosophical nature—a balance not a sickness'.

Indeed, it is around the particular kind of balance that Chadwick's interest in Kristeva's *Black Sun* can be pursued: for here, the balance is neither static nor rational, it is a balancing, a process, announcing an opportunity to shake up our received understanding of the world and, returning to Elizabeth Grosz's suggestion, to exercise our agency by deciding how much to accept that received understanding, and how much to refuse it. It is around this balance that Kristeva's distinction between object and thing is introduced. In a long note that Chadwick highlights at this point, Kristeva refers to a gap that can open between thing and observer where this kind of exercise of agency might occur. Kristeva spells out the difference around this exercise: 'following upon Freud's shaking up rational certainties, I shall speak of the *Thing* as being the "something" that, seen by the already constituted subject looking back, appears as the unspecified, the unseparated, the elusive, even in its determination of actual sexual matter. I shall restrict the term *Object* to the space-time constant that is verified by a statement uttered by a subject in control of that statement' (*BS* 262n.7).[9]

Rereading, or perhaps misreading, this distinction in specifically architectural ways might again raise the question what is it to *construct 'Thing'*? Indeed, can '*Thing*' be constructed at all, and if so by whom? The traditional claim and ambition of the architect would be to construct *Object*, such that they already enjoy full subjectivity and not only 'utter' constant or consistent meaning, but in doing so set out to control how others ought to understand that statement. Chadwick was clearly mindful not only of the long history of architectural attempts at control, but also of the futility of trying directly to attack the architectural object. Having acknowledged this, the challenge of *constructing 'Thing'* must address the potential coexistence of *Thing* and *Object*.

This potential coexistence has a profound impact on the assumptions made regarding the emergence, development and constancy of meaning, far more than on the architectural *Object* per se: putting this more generally, in a way as to link to some of Chadwick's broader ambitions, it has a profound impact on the architecture of architecture, on the assumed framework of how meaning works, and architecture's role as both a metaphor for and an object within that framework. Reiterating the importance of Chadwick's interest in and repeated forays back to earlier periods of history, and notably her explorations of various configurations of metaphoric link that have previously between body and building and world, the impact of this *thing–object* coexistence is felt on the particular revised cosmology within which human and architectural bodies find or more pro-actively position themselves.

Although Chadwick's interest in this metaphor led to significant and disparate strands of research during her career, it must be emphasised that this interest arose from her particular political concerns regarding experience and identity. With this principal motivation in mind, it can be suggested that the foregoing issues are related around the conception of agency, such that *agency is the process that negotiates between thing and object across the body as site*. Although such negotiation can be related to and informed by previous cosmologies and associated architecture–body metaphors, the particular notion of agency as this emerges within Chadwick's œuvre demands the significant transformation of such metaphors to acknowledge the role of the thing.

There are various dimensions of this suggestion that need to be clarified. Or rather, accepting that the very nature of the body understood as site rather than object posits it as boundless, contingent and ambiguous, such that the 'dimensions' of any particular body are countless, a number of particular questions can be addressed in order to clarify significant dimensions at play in this process of agency. Echoing the distinction made by Tafuri between *co-authoring* and *planning*, the relevance of such agency to the everyday experience of architecture, on one hand, and to the work and responsibilities of the architect, on the other, will be different. Chadwick made a number of suggestions that attempted to articulate how these developing concepts of agency and body politics were relevant to and might have an impact on her own artistic production or 'planning'.

The emergence of these questions, the importance and difficulties of *constructing 'Thing'*, link more broadly with Chadwick's criticisms of rationalism, and particularly to situations where priority is given to the measurable. To measurable objects, and particularly the static object of architecture, there is a corollary in the normalised, measurable and controlled body; to repeat Grosz's warning, it is naïve to hope that these controls can simply be made to disappear. The challenge for agency is to operate within and against such constraints. In this context, 'Thing' becomes a co-requisite of fuller agency, emerging along with the uncertainty of body that Chadwick sought. Despite the realism and apparent modesty of such demands, her approach to and contesting of measure was not to replace previous systems with another, but to challenge the belief and value-system attached to measure *per se*, and instead to value that which was beyond measure. Indeed, Chadwick's conception was that agency operates across a field that is able to not only accommodate but also to be organised around difference. In much the same way that her approach to the creative process developed as a *total pattern* that enjoyed a harmony involving *the most astonishing [...] mixture of cleanness and uncleanness*, the field through which agency operates is similarly heterogeneous, patchy, riddled with gaps, and enjoys harmonious difference as first principle and not just as liberal concession within an otherwise stable, measurable and regulated world.

With these demands in mind, there must be serious doubts about whether *'Thing'* can be constructed at all, in any coherent or stable sense, by the artist or architect. Instead of answering this doubt directly, it is helpful to introduce a number of architectural issues from the early modern period that interested Chadwick. In addition to the significant shift in world-view that occurred during the seventeenth and eighteenth centuries, including the move to what Barker referred to as 'the tremulous private body', architectural theory and practice also enjoyed significant changes that addressed the figure of the body and the role of experience.

While such changes took place for complex reasons, two significant factors can be singled out here: the influence of the Newtonian account of the universe and the Cartesian account of the human mind and body, which if taken together have arguably provided the most enduring measures for the 'modern' period. Chadwick had an ongoing though awkward interest in both Newtonian physics and Cartesian dualism; her notion of the body as site, and her aim to *construct 'Thing'*, can be understood to contest both of these enduring measures. While both these accounts, in their own ways, contributed to the 'mechanisation' of the body, the impact on architecture was that previous cosmologies, within which the body played a central role, began to unravel; as architectural theorist Alberto Pérez-Gómez has argued, architecture consequently began to lose its ability to act as a link between microcosm and macrocosm, between body and universe.[10] Chadwick had no intention to reinstate earlier cosmologies, although she was drawn to examine and champion these sorts of big questions. Her particular interest in the change from a pre-rational to rational understanding of the universe is another example of her tendency *reculer pour mieux sauter*. Her jump forward carried with it a range of potentially contradictory characteristics gathered from the early modern era, though these are recombined or inform a very different kind of cohesion, most importantly a cohesion where authority has most clearly moved. Chadwick's approach to the *body-as-site*, and the operation of agency that this underwrote particularly with respect to the body's engagement with its environment, reinforced what for her was the contemporary relevance of both cosmology and bodily metaphor.

movement and senses

Whatever the extent of apparent similarities between the eighteenth century and our current situation, Chadwick was clearly drawn back to the significance, and particularly the architectural ideas and realised projects, of this period. Of relevance in the present context are the responses of architects to what we might call the demise of architectural authority as this had traditionally been vested in the figures of either divinities or the ancients. As an alternative world-view was gradually established, these traditional quasi-natural authorities faced competition from suggestions that architectural meaning might be culturally determined.

Sidestepping the complexities of this process, the opportunities opened up for those accepting the influence of the cultural over the natural led to an apparent rise in interest in the notion of the embodied inhabitant as a generating or ordering principle for architecture. Whereas the role of the human body had previously been central to the mediation of divine authority through architectural means, this body was only present as an idealised object. While the ability of this body-object to act as an ordering principle able to hold together such cosmic rationale (by providing a tangible link between microcosm and macrocosm) cannot be denied historically, it simultaneously acted as a brake on any kind of agency. As Chadwick's exploration of Siamese twins emphasised, the traditional adoption of such an ideal body-object as measure sets every person up as irreducibly monstrous, the *dialectical opposites of geometric regularity*, such that our self-perception is set as *a source of malaise* rather than agency.

The emerging eighteenth-century view seized the opportunity to replace this body-as-object with a version that emphasised the individual experience of architecture, although in practice the opportunity thus provided was limited to those who practised architecture or were well-enough positioned in intellectual circles to influence what might be accepted as the criteria for architectural practice. Moreover, the apparent potential for individual experience to be just that—individual and personal—was limited by the prescription of certain rules governing that experience; these rules, of 'Taste', were inequitably stacked in favour of those with sufficient social standing to be conversant with the rules in the first place. Nevertheless, the influence of sensualist philosophy in the eighteenth century, and its impact upon and role within what became known as 'architectural character', interested Chadwick. In particular, the various anomalies and contradictions surrounding 'architectural character' influenced her thinking on *body-as-site* and experience.

Architectural theorist and historian Louise Pelletier has explored aspects of this change in world-view in her book *Architecture and Words*, where she refers to a number of the contradictions that architectural theory and practice grappled with. 'Eighteenth-century architects began to explore the expressive power of architecture as the product of a *personal*, culture-specific imagination, but struggled to maintain its shared language so as to preserve its sense of purpose and "meaning".'[11] Although Pelletier's book gives a good general account of the replacement of the cosmic rationale for ordering architecture with that of an embodied inhabitant or observer, and thus of the valorisation of the role of the senses that occurred during this period, her work is particularly helpful in this context as her discussion is framed through a detailed examination of how certain architects approached theatre architecture, both in practice and in unrealised projects, in design and theory, as a device that itself might frame and contribute to the narrative cohesion of its occupants' experience.

Through the changing approaches to theatre design, Pelletier opens up issues concerning the experience of architecture that echo Chadwick's concerns and can be related to the latter's interest in *constructing 'Thing'*. Although historically non-coincident, Pelletier's selected focus on the late eighteenth-century theatrical experience raises similar issues to Francis Barker's *Tremulous Private Body*. As Pelletier argues, there remained at this point some ambiguity between stage and audience, some possibility for the audience to become involved in the action, to become actors themselves.

Widening her examination of the architecture of the theatre and its relationship with spectatorial experience, Pelletier traces the development of similar ideas (in tandem with the acceptance of role-playing in society) through architectural theory, novels and real architectural devices in order to explore the possible links between 'architectural character' and its influence on inhabitants. Like the better-known theories of Boullée and Ledoux, Pelletier's main protagonist, Le Camus de Mézières, sought to involve spectators in the completion of the architectural work. As well as expanding the role of the body beyond that of object, such an approach clearly moves the conception of architecture beyond that of the built object.

Before I discuss Chadwick's direct engagement with Boullée in the next chapter, it is worth exploring some of the general issues concerning 'architectural character' in more detail. While a similar interest in the role of the senses and in movement are directly legible in her realised œuvre, such issues—inasmuch as they played a part in architectural character—point at how this anticipates the problem that Chadwick grappled with, in terms of what part any of these might or ought to play in both our physical and conceptual 'construction' of the world, and how this might strike a balance between the senses and the mind.

Pelletier notes how Le Camus' work, in common with other architectural theorists of that era, moved the way in which architecture was expected to communicate expression by addressing the senses rather than just playing to the mind; light, colour, smell and music were all charged with mediating specific emotions. In addition to this direct and immediate play to the senses, the conception of architectural character was developed by setting out a linear route that occupants or observers were expected to follow around a building. Such discussion of framed, deliberate views is clearly relevant to the contemporary development in England of picturesque landscape. These examples of theatre and landscape (as theatre) raise other questions regarding authority, reason, and the extent of individual agency over institutional imposition that are focused on the body and bodily experience.

While the possibility for audience involvement came with pre-conditions that clearly delimited available experience both in terms of what experience was available, and to whom—the membership of such an audience was broadly limited to the bourgeoisie, and policed through the acquisition of 'Taste'—the potential of both the senses and movement was acknowledged by Chadwick. Although the eighteenth-century accounts were every bit as prescriptive as the architecture Chadwick addressed in *Model Institution*, the possibility that 'architectural character' could involve inhabitants was developed instead around the encouragement of their active involvement. As she developed issues concerning architectural experience around the possibilities of *body-as-site*, the range of senses and the role of movement expanded from these early-modern versions. Rather than subscribing to predetermined positions and emotional responses, Chadwick's thinking suggests that such issues be considered as part of the contingent establishment of architectural experience.

In a far more dynamic account, Chadwick linked sensual experience to individual memory and myth as well as external stimuli, and sought movement that was not simply physical, but that set out the contingent establishment of viewing positions as part of the act of exercising one's agency. Rather than the empirical application of Newtonian mechanics to everyday encounters and movements at the scale of the human body, Chadwick was exercised more by Newtonian explanations of planetary motion, as her marginal notes to Koestler's *The Sleepwalkers* suggest. Discussing examples of how the mathematical language of physics has been used to 'dress' metaphysical concepts in order to provide them with a certain currency or kudos, Koestler suggests that even within the accounts of the mechanistic universe that led to the establishment of the 'modern' world-view such as those of Galileo and Newton, there remain much broader and less-mechanistic readings. Within Koestler's account of weight and gravitational attraction in this context, Chadwick was particularly drawn to his suggestion that 'the word "magnetism" was used in a broader, metaphorical sense; it had a profoundly appealing ambiguity as another Janus-faced agency which pertained both to the world of the spirit and of matter' (*SW* 508).

Although Koestler's use of the term agency is a happy coincidence, this passage does signal important ideas in Chadwick's notes regarding the movement of people and the link between agency and experience; for Chadwick, movement was more interesting when considered within an ambiguous flux of attraction–repulsion that responded to both spirit and matter, rather than according to principally mechanical understanding of movement. Following this step back from simple mechanics, Chadwick's theorisation of movement jumped forward by developing ideas of attraction-repulsion in ways that demonstrate an explicit interest in quantum mechanics. Writing her 'Soliloquy to Flesh', Chadwick posited a mature account of her theoretical position towards the body as part of an extended apparatus that enjoys—and indeed is partly constituted by—constant interaction with a complex site:

> My apparatus is a body x sensory systems with which to correlate experience. Not exactly solid and real, I am nonetheless conscious, via physicality, of duration, of passing through. The sense of motion is emphatic, positing flesh-hood not as matter or image, but as process, a sequence of qualities of action [...] On impulse, I plan an incidence of self, in other words, a building site to develop in. As I proceed, things appear to change. The site curves around my presence whilst I in turn mould the geography of space. In mutual circumnavigation, the terrain waxes open, and following the path of least resistance, performs new convolutions. I mirror these curvatures. The architecture grows corporeal and I am enfleshed. (*SF* 109)

While the apparent triumphalism of this statement suggests that Chadwick took this notion of 'apparatus' to answer her ambitions regarding a reconceptualisation of the body, sensory systems and their relationship with architecture, even on her own terms it brings together ideas from such a wide range of sources that its ability to hold together, let alone develop to inform artistic or architectural practice, must be questioned. Although the 'mutual circumnavigation' that Chadwick suggested in 'Soliloquy to Flesh' posits the sense of motion as a process, as action, her demands raised elsewhere clarify the dimensions and modes that might contribute to such a process. Moreover, it should be reiterated that her intention was to address such an account to the difficulties of everyday experience, where mechanical-Newtonian accounts continued to hold sway. Developing her ideas in this sense, Chadwick was drawn to the notion of 'reverberation', through which a process of motion, conceptualised around attraction–repulsion, might be mirrored within the environment.

reverberation and quantum consciousness

Chadwick came across the notion of 'reverberation' in Bachelard's *The Poetics of Space*, which she was reading at the same time as works by Koestler, and Fritjof Capra's *The Tao of Physics: An Exploration of the Parallels between Modern Physics and Eastern Mysticism*. Her rationale for working through these together is clear: as Etienne Gilson writes in the Foreword to *The Poetics of Space*, 'Bachelard was resolutely turning from the universe of reason and science to that of imagination and poetry'. Although Chadwick highlighted this passage, her marginal note at this point, '+ memory', provides an early indication that her interest in or agreement with Bachelard was qualified. While this would extend to looking beyond science and reason, she sought to acknowledge and draw upon, rather than turn away from, these disciplines.

Chadwick made notes on 'reverberation' (*retentir*) as a concept where the world comes alive. Bachelard's 'reverberation' is borrowed from Eugène Minkowski; according to the lengthy editor's note to expand this, Minkowski, in *Vers une Cosmologie* (1936), argues that the world comes alive by filling up with reverberations;

> It is not a material object which fills another by espousing the form that the other imposes. No, it is the dynamism of the sonorous life itself which by engulfing and appropriating everything it finds in its path, fills the slice of space, or better, the slice of the world that it assigns itself by its movement, making it reverberate, breathing into it its own life. The word 'slice' here must not be taken in its geometrical sense. It is not a matter of decomposing the world virtually or actually into sonorous balls, nor of tracing the limits of the sphere determined by the waves emanating from a sonorous source. In fact, our examples [...] because of the very fact that they fill up with sounds, form a sort of self-enclosed whole, a microcosm. (*PS* xiii)

Chadwick underlined these lines, writing in the margin 'here, yes it is!' and then below, 'installation as memory'. That Minkowski's work itself reverberated so strongly with Chadwick is understandable: his position, influenced by Henri Bergson, was that the essence of life was participation, and that objects—'all that belongs to the material and palpable world'— were secondary qualities. This priority given to participation (or agency, to emphasise the link with earlier sections), operating via reverberation to link people and world, struck a chord with Chadwick: in the margins to the next couple of pages (*PS* xx–xxi) she dwells on the resonance and reverberation of the object *per se*, adding 'The objects [Chadwick is probably referring to the objects within her installation *Ego Geometria Sum*] as poetical studies/triggers', and 'object's sense not to be disentangled but felt + allowed to resonate'.

For Chadwick, the importance of not reducing—objectifying—the objects comprising our environment by disentangling them was to provide reverberation, or agency, with the means to operate. Bachelard's account of reading poetry, which itself echoes Tafuri's account of co-authoring mentioned earlier, is predicated on reverberation. While Chadwick notes the importance of this process to an '(awareness) of own past + own self' in the margin, she returns to the question of the creative process, emphasising the importance of the '*effect of object on others' (*PS* xix). Unfortunately, she does not go on to provide any detail of how she considered this effect might take place, how she might *construct 'Thing'* as that which remained prior to the disentanglement of object from world. In order to speculate about this process, it is helpful to return to the work of Elizabeth Grosz. Just as Grosz's approach to the body as essentially unknowable enjoyed a clear resonance with Chadwick's position, her consideration of 'things' can be read productively alongside Chadwick's rather enigmatic suggestions.

In her essay 'The Thing', Grosz observes the Enlightenment version of the thing as the measure or the mirror of what we are not: while most of these 'things' were associated with inert materiality, Grosz's stated interest is in the emerging notion of thing that links it with some sort of animism, 'an animated and potentially malevolent materiality, a biological materiality that is or may be the result of our unknowing (usually atomic or nuclear) intervention into nature, the revenge of the blob'.[12] Grosz goes on to suggest that the thing could play a role as non-living *provocateur* to the living, a suggestion that would sit well with Chadwick's demand that an *object's sense not to be disentangled but felt + allowed to resonate*. Although Grosz includes a warning that these varying associations of the thing must remain immanent, Chadwick's further investigations into the realm of our unknowing interventions into nature at a cellular level anticipate, and indeed go further than, Grosz's position. Grasped as both immanence and reality, Chadwick's thinking provides *more* reasons to accept Grosz's suggestion of continua between living and non-living, as well as extra dimensions that include the thing's capacity to provoke or trigger self-awareness and the exercise of agency.

Although this does not bring us much closer to *constructing 'Thing'*, it emphasises the importance of organising the creative process around an intention to permit and encourage resonance, to guard against the disentanglement of things, and to acknowledge the role of movement not only in a mechanical sense, but also according to the more complex notion of movement as a balance or struggle that involves attraction–repulsion. Rather than conceiving of the process of co-authoring as something that occurs between mind and object within a Cartesian framework of even, empty space, the prerequisites of reverberation are ambiguity on behalf of both the *body-as-site* and the object-thing. Following Minkowski and Chadwick, the movement of attraction and repulsion that is established, contingently, between these two, or more precisely now across these continua, becomes a microcosm, a lump of space and stuff that resonates.

As Chadwick followed both her interests and the logic of increasingly diverse systems of thought she drew upon, it became increasingly apparent that the impact of considering the *body-as-site* required a radically different world-view if it was to achieve any kind of accommodation. Developing around her interest in the interface between people and world, body and self, Chadwick became increasingly attentive to various aspects of new science, both in terms of its impact on the stability of traditional world-views, and its potential as a metaphor within her account of the body and world.

Approaching these developments tangentially, some of the important aspects can be introduced through her reconsiderations of issues concerning *body-as-site* as an ecology. Writing in her *Filofax*, she emphasised the scale-less mutuality of influence that might pertain during the process of reverberation:

> VL [*Viral Landscapes*] as eco-logy
> Felix Guattari; (see notes ICA talk)
> Eco-logic
> Ecology Gk.   oikos—house
>   logos—discourse
> study of 'personal' territories
> macro/micro of V Landscapes
> dissolve distinctions
> All spheres mutual interface
> —mutuality of influence
>
> i.e. anatomy—ecology
> Filofax

This *dissolution of distinctions*, while discussed earlier principally in terms of the *body-as-site* and its potential relationship with the '*Thing*', remained central to Chadwick's thinking on the body and self as this developed towards the formulation of *anatomy—ecology* just noted. Within this ecology, and influenced increasingly by her interest in the potential of contributions to modern physics, her account expanded to address the increasing importance she attached to memory and particularly to consciousness. Writing in 1990, it is clear that the conceptual approach to the 'apparatus' of *body x sensory systems* remains within this emerging ecology, but has now been joined with, and indeed become subordinate to, this interest in consciousness.

> But consciousness is an indissoluble synthesis of our thinking selves and our physical apparatus: our body and sensory systems. It is experienced not as something solid and real, but as passing through, as *motion*. Fleshood is more than mere object or image, more than assigned meaning. It is dynamic, in process, a variable exchange of relations. (*WD* 69)

As she writes of *Fleshood*, the close similarity with her account in 'Soliloquy to Flesh' cited above is apparent. Around this apparatus, the potential for inscribing consciousness as an easy part of this synthesis had been highlighted by several writers, where its potential to operate as part of the same process, governed by the same principles of attraction and repulsion, was significant.

Although Chadwick referred to new science, and particularly quantum physics, from her earliest notebooks, it remained initially as something of a metaphor either to provide a ready-made alternative to a Newtonian, mechanistic world-view that she contested, or to counter passive, static notions of the experience of art or architecture. While she was not convinced that this was within her scope to address, she increasingly gave time to investigating it, reading at first popular science books, and later more specialist sources. In her copy of Fritjof Capra's *The Tao of Physics*, Chadwick highlighted one reported suggestion by quantum physicists that consciousness might be involved in theories of matter. Although Capra takes this as an invitation to ground mystical experience, it fits more closely in Chadwick's developing thinking around the relationship between consciousness and the *indissoluble synthesis of our thinking selves and our physical apparatus.*

> Wigner and other physicists have argued [...] that the <u>explicit inclusion of human consciousness may be an essential aspect of future theories of matter</u>. Such a development would open exciting possibilities for a direct interaction between physics and Eastern mysticism. <u>The understanding of one's consciousness and of its relation to the rest of the universe is the starting point of all mystical experience</u>. (*TP* 318)

Approached thus, consciousness is no longer an adjunct to the material world, or a higher plane, but part of the continua through which experience operates, the most radical counter to Cartesian dualism. Chadwick was neither drawn by theories of matter per se, nor by the apparent claims for quantum mysticism. Instead, the relevance of consciousness understood in this way is that it extends the ability and scope of Minkowski's reverberation, so that if adopted as a metaphor for the creative process and experience of the environment it can inscribe or call upon a far wider variety, a greater modality, of ingredients or forces within that experience. This potential role for consciousness had been explored by Danah Zohar, whose book *The Quantum Self* addresses such possibilities directly. In addition to some quantum concepts that Chadwick highlighted early on— complementarity, flux, both/and, indeterminacy—she had cut out an article from the *Guardian* and kept it in the back of her *Filofax*. In that article, a review of the book launch, Walter Schwarz's summary of Zohar's argument provides a clear demonstration of Chadwick's interest in this work and its possible relevance to her thinking:

> [Zohar's] theory is that consciousness is a quantum-physical system, keeping every living thing in intimate and constant interaction with others, with nature, with history and with God. In quantum physics, Isaac Newton's comforting world of solid and separate atoms is replaced by a subtler realm in which matter can no longer be pinned down, showing itself either as a particle or as a wave. Particles interact so intimately with each other that they *are* each other.[13]

As with other ideas borrowed from science, Chadwick would have been encouraged by this increased proximity between consciousness and matter. Through her adoption of such ideas and their development to fit better with her own practice and theoretical position she would have been wary about the last claim, as it could be taken to suggest that interaction leads not just to synthesis but to a conflation that would be every bit as restrictive as the traditional accounts of body and self that she set out to contest.

Rather than underpinning the gaps and voids that were key to her transformative account of how the self and world might be constructed, and how this in turn ought to inform the creative process, the extent of this inter-particle interaction threatens to close the process down. Chadwick's emerging 'ecology' of body, self and world sought to exploit the possibilities of quantum consciousness for contingent rather than enduring syntheses. To return to Minkoski's terminology, Chadwick sought to establish the increasing range of continua in order to support contingent processes, discrete reverberations that enjoyed the fullness Minkowski demanded, and each forming 'a sort of self-enclosed whole, a microcosm'. Through such discrete reverberations, body and self emerge along with consciousness, thing and object.

The ability, indeed the need, for this reciprocal construction to remain dynamic, in process, *a variable exchange of relations*, was important for Chadwick. In the margins of Rupert Sheldrake's *A New Science of Life*, Chadwick reiterated and reformulated how her understanding of the body and its relationship with the world it both makes and inhabits is reflected in the creative process: 'creativity as process morphic resonance, or actualising artwork out of implicate order [...] installation: time/space = space field of formative causation for singular fixed elements g.m./ body' (*NSL* above 249 and 250 respectively).[14]

Although Chadwick was familiar with Sheldrake's work, she did not adopt his position wholesale. In response to his suggestion that the creative process would be influenced by quantum understanding in ways that would lead to 'successively higher-level' wholes, Chadwick repeatedly asserted that the self-enclosed wholes of reverberation would quickly dissipate. She highlighted the following section of a dialogue between Sheldrake and David Bohm, where the former argued that: 'the creative process, which gives rise to new thought, through which new wholes are realised, is similar [...] to the creative reality which gave rise to new wholes in the evolutionary process. The creative process could be seen as a successive development of more complex and higher-level wholes, through previously separate things being connected together' (*NSL* 252). Against this, Chadwick added, 'yes but a whole is only a part of a whole'.

In this sense, Chadwick is both more interesting than Sheldrake, and follows more closely the potential consequences of quantum physics for other disciplines. She argued less for a process that aimed at sublimation, and more for an account of experience as a process that just strikes up discontinuous, succession reverberations. Nevertheless, the rather enigmatic balance between a whole and the whole to which it is only a part raises important theoretical questions regarding Chadwick's position, particularly how to hold together various issues just raised without returning to the classical synthesis that Sheldrake intimates.

At this point, it is helpful to introduce the more recent work of the theorist Arkady Plotnitsky, who has considered extensively the potential contribution that quantum physics can make to the humanities in general. While Plotnitsky's principal concern is with epistemology (or rather, 'anti-epistemology'), his observations can open up this thorny issue of 'wholeness' in ways that indicate both the coherence emerging within Chadwick's notion of the *Fleshood* and its relevance and relationship with an emerging world-view.

Chadwick's world-view was similar to that which Plotnitsky refers to as a General Economy, wherein the dynamism of *Fleshood*, its situation in process or as a variable exchange of relations, anticipates the problem of traditional conceptions of the self. Plotnitsky writes: 'General economies—theories never identical even to themselves—are theories in a plural style or genre, self-differentiating and self-disseminating, making the very concept of the self profoundly problematic.' To avoid difficulties associated with a traditional view of self and world, amongst other things, Plotnitsky suggests we speak of 'extended' rather than global configurations, 'for the general economic loss in representation is also the loss of wholeness'.[15]

The following chapter will address ways in which such extended configurations can be developed by considering Chadwick's thinking on

Fleshood alongside her continuing—and somewhat paradoxical—interest in some of the approaches of eighteenth-century sensualist architecture, particularly those of Boullée.

4 'Multistability' and viewing position

Chadwick's thinking on the body and its interface with the world consistently rejected the notion of the 'whole body' (whether this referred to the human or architectural body), although she equally acknowledged the need for, and the difficulties posed by, the usual coherence of our everyday experience of both body and architecture. Notwithstanding the radical reappraisal that her developing conception of *body-as-site* involved, and the wide-ranging modern-scientific influences on her thinking, her realised and theoretical work maintained a continuing interest in Newtonian physics and related ideas that laid claim to 'easy' explanations of our everyday experience and understanding. While she frequently voiced her own concerns regarding this interest, almost despite herself, she seemed to be drawn back by the siren song of Platonic geometry and Newtonian mechanics.

wholeness and the everyday

It is worth repeating Chadwick's oblique response to Rupert Sheldrake: *a whole is only part of a whole*. Although they would agree on the importance of the creative process and its wider applicability, and on the way this process operates by bringing together previously unconnected things to make 'new wholes', Chadwick's comments signal her differences with Sheldrake's overarching presupposition that such process leads to progress and synthesis. But what *kind* of wholeness is at stake? How might this kind of wholeness affect an observer and their potential relationship with a particular environment, a particular architectural or artistic work? What impact does this understanding of 'whole' have on our understanding or view of the world?

Chadwick's position did not oppose synthesis, provided this occurred along the lines set out in the previous chapter, affected by forces of attraction and repulsion. Just as she was most exercised by static accounts of the body, of architecture, and more generally of accounts that are predicated on Newtonian-mechanistic and singular versions of the universe, her riposte *a whole is only part of a whole* hints at operative, extended and contingent wholes that might be produced by a transformed approach. To reintroduce some of the key concerns from the previous chapter, this could be rephrased 'an object is only part of a "Thing"'.

This emphasises her desire not for less, but for more wholeness, not predicated on prior division of the world into discrete spheres of knowledge, but on the acceptance of what both Plotnitsky and Chadwick, both via Bataille, would refer to as a General Economy. This General Economy is a wholeness that remains prior to representation, and from which all representations, discourses, or bodies of knowledge are drawn. Chadwick's complaint was that typically, dominant disciplines denied their reliance on, or even the existence of, this General Economy; they denied that there might be areas that remained outside their control or survey. Writing in a notebook, she characterised this problem as the divide between scientific and non-scientific means of accounting for the universe.

> Science not only way of gaining access to truth of universe. Access nature of reality thro' non scientific means.
> What left out – to heal divide of art science—might be consciousness/ subjectivity/ lived time IDENTITY
> 2003.19/E/8.143

Although her aim to *heal the divide between art and science* might seem too obvious, the suggestion that it might be *IDENTITY* that could provide the means to achieve this is significant, as it draws in all the issues raised in the previous chapter concerning the body, particularly as this was reconsidered around the operation of agency. The continua that were discussed there, while not coterminous with the General Economy, emphasise that the process of agency and the various dimensions of its operation that could be called upon or activated by a particular instance of reverberation operate prior to or with partial acknowledgement of the available 'truths', and outside the 'laws' that govern their accepted relationship and possible combination. Each operation of agency produces *a whole that is only part of a whole*.

This consideration of wholeness, and the intention *to heal divide of art science*, shares several important aspects with the work Plotnitsky has done on bringing together science and the humanities; in his view, the traditional separation of science and humanities (and the traditional hierarchies of knowledge they produce) relies on a model of understanding that quantum science has demonstrated to be untenable. One of the early insights of quantum science concerned the relationship between the observer and the world they observed; the quantum account of this relationship had a strong impact on Chadwick's thinking, complementing her views on the body and identity politics, as both shared a demand for active participation. 'Spectators as "active" body—participatory, away from fixed position' (*Filofax*, c.1987).

The impossibility of remaining an impartial observer was hugely important for Chadwick. Her reading of Capra's *The Tao of Physics* demonstrates the relevance of quantum science for her developing conception of the body and its inevitable interrelationship with the world. Against the section on 'The Unity of All Things' (Part III, Chapter 10), Chadwick highlighted the following:

> In atomic physics, then, the scientist cannot play the role of a detached objective observer, but becomes involved in the world he observes to the extent that he influences the properties of the observed objects. John Wheeler sees this involvement of the observer as the most important feature of quantum theory, and he has therefore suggested replacing the word 'observer' by the word 'participant' [...] 'To describe what has happened [after a scientist has taken a measure] one has to cross out that old word "observer" and put in its place the new word "participator." In some strange sense the universe is a participatory universe.' (*TP* 145).[1]

Chadwick then added in the bottom margin

> ∴ influences observed world.
> observer=participator
> ∴ scientist → artist?
> creates + manipulates properties of particles.

Chadwick's notes here suggest that the ideas developing were not simply considered a possible alternative to traditional approaches, but were in fact becoming something of an imperative. In his own discussion of similar issues, Plotnitsky cites a significant passage from Niels Bohr's *Philosophical Writings*:

> the finite magnitude of the quantum of action prevents altogether a sharp distinction being made between a phenomenon and the agency by which it is observed, a distinction which underlies the customary concept of observation and, therefore, forms the basis of the classical

ideas of motion [...] an independent reality in the ordinary physical sense can neither be ascribed to the phenomena nor to the agencies of observation.[2]

Plotnitsky goes on to consider the impact this has on notions of 'wholeness', arguing that around the observer–object conjunction (or perhaps more properly now, the agency–phenomena conjunction), this is ambiguous. It is an always-irreducible interaction, which 'forms not a unity, governed by a classical economy of synthesis, but a complex and shifting complementarity'.[3]

Despite her frequent protestations that modern physics was 'beyond my scope' and so on, this limitation—if in fact it did apply at all—was perhaps limited to Chadwick's realised work. As her interest in and research into quantum mechanics developed at one remove from her realised projects, it enjoyed both a coherence and a wider potential: its presence there is legible, and can continue to provide a significant relay between a classical understanding of 'nature' and the broader epistemological framework to which this belongs. Drawing significantly on quantum mechanics to provide a transformed framework for both epistemology and metaphor (and arguably for actual relationships around *agency–phenomena conjunction*), Chadwick's work provides a number of fruitful suggestions for architecture in particular, while at the same time raising a number of awkward questions that provide resistance to such a transformed framework, particularly in light of the success of traditional Newtonian accounts in providing convincing 'knowledge' of the world that accords with an everyday experience.

Mindful of this, Chadwick implicitly approached the everyday as a site where both traditional and quantum world-views must play out their differences. Niels Bohr shared a similar concern, remarking that 'we' must 'use everyday concepts' in all descriptions.[4] To recall again Chadwick's concession that *buildings [are] stronger than people*, in addition to the everyday, common sense understanding of this, it can be taken as slightly less certain, as a statement of something that we take for granted but that might perhaps be otherwise. *Model Institution* epitomised the problems and logical conclusions of systems established in the seventeenth and eighteenth centuries, when the environment was reduced to the measurable certainty of normalised geometry. But as Chadwick asked there, can the everyday also provide a site of resistance against this static materiality, against the apparent autonomy of buildings? Her work mounted perhaps its strongest and most sustained challenge at this realisation; she opened up ways in which our experience of buildings might be expanded, while simultaneously shifting the key threshold of autonomy away from body, building, mind and so on, to an altogether different scale.

Above this threshold of autonomy, Chadwick pursued the possibilities of interconnectedness—or wholeness—and the alterations this might bring to everyday understanding. Narrowly Newtonian approaches prevent such interconnections or quantum wholeness, they launder the everyday of its ambiguities. What the everyday can offer is General Economy, although it has come to present as common sense what is in fact only one response, discounting a wide range of stimuli and predisposing the 'observer' to remain beholden to an established world-view or epistemological system. In contrast, the 'complex and shifting complementarity' of the quantum view presupposes the impossibility of such absolute predictability. Instead of supporting the autonomy of environment and observer, it operates a model of understanding that is radically contingent, that begins with the interaction, or interconnection, of agency–phenomena. As Chadwick's notes emphasise, this signals not just a revision to the received subject–object relationship, but a step change, a complete reconfiguration of the conception of this relationship. *Dissolution of boundaries of self, […] Self as event not matter […] Self as particle.*

Above and beyond (or before) these considerations of an expansion to the possibilities of experience, it is important to reintroduce Chadwick's determination to *construct 'Thing'* in this context, and to be mindful of the distinction between the experience of architecture, even with this transformed notion of agency, and the distinct role, potential and responsibility of the architect.

In particular, the latter must accept that the threshold of autonomy no longer provides any justification for separating the architectural object from those events that bring it into play. The 'strength' of this object must be tempered through attention given to the multiple and conflicting, quasi-quantum events that are inseparable from the phenomena itself. To pursue the logic of this quantum understanding, the architect is not faced with a choice between designing a built object that is conceived of as either static or open, but must accept that the object building does not attain any 'reality' until it is animated, 'represented', as part of an event that brings it into existence along with, but only for, the agent of that event. The demand of quantum mechanics that phenomena are imperceptible (indeed, radically unknowable) until they are effectively 'used up' in the process of being registered is clearly counter-intuitive when considering the strength of buildings. And yet when considered more by analogy, such that architecture is conceived of not as a discrete or static object, but a process or a framework around which such events can continue to occur, then the architect's role is to design this process, and thereby to consider the implications this has regarding the exclusion from access to the various processes of building. At the scale of an everyday encounter with the designed environment, this places more demands on the framework within which such work is understood. Chadwick worked theoretically and practically to bring together the incompatible, the conflicting contradictions and richness that such a framework would offer; one of her worries was that while the everyday encounter with architecture might provide an arena for such a new approach, received conventions of knowledge and behaviour might prevent this from flourishing.

> There must [...] be boundaries and limits to knowledge and meaning. Can we cross these boundaries and explore the territories beyond? And if this subjective terrain can be represented, does it then collapse full circle back into the order of things—become reified? (*WD* 68)

Giving voice to her concerns here, the potential of pursuing a quantum analogy for artistic or architectural production—the representation of subjective terrain—may well be recuperated by the strength of the conventional order of things that we take for granted in the everyday. Nevertheless, Chadwick was convinced of the need to cross the boundaries of accepted meaning, venturing into unknowable territories, considering possible structures of knowledge and meaning that might resist collapse or reification. She found one enduring source of interest for these explorations in *vanitas* artworks.

vanitas

At first sight, Chadwick's interest in the *vanitas* genre would appear to have little to offer the present consideration of quantum mechanics. The *vanitas* tradition, at its most productive during the seventeenth century in both Holland and France, worked by gathering together various objects, both precious and ordinary, driven by a clear agenda to encourage its audience to look beyond the everyday appearance of things. While this ambition has some resonance with Chadwick, she was more particularly drawn to the ways in which *vanitas* works operated to expand accepted experience rather than simply replace it. As she noted in the margins of her copy of Alberto Veca's *Vanitas: Il simbolismo del tempo*, it involved 'new + innovative medium tog.[ether] with tradition symbols/ images' (*VST* 166).

As Veca makes clear early on in his essay, 'it would be rather limiting and overhasty to define a *mememto mori* simply as a painting containing human bones' (*VST* 172). Although the human skull 'is probably the most explicit and recurrent object in the *vanitas* type of seventeenth-century still-life', Chadwick's interest was in the sheer range of stuff that was brought together in such work, and the way this gave new life to legible symbolism. Veca's section on 'The Symbolism of Objects' was particularly significant for Chadwick; it parallels both the notion of *The Juggler's Table*, and her own disposition to collect disparate things together for symbolic reasons. Chadwick underscored and highlighted all of the following passage.

> The Vanitas is not only the representation of death, of devastating effects wrought by death and the march of time [...] this type of painting can be more clearly and interestingly seen as the representation of time, and hence as a challenge to the immobile image, to transitoriness and to the transformations it produces in reality. [... Clara Peters' painting] is a jumbled collection of precious things, an illustration of the desire to possess, of the extension of power and affirmative desire in the man who accumulates and finds in the varied collection of his *Kunstkammer* the reflection of his own desires. The objects are both artificial and natural, exotic and domestic. (*VST* 172)

This gathering operation characteristic of the *vanitas* tradition provides a timely reminder of the discussion of Chadwick's own working process and conception of the creative persona, particularly the creative operation of bisociation combining *apparently unassociated images*, not to mention its clear manifestation in realised projects such as her *Meat Abstracts* series [1989]. Chadwick was drawn to the combination of 'both vanitas + celebration of physicality' (*VST* 172), its operation that refers to the mind, the imagination and the senses, the ability of the genre to provide for both equilibrium and instability, and to support an experience that involved both actuality and transformation. As Veca notes, 'Even though the two universes are antithetical, (the warning should logically lead to the abandonment of pleasure), they seem to be able to coexist' (*VST* 174).

Just as the framework for the complementarity of quantum experience must hold both potential outcomes (in strict sense, wave or particle) as virtualities only one of which can be actualised, so Chadwick's account of the operation of *vanitas* has strong echoes of this process: inside the back cover of the Veca's book, Chadwick writes:

> <u>figures</u> suggest an allegorical meaning yet combined with objects/companions shift towards the vanitas tradition of symbolic meaning of objects/still-life
> where side by side composition objects/figure → creates a continuous stream of interconnections, a dialogue unravelling to reveal a new set of values—a unique conversation poised between love/death fixed at a

precise moment in this representation, from a timeless flux of changes.
[...]
Homo Bulla man the soap bubble.

The ability for *vanitas* to support the coexistence of two antithetical universes is most important here. As these antitheses were approached by Chadwick, the potential of the *vanitas* to *create a continuous stream of interconnections, a dialogue unravelling to reveal a new set of values* can be understood to have operated particularly within a framework that accommodated reason, irrationality and imagination.

Chadwick's most explicit considerations of these issues in an architectural context came through her reading of Boullée's *Architecture: Essay on Art.* Before this is introduced, it is helpful to draw upon the work of Boullée's Italian contemporary, Giovanni Battista Piranesi, which provides something of a missing link between Chadwick's interest in the rich Baroque *vanitas* and Boullée's apparently rational, sober neo-classicism. Although these two figures are frequently caricatured as the rational and romantic sides, respectively, of architectural debates regarding Enlightenment neo-classicism, neither fits this straightforward pigeon-holing. Indeed, Tafuri describes Piranesi as a critic who doesn't take sides, but who prophesies the dilemma of modern architecture, caught between rigorous and proto-romantic positions. Piranesi offers 'an agonising dialectic'[5] as a riposte to what Tafuri describes elsewhere as 'the "naïve dialectic" of the Enlightenment [that] still sees the synthesis in the form of universality and still tends towards non-contradiction'.[6]

In Piranesi's well-known *Campo Marzio* (The Field of Mars, 1761–2), for example, rigorous scientific study is combined with arbitrary, inventive, imaginary restitution (the deliberate misrepresentation in scale and location of rigorously undertaken archaeological reconstructions). In this sense, the *vanitas* genre and much of Chadwick's work share an approach. Fragments from various pasts are recomposed as a question for the present. However, in contrast to the general acceptance of geometric rationality as a measure, symbol and guarantor of universality on the part of Piranesi's contemporaries, it is not just the means that are called into question by the *Campo Marzio*, but the broader epistemological beliefs underlying them. In both the *Campo Marzio* and the *vanitas* genre, the presence of scientific instruments or techniques symbolising the power of human rationality over the world is tempered by reminders of the march of time or that which escapes human control: *Homo Bulla man the soap bubble.* The power of rationality is seen to be unable to maintain effective hold over 'real'—or what we might call lived or everyday—space.

It is important to emphasise that it is not principally mortality that is addressed here, but the broader understanding of our place in the universe and the construction of meaning. Tafuri emphasises the profound impact this has, replacing the certainty of rationality and measure within a Newtonian universe, not with another certainty, but with a radical not-knowing: 'History no longer offers *values* as such. Subjected to a merciless inspection, it is revealed as a new principle of authority, which as such must be disputed [...] It is the experience of the subject that establishes *values* [...] In both the *Carceri* and the *Campo Marzio* History and Nature become *detached* from the subject, not to open up a new universe of values, but rather to present this radical divergence as the only possible value.'[7]

Although I do not want to suggest that Chadwick was a latter-day Piranesi, her approach to work did involve something of the 'agonising dialectic' that Tafuri reads, inasmuch as she sought to open a space where people could respond to such radical divergence of ingredients and establish value through the exercise of their own agency. Despite all that has passed between the Enlightenment and our own time, Chadwick's work can still be understood as the opening of a space within the mechanised universe inherited from Newtonian physics, and the broader assumptions this has led to regarding our encounter with the world. Such an 'agonising dialectic' is not expected to reach a synthesis, no kind of higher knowledge where art is used up *en route*. Instead, the resonance that she sought to instigate echoes Tafuri's suggestion regarding Piranesi; that his work invites us on a voyage from which it is difficult to return. Chadwick's concern emphasised the contemporary relevance and importance of work that supports this kind of radical divergence for the exercise of individual agency. With echoes of the *vanitas*, Chadwick called on experience that could embrace conflicting, antithetical universes. This antithesis must not, however, be taken as licence for non-meaning or radically isolated individuality; it seeks a balance between stable framework and a demonstration of the contingency of such stability.

multistability

Chadwick charged *Fleshood* to act as locus for individual agency and experience, a locus that was resistant to generalising accounts of philosophy or theory, and the potential reduction of experience to that which could be represented or accounted for. Moreover, this brings a warning against attempts to design for or normalise these representations, whether in artistic or architectural work. This awkward relationship with theory is encountered in operation at two different and interrelated scales: between a subjective experience that may well be able to, or more strongly may need to, circle back to the order of things as either representation or value (or both), and a far broader socio-cultural account of experience.

Much as Chadwick privileged subjective experience, she also sought ways in which its various scales, or even modes, of operation could be understood to operate together. While her interest in concepts such as Koestler's *total pattern* provided support for the bisociative act, more recent work in modern science and philosophy of science can help develop the broader concern of her work, that it was not sufficient to simply alter the theory that accounts for practice or experience, but that the relationship and hierarchy of terms within this relationship needed to be reconfigured. Following Plotnitsky 's suggestion, it is important to acknowledge both this general awkwardness, and the fundamental revision in approach, by speaking of 'extended' rather than global configurations. Rather than conceiving of subjective experience as a possible moment of 'divergence' within an otherwise constant, global whole, Chadwick's work posits that the 'whole' itself must be based on, rather than simply accommodating, radical divergence.

This awkward balance between competing ingredients, and the need or ability for individual experience to establish 'value' within a configuration based on radical divergence, has recently been approached through the notion of 'multistability'. Although the concept was developed within the scientific community, it has begun to demonstrate its broader applicability in a way that echoes Chadwick's own close interest in scientific matters, and her subsequent *leap forward* with these to redeploy them more metaphorically in other contexts.

On its own terms, multistability is a system property, and has been used successfully to describe the behaviour of systems that are neither stable nor totally unstable, but that alternate between two or more mutually exclusive states over time. Although perhaps the best-known examples it can be applied to are optical illusions such as the Necker Cube (1832), the Poggendorff Illusion (1860), Hering's Illusion (1861) Rubin's Vase/Faces Illusion (1915) and so on, where vision science has recently used accounts of multistable perception to characterise the conflicting readings that can be brought about by these visually ambiguous patterns, its applicability is far broader. Multistable behaviour has been identified in a variety of systems in different disciplines of science ranging from systems biology, biochemical networks and neuroscience, chemistry, to semi-conductor and laser physics.

Broadening its potential from these very particular disciplines, it has been increasingly suggested that multistability plays a significant role in some of the basic processes of life. Although within such disciplines multistable behaviour is linked to the coexistence of a number of final states, its impact upon the structure and expectations of knowledge as it develops to address these broader processes of life is most significant. Just as Chadwick drew upon specific insights of scientific research for material that supported her own work as both direct ingredient and as metaphor, so multistability offers both direct and metaphoric assistance here, pointing up a potentially new 'extended configuration' as a basis for contingent knowledge, and a configuration that offers to link the implications of Chadwick's *Fleshood* with the experience of one's environment.[8]

As such, multistable behaviour echoes the demands of quantum mechanics cited by Chadwick, extended and developed by Plotnitsky, regarding the impossibility of sustaining the classical notion of an objective observer who might observe an event or environment from afar and with disinterest. Discounting the emphasis on 'final states' in scientific accounts of multistable behaviour, the broader applicability for architecture lies in the potential impact this has on assumptions about knowledge, authority and value if architecture is approached as a multistable system.

Multistable behaviour that occurs within a system thus conceived does so against a background, or with the acceptance, of a General Economy of possibility. In contrast to traditional conceptions of architecture, to explore it in this way is to accept that there can be not simply two or more mutually exclusive states over time, according to the stricter understanding of multistablity, but that two or more mutually exclusive states or experiences can coexist, and that one person's experience can itself alter radically over time in the same location. Accounting for multistable behaviour in architecture maintains a long-serving architectural interest in viewpoint (even if this is only taken up explicitly in certain examples), but requires this to be transformed in order to address how viewpoint, or more precisely the position of the viewer, can shift to reveal different readings, and that echoes quantum acceptance that these other readings can never be recuperated. *It could have been otherwise*, but won't be: each subjective experience reconciles the 'radical divergence' to establish value but for that moment only.

Despite talking up multistability, there remains (as with other quantum informed concepts) a difficulty not only in demonstrating its applicability to everyday experience, but more importantly in overcoming the obstacles that arrive in the wake of classical accounts of Newtonian mechanics. The challenge is to go about working within the quantum system of that bit of spectrum covered by the classical, roughly the aspect of the universe perceptible to the human eye. While this is not to suggest that 'common sense' understanding is replaced, to accept multistable behaviour can offer encouragement to see the normative, static environment differently, and thus to engage with rather than just submit to the strength of buildings.

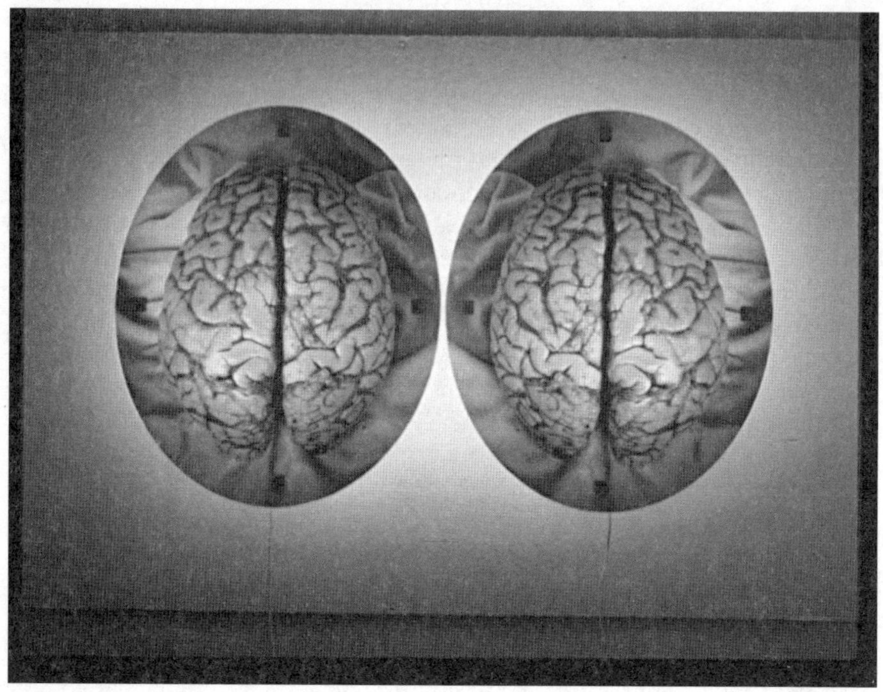

8 *Eroticism*, 1990.

Within this multistable system, objects—the built environment, bodies—are clearly located, but there also exist many other forces that can become ingredients to subjective experience. To repeat Chadwick's demand of *Fleshood*, 'it is more than mere object or image, more than assigned meaning. It is dynamic, in process, a variable exchange of relations' (*WD* 69).

Chadwick emphasised the ability of such a dynamic—we might say multistable—interpretation to strike a balance between the differing demands of Newtonian and other worldviews. While this reiterated her position that to exercise *Fleshood* is to avoid the reduction to assigned meaning, to avoid interpretation or behaviour according to established rules, it is striking that these comments come within notes she made while reading Boullée, an architect who appears to exemplify an approach to architecture as (pure, Newtonian) object.

static complemented by dynamic
finite by infinite

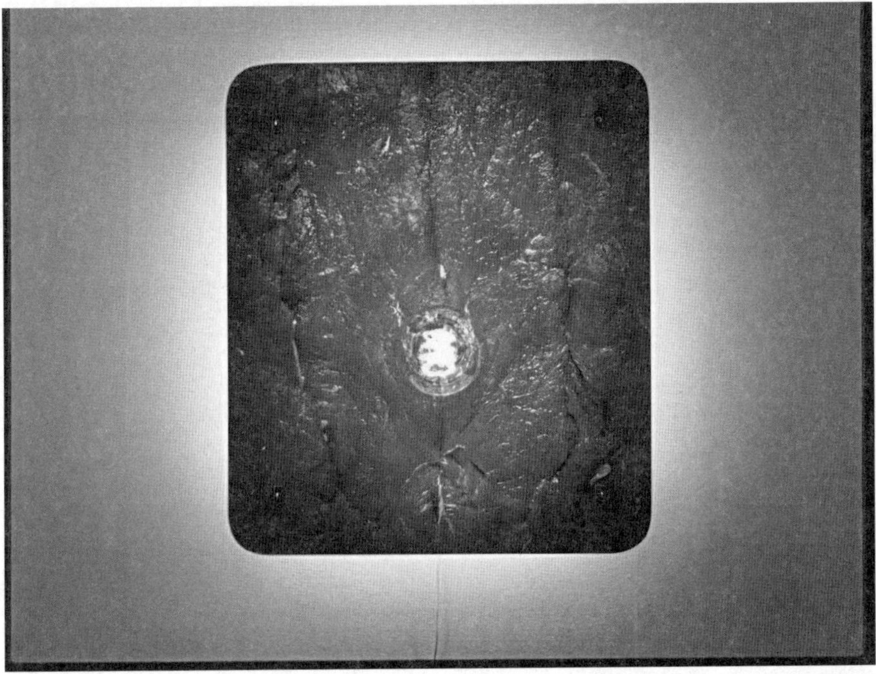

9 *Enfleshing I*, 1989.

In various photographic series from around this time, Chadwick contested binary definitions of self traditionally established around male–female, human–animal, inside–outside, and played on the various artistic traditions that have supported these binaries (from medical illustration to photography, reinforcing a sensory separation between vision and touch): instead, she offered a *'tactile photography, the very sensitizing of surface itself'* (*SF* 109).

Ordered immensity expresses Newtonian finite world → transcends it by
stressing variety + dimension of change of universe.
Dynamic interpretation finite/infinite resolved
    i.e. love/ desire
    soul/body
2003.19/E/6.26

Although Boullée is widely known through the extensive reproduction of his 'Visionary' projects (which clearly appealed to Chadwick's enduring appreciation of pure, Platonic geometry), her research notes indicate that she was more interested by aspects of his theoretical position set out in *Architecture, Essay on Art* (commonly referred to as the *Essai*). In the *Essai*,

Chadwick was drawn to the attempts Boullée made to reconcile or balance 'symmetry' and 'variety' in ways that would be directly available to experience, but which also addressed the relationship between art, architecture, truth, and the arguments over the authority of nature or history.

> Architecture, Essay on Art: Boullée
> Art, product of mind, imitation of nature/truth
> <u>sphere</u> (most perfect) always perceived as uniform, changeless, immutable
> stereometric
> —<u>symmetry</u>=order/perfection
> —<u>variety</u>: stimulating, new life/gives pleasure
> 2003.19/E/6.27

While Chadwick is drawn towards the issues that Boullée juggles with, and extends the possibilities of his argument beyond the limits that he sketches out, her notes also move between the *Essai* and other artistic and architectural movements that sandwich Boullée historically. This extension embraces the potential conjunction of symmetry and variety, which is relayed and expanded to acknowledge her central interest in the relationship between mind and body, reason and intuition, or between technocratic approaches to architecture that Boullée criticises, and the broader artistic approach that he advocates. She posits this extension early in her notes on the *Essai*:

> soul: neoclassical—monumental, symmetry, perpetual, austere
> body: rococo—transient, asymmetrical, rich, picturesque, graceful
> 2003.19/E/6.23

Chadwick's conjunction of Boullée with the rococo and picturesque might appear a striking anomaly. (However, on Boullée's own account of and support for 'Good Taste', the rococo would seem to provide this in spades, in stark contrast to his own visionary projects.) In fact, as his modern editor Helen Rosenau notes in one of her introductory essays, his position—in true multistable form—provides for and overcomes this contradiction. It is worth quoting Rosenau's argument at length:

> Boullée's *Essai* is characterised by two seemingly contradictory, but in reality supplementary, points of view. In his designs and descriptions of the Newton Cenotaph, for example, he represented a finite world. On the other hand, in his thoughts about the immensity and infinity of nature, as well as his concern for human relationships, he

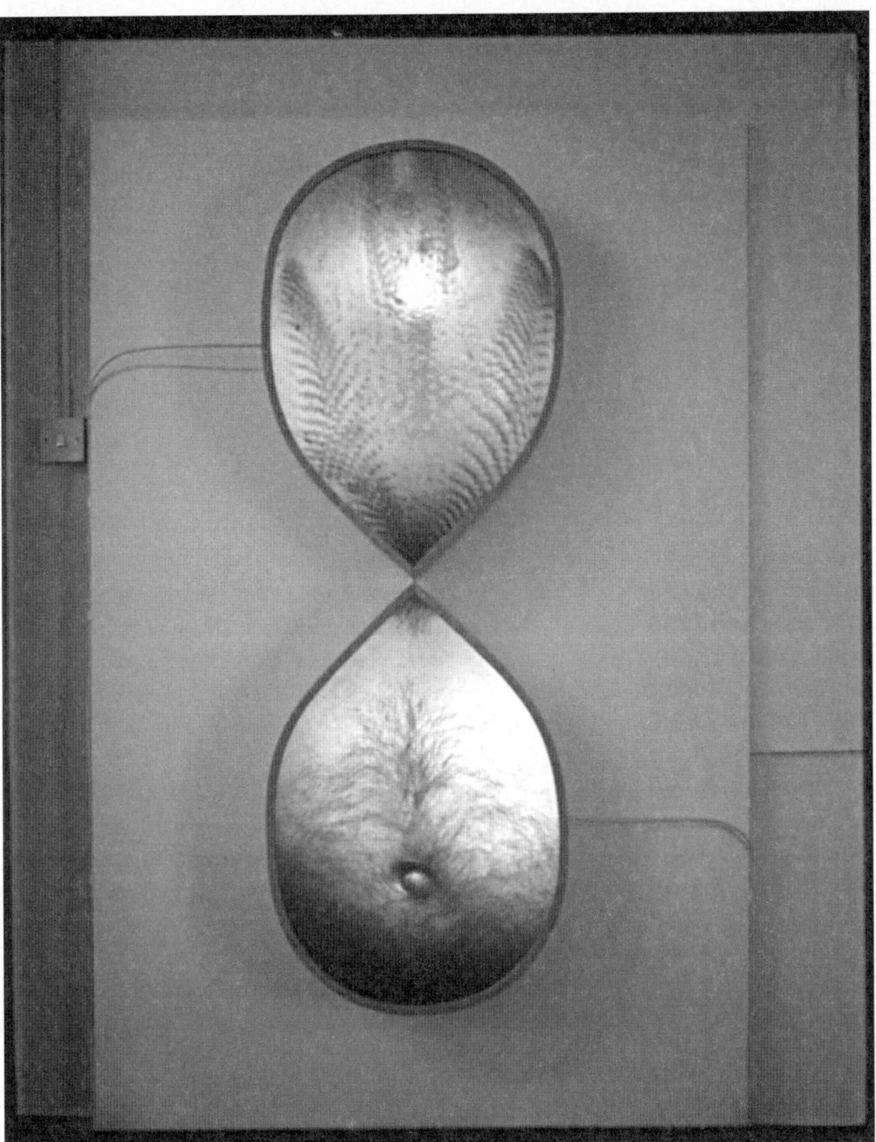

10 *The Philosopher's Fear of Flesh*, 1989.

transcended the limits of his time and stood for a modern interpretation of the coordination of the diverse aspects of human knowledge. A static view of the world is superseded by a dynamic one, the finite by the infinite. His theory of symmetry may be regarded as the fulfilment of the Renaissance view of art, as well as the precursor of the expanding conceptions gravitating towards symmetry, which characterises contemporary thought.[9]

Chadwick's interest in and close reading of Boullée's *Essai* are most easily understood as being motivated by the potential offered by this supersession of finite by the infinite, static by dynamic. Although he provided an example or an armature around which her interest in rococo and picturesque stuff could be included, Boullée's principal argument stopped short of where Chadwick would go. Nevertheless, the key issues that interested her were those Boullée explored in the relationship between person, architecture and nature.

Boullée's opening complaint was against architecture being reduced to technological understanding. Attempting to broaden this conception, Boullée placed greater importance on how our reactions to an object are related to how that object affects us, a quality he refers to as *character*. 'What I call character is the effect of the object which makes some kind of impression on us' (*AEA* 89 [84r]). An important aspect of *character* links Boullée's *Essai* to broader trends in the aesthetic theory of his time: indeed, he cites John Locke's *An Essay Concerning Human Understanding* to make his point that that everything, "'[a]ll our ideas, all our perceptions come to us via external objects. External objects make different impressions on us according to whether they are more or less analogous with the human organism'" (*AEA* 86 [77v]).

Although Boullée goes on immediately to qualify Locke's analogy, commenting that the closer something resembles the human organism the more *beautiful* it will be considered (and thus providing the fulfilment of the Renaissance view of art that Rosenau observes), his discussion of the human organism is limited to notions of symmetry, regularity, and geometric proportion, and this clearly reduces the range of possible impressions external objects can make. Rather than getting caught up in the detail of Boullée's discussion, my interest here is in how Chadwick's own development of the body picks up and transforms her interest in Boullée's theory. To his frequent celebration of variety within symmetry, she suggests a more dynamic interpretation of this relationship, one that starts with the body, can have a dramatic impact on how the external objects of the universe can be encountered:

> Ordered immensity expresses Newtonian finite world → transcends it by stressing variety + dimension of change of universe.
> Dynamic interpretation finite/infinite resolved
> 2003.19/E/6.26

(Re)introducing the more rococo body sympathetic to *Fleshood*, Chadwick suggested how Boullée's reliance on the organism might be transcended by drawing out the potential within his own position for a more multistable reading. Reading Boullée's *Essai*, Chadwick repeated several times Boullée's mantra combining regularity and variety, and noted the role he accorded the movement of people around architectural forms, where the encounter with variety within an overall stable and clear form would, he argued, instil curiosity and motivate exploration. Although Chadwick's own work clearly set out to encourage movement, curiosity and exploration, the appeal of Boullée was tempered because in the end, these were all to occur, for the users of architecture at least, within a clearly regulated physical and normative environment. This was the balance he struck between imaginative and rational engagement, where movement, imagination and exploration were to remain within the rules dictated by God, and passed on through nature's forms for the attentive architect to learn from and use in order to 'make effective nature' (*AEA* 88 [84r]).

Nevertheless, there are a couple of situations in Boullée's *Essai* when he acknowledges that these rules are either not reached or are completely passed over; these situations concern common sense and *force majeure* respectively, and both are relevant to the present discussion of multistability. Regarding the former, Boullée admits that the role he accords to human intuition operates *before* the work of scientific explanation: theories of solid geometry, musical harmony and so on provide a fairly redundant account for what we already know. The second situation arises when Boullée discusses 'inspiration' in the *Essai*'s 'Notes'. He explicitly links inspired moments with a kind of quasi-divine state, where 'a power beyond our control [*force majeure*] drives us and makes our faculties divine, if I may be allowed to use such an expression' (*AEA* 113 [144r]). Between these two moments of quasi-divine excess and everyday habit, regularity is set and variety is sanctioned. Chadwick's work suggests that the two situations marking its extremities are actually available across the whole range.

Boullée's acknowledgement that it is possible to operate outside the rules, outside a limited stable framework, is important, but to reserve this *force majeure* for artist- or architect-as-genius would be as much an anathema to Chadwick as overlooking the importance of people's everyday, habitual impressions. Her demand → *transcends it* [Boullée-Newtonianism] *by stressing variety + dimension of change of universe* does not so much extend the range of regularity within which variety is sanctioned, as offer *dynamic interpretation* where one's response to environmental 'impression' can be understood according to the model of multistable behaviour, and thus can exceed the rules at any point, not just at the extremities. Irrational and rational ingredients can be combined in any situation. As such, 'impressions' would no longer be beholden to rules established by others in advance, but subjective experience would operate to establish values from a multistable system based on 'radical divergence as the only possible value', to repeat Tafuri out of context. The variety available within multistable behaviour offers to sustain curiosity and encourage investigation, a kind of compensation for the moment when subjective values *fall back, become reified*.

Although multistability as a term was not really in circulation in this sense during Chadwick's lifetime, it can prove helpful as a matrix across which a variety of her disparate theoretical investigations concerning the body, *Fleshood*, and wholeness can be combined with her thinking on the creative self and the creative process. Moreover, it can support further investigation into the potential architectural impact of her thinking, particularly around the role of our perception of (or the impression made by) external objects, both artificial and natural. Operating and acknowledging 'the agonising dialectic', where neither history nor nature offers to provide certain 'value' any more, it can also make sense of, or at least organise, the following chapters that explore various related investigations that Chadwick undertook.

As a kind of parallel to Boullée's approach to architecture through his *Essay on Art*, I want to introduce a concept that Chadwick adopted to explore the combined promise of art and the issues of identity politics set out above. Instead of the quantum mechanical insights that Plotnitsky, for example, has combined with work in the humanities, Chadwick found greater support from contemporary work in biology; in particular here, she approached the variety of ingredients operative in her understanding of *Fleshood* analogously to the particular operation she described as the dissensual interaction between virus and cell:

> dissensus [...] decentres identity + proliferation of dissensus not destructive [...] territory for new subjectivity composed of non hierarchical coming together on micro-macro scale that is non damaging, a relation of incompatible elements that is not seen as destructive between landscape/arch
>   body/non-biology [...]
> A biology of desire
> Identity as insecure, shifting
> 2003.19/E/8.8[10]

Although the details of her interest in biology will have to wait, it is useful to introduce *dissensus* here because it represents the most developed and expansive statement of Chadwick's theoretical thinking on experience, architecture and identity, and posits this in terms which, while not offering architecture any easy answers, do indicate the extent of the challenge that her work can issue to architecture. That said, it is worth emphasising the insecure, shifting character of Chadwick's theoretical notes that is indicative of the kind of independent place these took within her œuvre. Although she never attempted or was drawn to provide any theoretical completeness, *dissensus* is clearly commensurate with a number of the significant issues discussed in the previous chapters and can demonstrate a theoretical coherence between them. Chadwick's interest in bisociation, borrowed to approach the creative process for artist and observer alike, and in *total pattern*, borrowed to set out the work of installation, or the notion of 'multistability' that I have borrowed from elsewhere, all operate with a dissensual *relation of incompatible elements*.

Notwithstanding its ability to complement these issues, Chadwick was initially drawn to *dissensus* as part of her considerations of the limits of autonomy, where the cellular emerged as the scale above which she believed there could be no autonomy. Traditionally in architectural discourse, discussions of autonomy have been reduced to questions regarding form: in contrast, Chadwick's work suggests that this ought to be reconsidered by addressing architectural experience in ways that called into question the role of the self (as site) and the links between the mutually reinforcing metaphors of architecture and knowledge.

Indeed, a central support of the perception that *buildings stronger than people* is this mutual reinforcement: but as Chadwick understood *dissensus*, there always exist multiple possibilities within every architectural situation, possibilities not simply for action within static physical or epistemological environments, but for actions that acknowledge the insights of quantum-mechanical informed positions and undertake to establish a contingent wholeness that only ever remains part of a whole. Such an architecture has never been nor will ever be completed: it forms part of the continua that also included the *body-as-site*.

Chadwick's theoretical and realised work explored how *dissensus* could involve and work constructively with the established rules governing how we 'ought to' behave in an environment: she stressed that her *dissensual* technique was evolutionary not revolutionary, for to operate successfully it needed to identify the possibilities offered by 'strong' environments, to identify spaces and techniques of resistance, and then maintain the legibility of this situation that *dissensual* response went on to criticise. This legibility was for her an artistic responsibility, summed up in her account of this working process as a *creative + manipulative theft*. For Margret Grebowicz, reviewing a range of *dissensual* responses in various disciplines, it is enough to articulate dissent against a strong environment, that this in its own way produces new knowledge and involves the active exercise of agency.[11] The difference between these two positions illustrates perhaps the difference, following Tafuri's distinction, between the responsibility of the creative persona understood as 'planner' and the opportunity of the creative persona understood as co-author. While both positions might follow the analogy of *Le Bateleur* and draw upon an understanding of the universe that exceeds the rational, the traditional assumptions of the artist, or perhaps with greater difficulty here, the architect, are seriously unsettled. While both stand to gain, the demand this places on architecture is to expand its practice well beyond the conventional design of autonomous building. To repeat Chadwick's remark, practice must change to *construct 'Thing'*, not a physical object but an approach to architectural experience that can accommodate a far wider range of dimensions.

Part Three: Artifice and nature

5 The grotto and architectural conceit

Writing notes in her *Filofax* sometime in 1988, Chadwick addressed the concept of nature thus:

> I am confused as to what precisely is natural any more.
> Natural is really a 'moral' concept.
> there can never be 'Nature'
> only questions of what is <u>relatively</u> natural

If we accept Chadwick's assertion that there *can never be 'Nature'*, what are the consequences for architecture? Given the current willingness of many people to accept arguments that climate change is not happening, or to refute that it, along with other examples of environmental degradation, has anything to do with human action, Chadwick's suggestion that 'Nature' doesn't exist could be a very dangerous proposition. While some might take this as an opportunity to continue ignoring such links, her œuvre demonstrates a desire to emphasise their importance, to examine and strengthen them. By addressing her 'confusion', Chadwick worked to explore how human beings might be considered more as part of a continuous and complex environment. Just as she challenged other binary divisions in favour of an understanding that became organised around continua, so her work addressed the accepted division of nature and artifice, calling into question the role of nature as an autonomous realm, as one of her later notes emphasised:

> the organic as integrated within us
> thoughts / brain / theory—all organic
> rather than natural or artificial [...] "all flesh is grass"
> 2003.19/E/11.6

Typically for Chadwick, though, her apparent rejection of 'Nature' did not simply cause its long history to be forgotten. She asked, in many locations and contexts, what is nature now? Reflecting on her 'confusion' caused her to consider the *'moral' concepts* that have determined the role of Nature in various ways through human history. Instead of trying to single Nature out, give it a role as 'other', Chadwick's thinking developed around an active, non-singular and non-predictable concept. She approached nature as part of a multistable system, where the only questions that could be asked regarding 'nature' were addressed to what is *relatively natural*.

In order to organise some of the salient *questions of what is relatively natural*, it is helpful to refer to Chadwick's interest in the grotto. As an architectural category, the grotto can boast a long and rich history in both realised example and theoretical discussion, through which competing versions of the relationship between architecture and nature have been explored and tested. Her own work, and the present book, echo something of this relay between a close interest in the grotto itself, and issues concerning the relationship between architecture and nature in general.

The grotto proves to be a kind of limit case, not only literally and figuratively outside 'proper' architecture, but also as liminal condition or boundary state between different worlds. Its appeal for Chadwick is easy to comprehend, and it provided her with an enduring point of reference through which questions concerning the *relatively natural* could be explored, and to which other research—for example, her interest in other historical and mythical architectural examples such as the Garden of Eden and Jerusalem—could be referred.

Much of Chadwick's research into the grotto relied heavily on Naomi Miller's 1982 book, *Heavenly Caves: Reflections on the Garden Grotto*. Although Chadwick's copy was heavily annotated throughout, it is useful here to begin by citing at length from Miller's Epilogue, as this gives a strong sense of the vast range of stuff that is run through the grotto. Additionally, the Epilogue also lends support to the grotto's relevance in contemporary situations: discussing Frederick Keisler's *Grotto for Meditation for New Harmony* (1964), Miller observes the currency of these enduring issues:

> Keisler's rhetoric [on the grotto] is twentieth century, but his ideas connect with the ancients. From Homer to Joyce the grotto has been the locus of mysterious forces, of unanswered questions, of states of being and becoming. A component in the garden, both earthly and divine, it is the far side of paradise and the paradise within, the beginning and the end. A fancy, a capricious toy, it is born of nature and spun by art ['and forged on technology's anvil', Chadwick adds in the margin at this point] for delectation and delight; it is elusive and

remote and infinite in its potentials. Perhaps like the proscenium of the theatre, the grotto is above all a metaphorical portal, an entrance, a place of passage. To enter is the significant act; for to enter is to acknowledge the distance between outside and inside, between reality and illusion, between nature and art. Like the theatre, the grotto is a gateway to wonder and to knowledge [...] But like the labyrinth, the story has no end. (*HC* 123)

Although Chadwick clearly shared Miller's enthusiasm for this topic, for her the significance of entering the grotto, both literally and figuratively, was more than just to 'acknowledge the distance between outside and inside, between reality and illusion, between nature and art'. It provided an opportunity to *test* the distances—or more tellingly, the proximities—assumed to exist between these various paired terms, as well as to enjoy the ambiguity that the grotto involved. Indeed, '[a]mbiguity was the key' (*HC* 35) to sustaining the grotto itself, Chadwick's interest in it, and her broader explorations of *what is relatively natural.*

In chapters leading up to this point, Miller traces the idea and realisation of the grotto in Western civilisations from antiquity. Chadwick highlighted several occasions where Miller links the grotto's elusive form to the relationship struck between nature and art. For example: 'A particular feature of landscape and garden, the grotto is a commonplace ubiquitous in antiquity and prevalent in classical sources [...] Because the grotto may be viewed in a myriad of contexts [...] it constitutes an elusive art form [...]— the grotto is, above all, a metaphor for the cosmos. Variety of forms is almost as vast as variety of functions, with nature versus art as the leitmotif' (*HC* 7).

Chadwick made reference to this contest in a number of her notebooks, although importantly she marked it as a combination rather than a contest:

Nature + Artifice: the Grotto
Art as Nature's Ape
2003.19/E/7.69

Figuring the relationship *Art as Nature's Ape*, she worked to explore this combination around the grotto's characteristics of ambiguity and conceit.

nature's ape

Miller explores what she bills as the contest *nature versus art* through a wide variety of different configurations. She points out that although classical grottoes were so closely related to natural sources or springs that there was no distance between nature and art, 'time soon transforms [the grotto] into an elaborate architectural conceit. Art imitating and surpassing nature: the theme is constant from Pliny to Palissy to Pope' (*HC* 10) and she examines the changing balance within the relationship, including the particular manifestations and (awkward) consequences this had for architecture.

> No structure more effectively illustrates the mockery of architecture—almost its very negation—than does the garden grotto. As John Sherman has written, it is this essential duality between art and nature that makes the grotto such a perfect specimen of mannerism [...] Nowhere is this art/nature dichotomy better expressed than in Tolmei's letter [...]: 'The *ingenioso artifizio* newly rediscovered of making fountains [...], where [...] some appear as natural artifice, and others as artful nature' (*HC* 43–4).

In spite of the changing realisation of grottoes, Miller implies they all share the logic that nature and art, or human artifice more generally, are separate spheres. Moreover, the grotto's privileged position, given its licence for conceit and its inherent ambiguity, makes it a good architectural vehicle for testing out the balance of this *art/nature dichotomy*, the assumption is that art, or architecture, is the dominant term of this pair.

Chadwick's assertion that *there can never be 'Nature'* clearly pulls the rug out from underneath such assumptions. She makes a related remark regarding the relativity of nature in another notebook, where she notes *Art as Nature's Ape* and—importantly—*vice versa*. The context of this remark is also important, as it links her thinking, and the implications of her thinking, to broader issues her work addressed:

> Essay—on still life/vanitas
> Art as Nature's Ape + vice versa
> [allegory]
> Nature/ Architecture: the Grotto
> Desire & Sexuality—Jouissance—
> Simulacra – Mirror
> 2003.19/E/6.145

The reciprocal aping that takes place between nature and art, nature and architecture, echoes issues already discussed such as the ability of *vanitas* to support the coexistence of two antithetical universes in order to *create a continuous stream of interconnections, a dialogue unravelling to reveal a new set of values.* As her thinking on *questions of what is relatively natural* developed, it became clear that this too went beyond just juggling the same stuff, but intended to have an impact on epistemology, on the ways in which our world-view is constructed and maintained.

It is possible that Chadwick borrowed the phrase 'Nature's Ape' from Giovanni Battista (or Giambattista) della Porta. In *Natural Magick*, written in 1558, della Porta's account of the relationship between art, the artist and nature bears on three important considerations that Chadwick made in her own thinking on this topic. Much of della Porta's *Natural Magick* is devoted to bringing about change, to the production of the new. As a key figure in this process, he portrayed the magician as both artist and nature's assistant:

> Art, being as it were, nature's ape, even in her imitation of nature, effecteth greater matters than nature doth. Hence it is that a magician being furnished with art, as it were another nature, searching thoroughly into those works which nature doth accomplish by many secret means and close operations, doth work upon nature [...] and either hastens or hinders her work, making things ripe before or after their natural season, and so indeed makes nature to be his instrument.[1]

When della Porta was writing, roughly contemporaneous with the emergence of *Le Bateleur*, it was believed that the magician was able to gain access to nature's *many secret means and close operations*. Although della Porta's assertion was that human agency was more powerful than nature, that it could effect 'greater matters than nature doth', nature itself was also considered active, it was granted a kind of agency or animism. If, for example, natural objects contained enough *spirit*, they could pass it on to other objects in their vicinity. As Carolyn Merchant observed, this capacity was a result of the various properties that combined to make up natural objects, and art's position as nature's ape can be understood as a response to this conception: 'The tripartite distinction between matter, spirit, and soul was the foundation of the Neoplatonic hierarchical structure [of nature]. Operating within this hierarchy, the magus could draw down the celestial power to marry inferiors to superiors, and therefore to manipulate nature for individual benefit.'[2] The individuals who benefited from this were, of course, the initiates of the system itself, located in the upper levels of the social hierarchy (itself posited as quasi-natural). Recalling Chadwick's acknowledgement that the *natural is really a 'moral' concept*, her awkward interest in the characterisation of art as nature's ape can be explored further. While she would have gone some way with the concept typified by della Porta, particularly in terms of the active role granted to nature, her qualification + *vice-versa* suggests she would have had a very different view of the moral responsibility of 'magician' as artist and the consequences this has had.

In contrast to the high social standing of this magus, Chadwick's own identification with the creative persona as *Le Bateleur* or The Juggler opens an alternate position and possible response regarding these issues of nature's ape. This position reflects Chadwick's complex interest in the developments of artistic and scientific movements towards the Enlightenment period. While della Porta's understanding granted nature an active aspect, his advocacy that nature should be *instrumentalised* foretells the gradual wane of this aspect, in parallel with which the remit of nature's ape was reduced to focusing on the empirical. By the Enlightenment, it was held that the magus turned empirical scientist was able, through experience and calculation, to observe divine or universal order directly in the natural world. The responsibility of the 'ape', the artist or architect or indeed scientist, was held to account over the speed up, slow down, or general manipulation of nature. *Nature as a 'moral' concept* rested firmly with the human, administered increasingly by the quasi-divine figure of the scientist.

While the magus-as-quasi-scientist knowingly aped nature in the active, controlling way typified in della Porta's text, copying and manipulating nature's processes in order to perfect and hasten them or to slow them down, *Le Bateleur* looked elsewhere, 'failed to' capitalise on the potential of this insight, failed to see the significance in, or potential to instrumentalise, the world around him. This leaves the stuff he confronts, or juggles with, as active ingredients in the process; nature in this arrangement remains active, it exceeds measurement and partly evades the scientist's gaze.

There are certain parallels between *Le Bateleur* and the grotto: both were figures with a peripheral position in society, and enjoyed a somewhat ambivalent reputation. For Chadwick in particular, they exemplified the potential of the 'wrong' use of insight. Indeed it could be suggested that the grotto played a role for Chadwick as a kind of Juggler's Table involving different dimensions, it played a role variously as a metaphor and site for the creative act, and as a vehicle for creative imagination. As Miller stresses: 'we can hardly discount the grotto's function as *musaeum*, particularly in the sense of *domus nympharum*, a source of creative imagination' (*HC* 84).

As an architectural vehicle, the grotto was something of a theatre, it provided an opportunity for the increasingly rigid architectural rules of the Enlightenment to be questioned.[3] While the fuller agency of nature suggested by della Porta's position two hundred years previously would no longer be sanctioned, the architectural play of the grotto did operate with nature as a 'moral' concept, it thrived on maintaining an ambiguity between artifice and nature, an ambiguity that would not have been accepted at the centre ground of architectural or scientific discourse at that moment. Approaching this issue from a different direction, the grotto as a source of *creative imagination* provided art with an opportunity to ape nature in ways that addressed irrational temporal structures. While della Porta was explicit about art opening as another nature, where human knowledge could hasten or hinder Nature's work, the grotto operated another time qualitatively different from this speed up or slow down.

nature's time

Chadwick's interest in architectural thought that sanctioned *creative imagination* included other examples in addition to the grotto, including utopian and mythical architectures. Her interest lay not so much in these on their own terms, but in ways such 'other' architectures had been related to more ordinary concerns. In common with her attraction to the grotto, these informed her thinking on the relationship between artifice and nature, on alternative approaches to nature's ape, and on the relationship between architecture, knowledge and power.

In her copy of Thomas and Mary Markus' 1985 exhibition catalogue *Visions of Perfection*, Chadwick marked the role of mythical architecture on Tony Garnier's utopian scheme. Thomas Markus writes: 'a kind of Paradise Garden appears at the core of the modern industrial city. Tony Garnier in his *Cité Industrielle* (1917) shows numerous examples of the harmonious blending of nature with factories, houses and public buildings' (*VP* 13). Chadwick writes in the margin at this point 'Nature + artifice as human utopian system: eg. O.M. [*Of Mutability*] Eden + Jerusalem combined'.

Chadwick's combination puts a particular spin on Garnier's 'harmonious blending': to recall the argument from Chapter 1, the appeal of *Le Bateleur* for Chadwick lay in an ability to achieve Paracelsian harmony that combines and balances difference, rather than to be generated by or reduced to one unified system. With this in mind, her interest in and treatment of utopian architectures signals another divergence from the broad development of art as nature's ape. As Carolyn Merchant argues in *The Death of Nature*, della Porta's assertions regarding an instrumentalised nature, reduced to a knowledge available to human thought, were clearly incorporated by Francis Bacon in his famous utopian novel *New Atlantis* [1626], where they took on a more explicit role as techniques for acceleration or slow down of nature, or for its control more generally. While the role of these assertions as a precursor for empirical science has been mentioned, examples abound of a kind of power creep, an extension of the power of knowledge from humans over nature to certain powerful humans over other less powerful. As Markus notes, this is a characteristic paradox that haunts many utopian architectural schemes:

The architecture of utopia is not only fascinating in itself, and in the influence it has had on an ordinary non-utopian architecture, but it also raises a fundamental question about architecture itself. Since the driving force of architecture is the desire to create stable, and long-lasting order, it has built into it the same duality as that embedded in utopia: the need *for* and the dangers *of* systematic order. This requirement for order not only represents a fundamental human need, but can also be used by any group possessing political power or economic power to impose *its* order on those without such power. (*VP* 9)

While Chadwick's *Model Institution* manifested the Orwellian menace that lurks in Markus' warning, her thinking on the grotto and the various utopian and mythic architectures that interested her was directed towards the potential these held for transforming the links between power and order. In particular, her work attempted to sidestep the desire for stability that Markus identifies as inherent in architecture, by exploring other possible arrangements that could respond to the relationships concerning stability and longevity in different ways. Her interest in *Nature + artifice as human utopian system*, for example, not only emphasised her belief in the reciprocity of the artifice + nature relationship rather than the separation set in train by work such as della Porta's, but also considered another potential separation that Markus refers to as the double power of utopias. He observes their 'double function of critique of the present and vision of the future [which] gives them a paradoxical double power' (*VP* 8).

Double power, for Chadwick, is only a potential, rather than the firmer property that Markus suggests: there is no power if these two aspects remain apart. Thus, in addition to the duality of 'order' just noted, Chadwick's position embraces this double power: together, they indicate the potential for combining that which is commonly accepted as 'reality' with myth, imagination, and the irrational. The tension Markus alludes to can be more clearly understood, when approached through Chadwick's work, as a tension between the real and the ideal, between an architecture in-time, and a utopia that that stands out of time.

In common with other instances of her thinking where she emphasises the importance of *doubling* as way of overcoming the traditional separation of terms in binary formulations, her consideration of the role of utopia addresses how this might similarly be extended or transformed. Although nature appears as a marker for promise or perfection in Chadwick's allusions to *Eden + Jerusalem* and so on, it is one that is always accompanied with a warning such as the *vanitas*.

Architecture has a long tradition of aspiring to the character of myth, standing above time by extricating itself from timely issues epitomised in the *vanitas*. This aspiration is legible in the examples that Markus provides.

The process of purification is addressed more explicitly by another of Chadwick's sources, Joseph Rykwert's *On Adam's House in Paradise*. 'The primitive hut [...] as Laugier conceives it, is a pure distillation of nature through unadulterated reason, prompted only by necessity' (*AHP* 48). Rykwert examines the motivation for this process, and cites as examples some of the big names of early twentieth-century architectural modernism, Le Corbusier, Frank Lloyd Wright and Adolf Loos. There is a parallel between the way these architects drew on the 'pure distillation of nature' as justification for their own work, and Garnier's reference to Paradise that Markus refers to. All of their radical architectural proposals operate by going out of time to draw upon some mythical 'origin' or architectural first principle. The danger with this approach, as Markus notes, is that 'Many Utopias have a timeless, a-historical character and, consequently, ignore the dimension of time. Being conceived beyond time they disregard the need for change, decay and renewal or simply growth' (*VP* 7–8).

Chadwick's response, *History/atemporality + utopia* (added in the bottom margin at this point), indicates the way in which her work differs from most architectural treatment of myth and utopia. Rather than drawing on a pure, distilled origin to legitimise proposals that are similarly timeless, her approach was to combine the atemporality of myth with issues grounded in time. One thread of this approach was to put nature back into doubt; I am here back at Chadwick's confessed 'confusion', and the ways in which her *relatively natural* questions were able to contest this 'pure distillation of nature'.

It is no coincidence that Laugier's work on the primitive hut had such an impact when it was published in the middle of the eighteenth century, a time when architecture, as with many other disciplines, was undergoing radical change. This transitional period, referred to by Tafuri as a hinge between two different, and incompatible, universes, was of particular interest for Chadwick, for much the same reason that Tafuri gives: 'By referring to it, one can cautiously test the ground both up to the thresholds of the tradition we live in and towards a past that is recoverable as such, but with which one can still deal through its formal re-evocation.'[4] While Chadwick juggled with work from both sides of this hinge, rococo, neo-classicism (the pin of the hinge itself), and the picturesque, her enduring interest in the grotto, as an example in the margins of more lofty architectural debate, can be understood to have provided more latitude, literally and figuratively, when it came to the 'distillation of nature'. As Tafuri observes: 'Architecture, from absolute object, becomes in the landscaped context, relative value: it becomes the medium for the description of an edifying play.'[5] Chadwick herself noted in the margins of Miller's discussion of the picturesque grotto 'Integrative spirit of

architecture entwined with Nature + old with new. Classical with Modern'
(*HC* 80).

While this reflects some characteristics of the picturesque grotto, it also
stands as something of a manifesto for Chadwick's own position regarding
the possibilities of architecture. As the account of her identification of
creative self with the figure of The Juggler indicated, she believed that this
kind of 'edifying play' was very serious, and that it provided an opportunity
to sidestep the purification undertaken by 'proper' architecture. Just as *Le
Bateleur* looked the 'wrong' way, downwards, against the 'proper' aspiration
to progress towards 'higher' knowledge, Chadwick explored the potential of
the magus-as-nature's-ape if they approached these landscape, utopian, and
mythical examples the other way. Instead of the grotto being some kind of
froth thrown up by architectural discourse, mere play, it ought be
understood as representing a locus through which the purification and
distillation of nature could be contested. In contrast to the universalising
tendencies of the Encyclopaedic age, Chadwick saw in the grotto an
opportunity to address the individual needs of individuated citizens, a locus
in which the repressed secrets of the distillation process itself might be
explored or uncovered, and the relationship between artefact, nature and
history renegotiated.

nature's mirror

Throughout its long history, the grotto has been associated with other
subterranean places, such as catacombs and crypts, as well as ruins, where
buried secrets were believed to be hidden. In addition to its ambiguous
status regarding nature, this provided Chadwick with an opportunity to
extend her treatment of *questions of what is relatively natural* to include human
nature, and thus to expand the remit of Tafuri's two universes to include
other realms in addition to the historical periods that he indicates.

In addition to the role of the creative archaeologist's search for origins
or roots (epitomised for Tafuri in the figure of Piranesi thanks to the
latter's combination of rigorous scientific study with imagination or
arbitrary restitution), Chadwick's approach shares and repeats this interest
while supplementing it with an emphasis on the role of individual memory,
search and imagination. Her work reinforced the relevance and importance
of a renovated cosmology to the process of positioning oneself in the
world. Through her architectural explorations of the grotto, she attempted
to instigate a transformed method of looking and searching that was based
on imaginative combination. In doing so, she drew out another enduring
theme in the grotto, namely the role it has played in establishing and
communicating cosmological understanding. Indeed Miller emphasises on a
number of occasions, all highlighted by Chadwick, that 'the grotto is, above

all, a metaphor for the cosmos' (*HC* 7); '[it is] the creation of a cosmos in miniature, a nature that is cultivated and controlled [...] an elaborate architectural conceit' (*HC* 10).

While the architectural adoption of the primitive hut has already been mentioned as 'pure distillation of nature through unadulterated reason', Rykwert discusses a number of other instances where its role as an individuated model is also significant, and where it comes closer to Chadwick's interest in its potential. As with the grotto, the primitive hut did also operate in many instances as a microcosm with the inhabitant at the centre. Rykwert remarks on these features where the primitive hut provides 'a coherent, formally self-contained "map"; and it refers to the initiate's body—he identifies himself with it when he embraces it—to sacred history, the hierogamos and the cosmic order' (*AHP* 188).

This ability for individual identification was, for Chadwick, a significant property of these architectures. As she intimated in the margin of *Heavenly Caves*, these cosmological qualities not only lead outward into the social world of shared history or into the wider cosmos, but also lead inward to address dimensions of a different 'nature' ignored by architecture: 'Withdrawal into illusory world as communion with interior world of desire—one's own inner nature' (margin to *HC* 11). The potential to position architecture in a different relationship with these various natures was an important aspect of Chadwick's thought. It would involve a reintroduction of the idealised into conversation with the everyday: of the commonly hidden aspects of body, memory and cosmology with the 'rational' dimensions of nature that survived distillation. In a complex list of forces or dimensions that would form part of this relationship, that would acknowledge 'nature's' relativity, Chadwick included the following:

<u>Desire + Love</u> Sexuality/ Narcissism Jouissance
<u>The Mirror</u>: simulacrum
Vanitas/ Still Life
Mutability
<u>Nonesuch Place</u>: Architecture of Fabulous Loci Dreams
Nature + Artifice: the Grotto
2003.19/E/7.69

Chadwick linked the role of the grotto as locus for individuated cosmology with its previous capacities, and its potential, to operate as a mirror to nature. Her interest in *The Mirror: simulacrum* expanded well beyond the limits of the grotto, although the limitations for reflecting both outwardly as well as *one's own inner nature* on the relevance of this potential can be approached initially by considering the metaphorical and physical mirroring that the grotto has been charged with.

As nature's ape, the grotto had at times moved far from the simulacrum that Chadwick included in her wish-list given above. As she highlighted in Miller's analysis, some of the most successful 'mirroring' occurred when artificiality was most manifest: 'It is poetic irony that the back to nature movement of the eighteenth century resulted in grottoes so far removed from the natural mode. Still, they became metaphors of nature if we consider them as openly in revolt against the formal garden, understood as contrary to nature herself [...] To produce the illusion of nature by artificial means was the goal' (*HC* 93). At such moments, successful mirroring was brought about by grottoes that were literally made as machines. The mirroring can be considered to occur in two contrasting but complementary ways, with the grotto understood as a machine for both literally and metaphorically observing both inner and outer worlds.

In a couple of places Chadwick writes *Camera Obscura* in the margin of *Heavenly Caves*, and again inside the back cover, but this is not the only optical device that was associated with or incorporated into the grotto; telescope, mirror and microscope are also mentioned by Miller. Listing a number of optical devices in Pope's Cave, Miller emphasises the knowing doubling at play in this particular example, and by extension in other realised and theoretical works. 'That Pope was aware of all the metaphysical associations of the cave, of its connections with Plato's cave, Locke's "dark room" of understanding, and Plotinus's notion that the mind gives "radiance out of its own store" (*Enneads*, 4.6.3), is apparent in the titles of the caves in Pope's own poetry; the Cave of Spleen, Cave of Poetry, and Cave of Truth. Here, grottoes were understood as "the haunt of frugal virtue, philosophy and true wisdom"' (*HC* 83).

Despite the importance she accorded these associations or overtones (indicated by the sheer size of the asterisk she added in the margin here) Chadwick's work suggested that she was dissatisfied with the way nature was looked at, not only in terms of the empirical scientific observation already discussed, but also in terms mediated by these grotto metaphors. Introducing her own 'grotto', *The Oval Court* (part of her installation *Of Mutability*), Chadwick acknowledged the role accorded the mirror together with its limitations, before suggesting the extra reach desirable for a 'palpably real' experience:

> Within each event the position of things is given, but the emotive momentum is left hanging. It may be perceived literally as an outwardly manifest reality, a mirror, or experienced by the eye alone, but will only become palpably real if felt deep within the reflexive domain of

introspection. Open to speculation yet unfathomable, as oracle I draw the breath of stimulus itself. The temporal field has dispersed into sensory shallows. I am merely a tendency to exist, scrolls of pure conjecture enunciated inwardness. (*OM* 29)

The awareness of all the metaphysical associations of the cave, played out as metaphor in Pope's grotto as in countless others, did not satisfy Chadwick's ambition for the grotto's potential as a device for understanding or supporting such experience. Just as her *questions of what is relatively natural* operated by expanding the range of nature's ape and nature's time based on an increasingly rational basis for these links, so her interest in such mirroring targeted the presuppositions that lay behind the organisation of the metaphors themselves. Chadwick's theoretical position is in this respect anticipated by Tafuri. It is coincidence that he likens the Futurists with the artist-magician, but as he goes on with this point, accusing them of stopping short of the logic of their approach, a stronger similarity with Chadwick's own observations is apparent: 'faced by this *new universe of artificial "things"*, used as basic material for their artistic work, they still behave with a mentality anchored to the principle of *mimesis*'.[6] While Chadwick's appreciation of Pope's grotto is clear, she kept this in context. For her as an artist, to work with a mentality anchored to the Enlightenment universe of natural 'things' would be to repeat the approaches she criticised regarding a nature taken out of time. But it should also be asserted that Chadwick's nature (or relative nature) includes far more than that granted by Tafuri.

In terms of the machines and metaphors of looking with which Chadwick's theory operates, her approach to the grotto, as a contemporary architectural consideration that could address appropriate cosmologies, drew upon and transformed previous models. The traditional sources for metaphor were simply no longer appropriate. Moreover, the simple *replacement* of one paradigm with another (the basis for and the problem with Tafuri's criticism of the Futurists just given) was equally problematic. There was a need to gather in a greater range of different ingredients to understand looking properly, and her work endeavoured to include a wider spectrum of approaches. Artist and theorist Victor Burgin has explored directly some of the issues concerning looking that can help bring Chadwick's wide-ranging considerations of these topics into focus here.

Burgin's underlying complaint is the all too frequent conflation of psychical space with the space of visual perception. He notes various *camera obscura* metaphors, not from the Enlightenment phase when optical devices acted as metaphors for the relationship between self and world (for cosmologies, if you like), but metaphors that run through the work of more

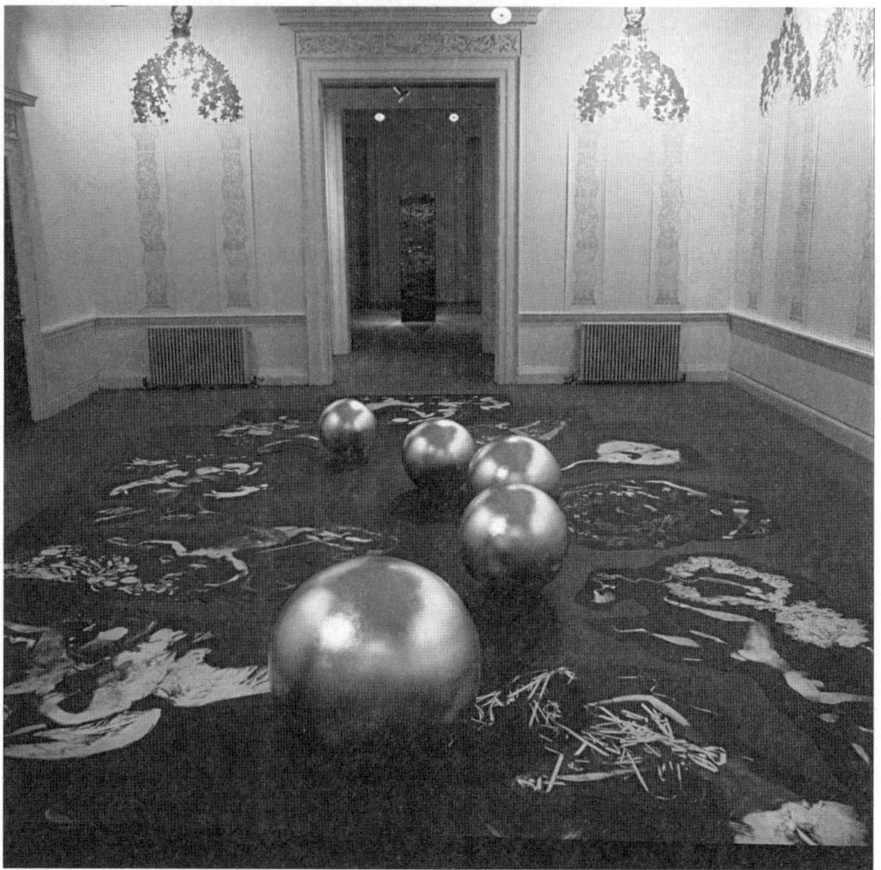

11 *Of Mutability*, 1986–7.

Installation for the Institute of Contemporary Arts (ICA), London, where it occupied the Upper Galleries. Here, the reflecting pool at the centre of *The Oval Court* with *Carcass* just visible through the door into the adjacent gallery. Computer-drawn Solomonic columns line the room, topped with swags of foliage and images of Chadwick weeping. (opposite) Detail of 'Leda and the Swan', one of twelve different scenes comprising *The Garden of Delights* at the centre of *The Oval Court*, made from complex collages of blue photocopies.

recent writers such as Karl Marx, Jacques Lacan and Roland Barthes. In all such examples, Burgin believes the metaphoric application of the 'cone of vision', with the subject's eye or mind situated at the apex of the cone, has been responsible for 'a reductive and simplistic identification of looking with objectification. In so far as this metaphor is drawn from physiological optics, it is inappropriate to the description of psychological functions. In so far as it is drawn from Euclidean geometry, it is inadequate to describe

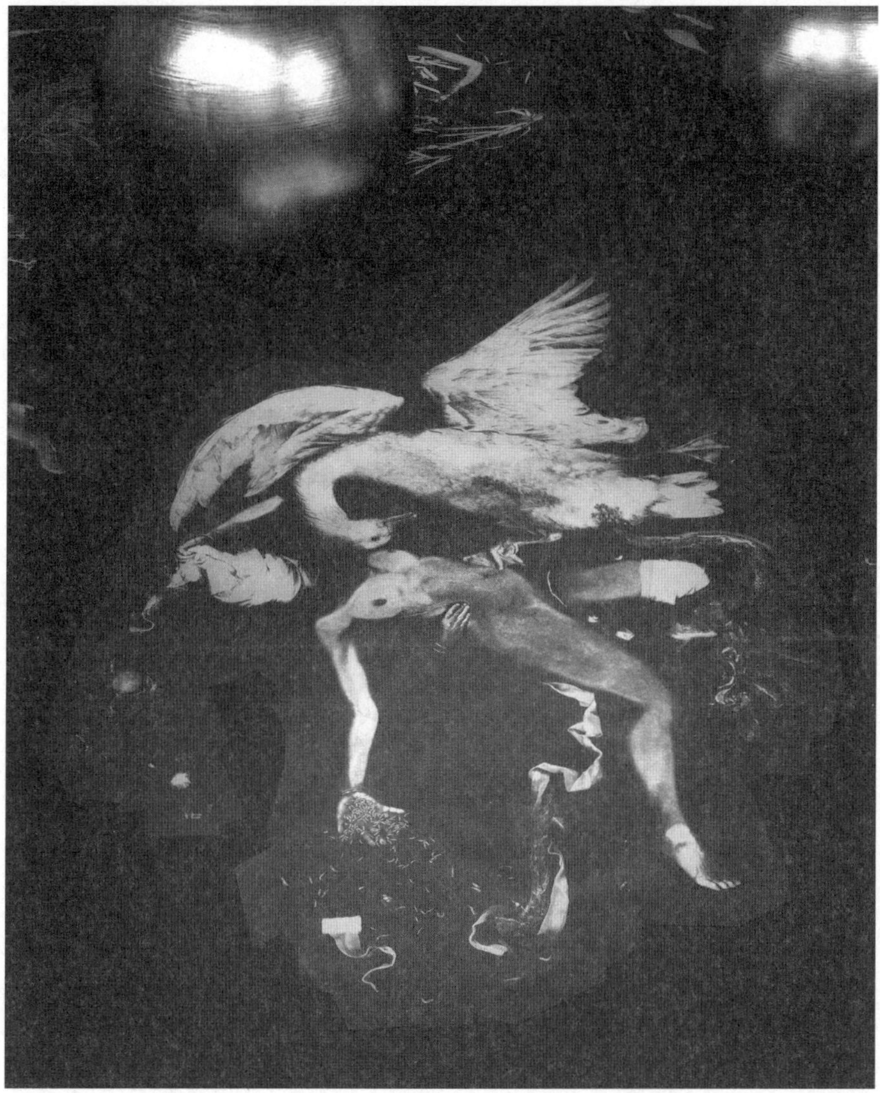

the changed apprehension of space which is an attribute of so called "post-modern" culture.'[7]

Burgin objects to the application of the visual cone, arguing that it flattens all sorts of other dimensions that are part of the experience of looking, and that it conflates optical and psychical space (Chadwick's *reflexive domain of introspection*). These in turn have an impact on our understanding of the viewer and the viewed, on the role of the unconscious. While there are positive aspects to the cone of vision model, particularly the way it reinstates the subject in the space of representation, its drawback is that it maintains the traditional subject–object dichotomy as a relation based on a separation between inside and outside. Burgin's suggestion is that looking can involve double aspects—both active and passive, sadistic and masochistic, of alienation and identification, and so on—that are especially relevant around mirroring.

This approach, with its emphasis on doubling, would clearly have appealed to Chadwick: this lends support to her complex, open architectural approach, it responds to her understanding of the importance and dimensions of a contemporary cosmology. Chadwick's thinking suggests a multi-layered conception of architecture, a different grotto, not as architectural conceit but as an artifice across which the *relativity* of nature can be explored. Her thinking around the grotto mirrors a fuller, more heterogeneous conception of nature, one that is supported by a number of points of view that exceed those modelled on the cone of vision, including the Keplerish-Archimedian point situated outside the cosmos that is traditionally sought by the architect, and the architect's 'other', the subject reduced to the eye, the Corbusian eyeball moving around 1.5 metres above the ground.

Although much of Chadwick's œuvre can be taken to contest the legacies of these points of view, she can be understood to have worked through them rather than simply rejected them. By championing the ambiguities that both positions overlooked on the way to their respective schemata for seeing clearly, Chadwick addressed both idealised and experiential schema for our relationship with nature. Again the grotto epitomised broader concerns regarding landscape, architecture, and their inter-relationship, through which differing approaches to both physical and mental landscapes were played out. While Burgin's analysis was directed elsewhere, his notion of a 'perverse space' provides a useful tool through which Chadwick's considerations of these historical situations, and thence our contemporary relationship with nature, can be opened up. In both schemata, whether looking from the cosmos to understand the world, or looking from within the world through to the cosmos, Chadwick sought the remainder, the stuff that had to be left out or could not be accommodated by the cone-of-vision model. Similarly to Burgin, she consistently demanded these and other relationships be opened up to address ambiguity, and include more multi-layered, and possibly irreconcilable, ingredients.

On several occasions Chadwick noted the interest in *variety* expressed by eighteenth-century architectural and landscape theorists. While this was frequently provided by quantity, the more important aspects of variety for productive, or 'perverse', ambiguity were encountered where this was categorical or qualitative variety within experience. As landscape philosopher John Dixon Hunt has shown, the vogue for almost endless variety that thinkers such as Pope demanded of their landscapes was due in large part to the work and influence of the philosopher John Locke (1632–1704). Locke, in *Of the Conduct of the Understanding* (published posthumously in 1706), discussed the notion that the human mind is initially empty, and is filled by a rapid succession of fleeting images. As Hunt observes, this model of the understanding influenced both the theory and design of landscapes, where endless variety was believed to provide the mind with a suitable environment in which to expatiate.

Although this direct mapping of the concept of the understanding onto 'real' landscapes (wherein wandering minds would through their experiences gather impressions, supplemented by reflection, to provide greater understanding) seems to mark an empirical situation that was provided for by picturesque landscaping, it was also influential over very rational positions and severe neoclassical compositions such as those of Boullée. This provision of variety could be accomplished within apparently 'formal' approaches, and Hunt goes on to provide illustrations of what he refers to as the 'Wandering Thoughts' camp being satisfied by apparently formal settings. (Indeed, the inclusion of variety within these settings served to highlight the formality and symmetry of their overall arrangement.)

Rather than having to choose between nature or artifice, the more sophisticated claims of this camp were for landscapes that included both: the mind would be kept even more occupied, as it would have to adjudicate between the effects of both. 'Varieties of garden not only became a means of declaring various psychological traits and habits, they were invoked to describe different kinds of imaginative skills.'[8] Although Hunt emphasises the importance of gardens as ciphers of the eighteenth century's broader aesthetic patterns, the sanctioned role of the imagination was limited to certain prescribed themes. Moreover, access to such gardens, and the prior knowledge required to unlock the stimuli for imaginative play, was of course limited by social position.

The important point here for Chadwick was not the difference across gardens, the variety of their variety, and therefore the difference between imaginative skills called upon, but the potential inscription of imagination in experience per se. While this was accepted—even in its limited form—in the garden and its architecture, it was generally limited to that arena. In the serious architecture of the city, debate on architectural character laundered nature of any ambiguity. In contrast, Chadwick voiced the possibility of an ongoing role for imaginative skill:

> Combine natural with fantastic
> Epic still life [...]
> Concrete realism + fantasy combined.
> 2003.19/E/7.55

Although expressed in rather bald terms, Chadwick's support for the combination of reason and imagination (which she repeated often) can be unpacked by considering supplementary work through Burgin's analysis of the cone of vision. Rather than the grotto, landscape, or architecture more broadly operating as a 'mirror of nature', Chadwick emphasised a need to think of what might be obscured by such a mirroring.

> The <u>Mirror</u>: behind silver, alchemical entry into Spirit through love [...]
> Paradise as a reflection of a dream [...]
> Oceanic feeling ~ expansion awareness—self dissolves as salt into water
> <u>Mirror</u> like apple gives self knowledge + self consciousness ego separates
> 'self' from 'nature', body from soul, consciousness from infinite
> Use mirror to return back through the eye into Paradise into unity by
> passive surrender into glass.
> 2003.19/E/7.64–3

In contrast to what Chadwick here implies is an active mirroring, she suggests a reversal, or at least a reconsideration, of what lies behind the mirror, what is cut off by the attainment of this version of selfhood. Just as Burgin expressly criticises such schemas for *self knowledge + self consciousness* because they rely on a reductive, single point of view, Chadwick similarly suggests an alternative, an expanded awareness with no defined viewpoint. Her terminology is dangerously misleading: 'passive surrender' and a suggested return to Paradise clearly imply a regressive, quasi-religious subjugation that belies the weight of her œuvre. Despite this, the motive here is clearer: taking her interest in the grotto through its potential as a complex 'optical' device rather than a simple reflecting surface, the balance that her thinking struck between active and passive mirroring developed according to the kind of 'perverse' optics that Burgin's work implies.

Her thoughts on Paradise are echoed in her reflections on the rococo Spiegelsaal, or Hall of Mirrors, in the Amalienburg palace near Munich (1734–9), which she visited in 1984.

> <u>Amalienburg</u> : Spiegelsaal: Room as art concept
> The dance, dizzy rhythms. "The world as idea"
> Rocaille as snow, melting spirit, allegory of spiritual love/thaw.
> Palace as paradise on earth –bought ∴ celebrates erotic
> 2003.19/E/7.61[9]

Chadwick's interest in the rococo was enthusiastic but qualified: any approach to the rococo was to be accompanied and complemented by an equally serious engagement with neo-classicism, and they nearly always appear together in her notes. For example:

> soul: neoclassical—monumental, symmetry, perpetual, austere
> body: rococo—transient, asymmetrical, rich, picturesque, graceful
> 2003.19/E/6.23

Chadwick's insistence on addressing these together reflected her deliberations on the separations just noted—*'self' from 'nature', body from soul, consciousness from infinite*. Moreover, her thinking was not simply a return to a pre-lapsarian situation, nor to instigate another dualism around these terms or the approaches they announce. It was to fuel her consideration of the contemporary relevance of this balance on our own relationship with the world and her questions of the *relatively natural*.

Her reaction to the Spiegelsaal, while it did emphasise the *bodily* characteristics she linked with the rococo, pleasure not power, can be understood to open towards the passive reflection she associated with *the Mirror*. The Spiegelsaal involves a mode of reflection that includes but exceeds optical reflection: while the overriding impression of this space derives from the mirrors, which in combination intensify the experience of the space by mirroring away to infinity in all directions, this was not entirely responsible for the 'dizzying' experience that Chadwick noted. Indeed, it was not just the silvered mirrors, but the architecture itself, that brought this about, and which provided a model for an alternate and extended mirroring of 'nature'.

A typical account of rococo architecture, such as that provided by Christian Norberg-Schultz's book *Late Baroque and Rococo Architecture* of which Chadwick had a copy, underscores the characteristics that would have had clear appeal for her, such as its celebration of the 'earthly' or the 'low', its transitory rather than transcendent intentions. While these were clearly relevant, her response to this architecture elaborated on the processes of interaction, or mirroring, involved:

> Rococo cartouches for tactile + emotive sensation
> ornaments of non existent protean substance = emotion
> a substance resembling both inorganic + flesh /skin
> *Filofax* (notes after 'Early Baroque Cartouches', ornamentale vorlange blatter, Rudolf Berliner Klinkhand+ Biermann, 1981) Next dated entry 5 March 1988.

The indeterminacy of the substance of rococo architecture not only indicates the historical appeal of the rococo, but suggests why Chadwick felt it held contemporary relevance. Her reading of its ambiguous, *protean substance*, at once inorganic and fleshy, an architecture of energy and matter, comes closer to some of the insights of modern science than the stable Newtonian view underpinning Enlightenment architecture. She emphasised the appeal of this indeterminacy while comparing her own work with that of François Boucher (1703–70), a well-known rococo painter:

> Compare Boucher figure + mine
> My work about unification/dissolution not separating object/subject or image/viewer
> 2003.19/E/6.123

Chadwick's description of her work here echoes her interest in the rococo architecture of the Spiegelsaal, in contrast to the separation she observed in rococo painting. Indeed in this respect, the Spiegelsaal can take its place alongside the grotto in terms of the relevance it held for her thinking, inasmuch as the grotto has also been taken as enjoying a liminal state and location: 'the grotto is on the edge of chaos; it is the primordial substance [...] where all is subject to metamorphosis' (*HC* 30, 73). For Chadwick, the importance of both examples ought to remain central to our experience, rather than the protean or primordial substance of these situations either remaining marginalised, or being controlled by magic, science or religion. In contrast to the model of experience or perception she reads in Boucher's work, which exceeds its rococo style and could stand for the modern attitude of separation far more broadly, Chadwick's thinking juggles with these various ingredients in the framework of experience. Instead of considering the figure in nature, or in a 'naturalised' architecture (as nature's ape), which maintains nature as a separate category however defined, her understanding of experience called this conception of nature into question. Metamorphosis and chaos were not to be overcome by greater forces prior to individuated experience, but as the examples she found in the formlessness of the rococo and the grotto suggested, ought to be ingredients of experience itself.

As she stressed elsewhere, such experience ought to be offered *harmony*, but this harmony was conceived as a balance of attraction and repulsion, akin to Minkowskian reverberation. The *unification/dissolution* ought, she would argue, to remain as a kind of 'void' within all experience.

> The Void. The pulsing around a void~ the event horizon~ the 'field'
> Formlesness + perception
> energies as illusory forms, illusory patterns, mapping the passage through non-territories
> 2003.19/E/8.26

These various illusory forms or patterns can be understood to operate as the potential for 'passive' reflection Chadwick identified with *the 'Mirror'*. In combination with the active reflection that could be based on the cone of vision, passive reflection in itself needed a different schema and would challenge the cone of vision model with the separations it assumed and perpetuated. To weave this assertion back into the complex relay of relationships and metaphors that exist between architecture, nature, subject–object separation and human understanding is a complex process, and one I do not propose to undertake here. Haunting this process, though, is Burgin's insight that recent contributions to this discussion, which add more layers to the consideration of experience, continued to organise themselves according to an understanding of space that was based on this traditional visual model. His introduction of perverse space does not simply add another layer, but rather asks that the framework for considering our experience adopts a qualitatively different approach. While in common parlance, perversion carries overtones of a deviation from the norm, a deviation from nature and natural morality, we can do no better than repeat Chadwick's assertion that *Natural is really a 'moral' concept—there can never be 'Nature'*. Taken thus, perverse space does not signal a deviation or an alternative, but a co-requisite for experience where nature and the natural can no longer play a role as 'other' against which human experience or artifice is measured.

Miller discusses the grotto in terms that imply it was an architectural vehicle where perversion was sanctioned (to which other clearly circumscribed situations such as the festival could be added): 'It may be understood as the expression of the irrational in a superbly rational world, the element of chance in a highly planned cosmos, the notion of chaos within the ordered scheme [...] A counterpart to animate the rigid geometry of the Renaissance garden, the grotto could be construed as a natural or an artificial entity. Amid the ambiguity, illusion reigned' (*HC* 53, 58). Chadwick marks these passages heavily, although all indications are that she would turn this relationship around, and posit that the rational was only a moment of artificial, relative clarity in an otherwise chaotic continuum. Her 'denial' of nature was less along these lines of momentary and localised reversals of the accepted hierarchical relationship between nature and artifice (reversals that leave the main 'whole' undisturbed) and more concerned with exploring the alternate relationships derived across a continuum of void, the energy of illusion, the combination of concrete reality and imagination. In this sense, the grotto informed Chadwick's suggestions for a new cosmology, a new epistemology, where ambiguity and imagination had a central role to play, and which had a basis in not-knowing rather than the assumed completeness and cohesion, and ultimately the subjugation, of nature.

> body as a garden
> cultured nature [...]
> the organic as integrated within us
> thoughts / brain / theory—all organic
> rather than natural or artificial
> describes life
> flesh as flowers
> flowers as flesh
> "all flesh is grass"
> 2003.19/E/11.6

6 Architecture, the divinities and the authority of science

For Chadwick, the grotto provided a rich vehicle around which she was able to develop her extensive considerations regarding the relationship between architecture and nature. The *questions of what is relatively natural* that were explored in the previous chapter, while delimited there around the issues concerning the grotto, were also closely linked to Chadwick's broader interest in how claims have been made for authority and jurisdiction over our experience of and actions in the world. In this sense, 'Nature' represents one significant but not exclusive claim in an ongoing competition between differing models of authority. Nature's changing fortunes have occurred along with those of the divinities, the ancients, and science, all of which have been called upon, and continue to be called upon, by architecture.

While Chadwick's thinking on this ongoing tussle over authority was informed by research that was historically and theoretically widespread, her interest in the writing of Boullée provides an instance through which her position can be most clearly set out. Although Boullée was a well-known champion of Newton, both through his *Architecture, Essay on Art* and his well-known project for a *Cenotaph to Newton* (1784), Chadwick's considerations of Boullée's work nevertheless reflected her own ambivalent response to the impact of Newtonian science on our experience of the world. In preparatory notes for a lecture, she repeated her desire to move

away from Newtonian object to state flux temp. fixings
2003.19/E/8.139

It is important to state that Chadwick found material to support such a *move away* within Boullée's work itself. Boullée's architectural proposals were drawn up in a severe neoclassical architectural language that is frequently taken to epitomise the priority granted to rationality and the power of human reason during the Enlightenment period, a priority foretold in the title of Newton's most famous and influential work *Mathematical Principles of Natural Philosophy* (*Philosophiæ Naturalis Principia Mathematica*, 1687). Nevertheless, Boullée's writings display a far more nuanced and uncertain balance between the authority of mathematical principles and natural philosophy, and provide a much better reflection of the disputes over authority that took place in what was, after all, a period of great social, as well as scientific, change in Europe.

In the notes she made on Boullée's *Essai*, Chadwick remarked on Boullée's rationale for the dominance of Platonic forms that characterise his architectural language:

> circle/globe aesthetically full + satisfying: selected from natural forms based on Platonic perfect solids~ most perfect form
> Reasoned appreciation of function ruled by laws of nature: task to reproduce in structure idiom the <u>ennobling</u> impression Nature makes on man: perfect forms + hues based on changes of season.
> 2003.19/E/6.25

These observations indicate the continuing influence of the ghosts of previous authorities, and the push and pull experienced between them. Here, human reason, far from explaining nature, is ruled by nature's laws, which are themselves based on a metaphysical perfection explained by classical philosophy. While Newton's *Mathematical Principles* offered scientific laws (the Universal Law of Gravitation and the Laws of Motion) for the behaviour of the universe, and thus to demonstrate its unity, the universalising tendency of this work was tempered during the eighteenth century. The various philosophical and aesthetic responses to this rise of empirical science refused to grant science exclusive sway over explanations of our relationship with the world: the authorities of divine power, of the ancients, and of Nature continued to play a significant role, recombined into various new schema for power-sharing pacts. Boullée's work was clearly keyed into these broader contemporary concerns, and in this regard, it provided Chadwick with another opportunity to reflect on the tensions brought together in Tafuri's 'hinge'.

Boullée was explicit about the authority of nature:

> Oh, Nature! How true it is that you are the book of books, universal knowledge! No, we can do nothing without you! (*AEA* 89 [85v])

This comes from a section of the *Essai* tellingly entitled 'Programmes intended to establish that the Study of Nature is necessary to architecture'.

In the same section, Boullée emphasises that not only is Nature the source of universal knowledge, but that architecture must return to make natural effects:

> I cannot repeat too often that an architect must make effective nature. It is impossible to create architectural imagery [*tableaux*] without a profound knowledge of nature: the Poetry of architecture lies in natural effects. That is what makes architecture an art and that art sublime. Architectural imagery [*tableaux*] is created when a project has a specific character which generates the required impact. (*AEA* 88 [84r])

It is around this concept of 'architectural imagery' (*tableaux*), which is consequently developed by Boullée as what he calls the 'extended image' (*image étendue*), that it is possible to take up Chadwick's interest in and divergence from his position. Although this interest might be taken to be rather paradoxical, given her repeatedly stated interest in moving away from understandings of the world based on the stable Newtonian view, towards *state flux temp. fixings*, dirt, irrationality, matter, and so on, Boullée's *Essai* revealed for her something of its own paradox. In his working through of the necessity of the *Study of Nature*, Boullée is caused to lament that, despite the universal knowledge on offer in the book of Nature, few people bother to look and learn: with something of a sleight of hand, he then works through an assertion that architecture can be based on the authority of Good Taste.

good taste, nature and authority

> The art of making things agreeable stems from Good Taste [...] a delicate, aesthetic discernment with regard to objects that arouse our pleasure [...] Let us concentrate on architecture and we shall see that here Good Taste consists of providing more delicacy than opulence, more subtlety than strength, more elegance than ostentation. Thus it is grace that is indicative of Good Taste. (*AEA* 89 [85v])

'Taste' was an important aspect of many eighteenth-century aesthetic debates, although its relevance in the present context concerns Boullée's account of Good Taste and architecture, as Chadwick's thinking on Boullée's *Essai* is closely tied to this relationship. One of the principal themes of Boullée's work, which Chadwick raises on several occasions, concerns the balance between symmetry and variety:

Architecture, Essay on Art: Boullée
Art, product of mind, imitation of nature/truth
sphere (most perfect) always perceived as uniform, changeless,
immutable

stereometric—symmetry=order/perfection
—variety: stimulating, new life/gives pleasure
2003.19/E/6.27

Within this short note, the differing authorities of the human mind, of *nature/truth*, and of universal geometry, all come into play. For Boullée, as for many of his contemporaries, Good Taste was charged with negotiating between these. His reference to that 'delicate, aesthetic *discernment* with regard to objects that arouse our pleasure' is particularly important, for while 'Good Taste' was linked to Nature, it was more contingent than Newton's Universal Laws, and qualified by some sort of human judgement. As his modern editor suggests, Boullée was influenced by Montesquieu's article on 'Taste' (*Goût*) in the *Encyclopédie* (1757).[1]

While Montesquieu's article was not necessarily the last word on 'Taste', it posits the principal assertions, and something of the uncertainty, relayed by Boullée and picked up by Chadwick. According to Montesquieu's definition, Taste was not just a subjective preference akin to a preference or dislike for certain foods, it could be Good or Bad. Moreover, while Taste did acknowledge the Laws of Nature (an *imitation of nature/truth*), it was ultimately a human sensibility, and as such could be nurtured, and developed and its outcomes agreed upon by society. As William Ray has described it, the discernment of taste involved fostering 'the construction of consensual truth',[2] a truth that was within the power of people, rather than of nature, to determine.

In arriving at a consensus, the possible variations in Taste ought to be negotiated; it is here that the balance between order and variety can be understood to be in play. However, Montesquieu's definition downplays these potential variables in order to concentrate on 'common principles', a move that Downing A. Thomas argues is remarkable, given the rigour with which Montesquieu had addressed 'the question of the many physical and moral variables that were drawn out with such complexity in [Montesquieu's] *De l'esprit des lois* [*The Spirit of Laws*, 1748], an omission that is all the more surprising given how appropriate such variables would seem to be for the subject of taste'.[3] He goes on immediately to stress 'Montesquieu did bracket individual difference in the essay on taste— differences of which he was fully aware—[…] in order to identify common principles, such as the pleasure afforded by symmetry.'

Boullée followed Montesquieu in the emphasis given to symmetry in his account of how Good Taste should influence architecture, how symmetry and regularity should take priority within what might be referred to as his 'consensual truth' or laws of architecture. However, he did stress that an overall formal clarity could—indeed should—accommodate variety, provided the latter did not threaten the overall ease of recognition. In this respect, Boullée again echoes Montesquieu's definition of Taste, as Thomas notes: 'A well-ordered but varied presentation causes the soul to experience pleasure, as do appropriate uses of symmetry, contrast, surprise, grace, and so on—each of which forms a section in the *Encyclopédie* article.'[4]

Boullée's understanding of regularity was guided by Platonic forms, although as his *Essai* qualifies or develops this more explicitly towards Good Taste and beauty, he repeats a classical conception that operates an analogy between the human body, the building, and even urban planning. He comments that the closer something resembles the human organism the more *beautiful* it will be considered, and vice versa. In a later section on *Character*, Boullée reiterates this point citing John Locke's *Essai Philosophique*, stating that everything, 'all our ideas, all our perceptions come to us via external objects. External objects make different impressions on us according to whether they are more or less analogous with the human organism' (*AEA* 86 [77v]).[5]

At this point, Chadwick's response to the issues raised by Boullée's *Essai* can be developed through its engagement not only with 'Nature' but also with the role given to the human form as a paragon for Good Taste. In later notes, she repeats some of the central observations of Boullée's *Essai*, before asserting her own clear departure from his position:

> "Nature": essay on symmetry. Eye favours symmetry–chooses symmetric patterns both inside (within) as organ developing + outside (observed world)
> Desirable property because of function of eye preferring symmetry.
> Easier to recognise (effects evolution species)
> Egg as eye (Bataille)–re-read [...]
> FAVOUR ASYMETRIC [*sic*]–anti-eye
> 2003.19/E/8.108

Although there are many bits of Boullée's work that remain significant for Chadwick, her striking assertion *FAVOUR ASYMETRIC–anti-eye* announces an aspect of her thinking that explored alternate laws and authorities, laws that counter conventional arguments to take nature as rulebook, while maintaining her own strong interest in nature (as a relative question, of course). This interest in going *inside (within)* signals Chadwick's determination to look for 'nature' elsewhere and by other means, to identify and value different properties, and was a response to the shortcomings she perceived in various architectural schemata, not just Boullée's. The consequences of *FAVOUR ASYMETRIC–anti-eye* open up some of the roles that have been played by looking in a number of the most influential relationships that have been struck between the body, nature, architecture and authority. Several of these continue to have an impact upon the ways in which architecture is both taught and discussed today.

Chadwick's note to herself *(Bataille)—re-read* comes after notes she took on a selection of his essays published as *Visions of Excess*. Whatever her re-reading intentions actually were, it is interesting to consider Bataille's essay on 'The Deviations of Nature' in that collection. There, Bataille discusses the role that overlaid images can play in gradually transcending individual physical appearances; how '[t]he composite image would thus give a kind of reality to the necessarily beautiful Platonic idea', and how the common measure 'necessarily approaches the regularity of geometric figures'.[6] This discussion is particularly interesting in the present context, as the movement from individual to consensual agreement over beauty, or Taste more broadly, weaves a steady course between the regularity and authority of Platonic geometry, the book of nature, beauty and the limitations of individual variety. Moreover, Bataille's description of the build up of the composite image closely echoes Boullée's account of regular volumes (although they had very different motives).

Boullée asserts that 'the combination and the respective concord which are the result of all these properties [regularity, symmetry and variety], give rise to volumetric harmony' (*AEA* 86 [78v]). He goes on to locate these properties at the heart of his theory of architecture: 'As in nature, the art of giving an impression of grandeur in architecture lies in the disposition of the volumes that form the whole in such a way that there is a great deal of play among them [...] It is just such expanded images [*images étendues*] that I have tried to produce in several of my projects' (*AEA* 89–90 [86r]). The production and experience of expanded images (which themselves echo his description of *the combination and respective concord* of the properties of regular volumes) anticipate the composite images discussed by Bataille.

Although the thinking of Chadwick, Bataille and Boullée overlaps around this issue, they pull in different directions. Within the present context, it is relevant that Chadwick's decision to *FAVOUR ASYMETRIC–anti-eye* is prefaced by her summary of the empirical half of Boullée's rationale: *Desirable property because of function of eye preferring symmetry.* However much Boullée's projects might have been crushingly authoritative, his motivation to produce an architecture of expanded images (*images étendues*) was to replace the authority accorded to proportion with that of symmetry, and to allow some play between individual variety and overall 'consensus'. In this, his motives can be understood in the context of the broader debates of his time concerning Taste, where he subscribed to the notion that individual perceptions were acknowledged but handed over and absorbed into the composite image of consensual truth. Nevertheless, this 'truth' or judgement of Taste was the product of human culture, and Boullée strikes out for this while directly questioning the transcendent authority of proportion upon which architecture had for so long been predicated.

Boullée raises some interesting issues regarding the priority attributed to proportion in terms of the difficulty ordinary people have in grasping this 'rule'. Although he does acknowledge its importance, he proposes to emphasise symmetry instead, because of the relative ease with which it is evident, as Chadwick repeats *Desirable property because of function of eye preferring symmetry*. While Chadwick goes on to question the basis of authority based on the eye, she had some sympathy with his attempt to wrest the authority over looking from the metaphysical and to locate it instead in the physical realm. Given that the reality of the eighteenth-century importance of Taste was hardly one of full agency or democracy, it did mark an attempt to challenge the notion of 'genius' that artists and architects had been granted for centuries thanks to their ability to reproduce the natural order in their work. Boullée emphasised that this was his motivation in replacing the priority of proportion with that of regularity based on symmetry: 'In architecture a lack of proportion is not generally very obvious except to the eye of the connoisseur. It is thus evident that although proportion is one of the most important elements constituting beauty in architecture, it is not the primary law from which its basic principles derive' (*AEA* 87 [81r]).[7]

While Chadwick would not concur with the primacy Boullée granted to regularity, she was sympathetic to his attempt to call genius to account somewhat, to establish more of a self-regulatory role to genius that balanced between natural and acquired human taste. In classical mythology, genii were immortal like gods but felt passions like humans, and they occupied a realm between earth and sky, sent down by the gods to mediate in human affairs. Interestingly, in the light of the previous chapter, genii were reputed to inhabit grottoes, although as the Enlightenment kicked in, the more flighty aspects of this reading were downplayed, and genius became associated more with the human mind, strength of imagination and so on. Nevertheless, as he discusses 'inspiration', Boullée explicitly links inspired artistic moments with a kind of quasi-divine state, where 'a power beyond our control [*force majeure*] drives us and makes our faculties divine, if I may be allowed to use such an expression' (*AEA* 113 [144r]).

While Boullée's example links such creative moments 'upwards' towards divine authority, Chadwick's approach to the creative process and self would explicitly look the other way, 'down' towards the everyday. The potential to harness this *force majeure* explains to some degree Chadwick's enduring interest in Boullée, and her belief that *FAVOUR[ING] ASYMETRIC–anti-eye* hinted at a model within which two different modes of looking, two different sets of rules, could be 'resolved':

> static complemented by dynamic
> finite by infinite
> Ordered immensity expresses Newtonian finite world → transcends it by stressing variety + dimension of change of universe.
> Dynamic interpretation finite/infinite resolved
>   i.e. love/ desire
>   soul/body
> 2003.19/E/6.26

While her suggestion was that the *variety + dimensions of change* in Boullée could actually transcend the ordered, Newtonian world, the more important aspect of these notes lies in Chadwick's desire, hinted at here and expressed many times elsewhere, to resolve the Cartesian split between soul and body. This is particularly resonant given that Boullée's *Essai* cited John Locke's *Essai Philosophique*: Locke's argument, used by Boullée, that 'all our ideas, all our perceptions come to us via external objects' was a direct challenge to Descartes' move to grant certainty only to internal perception of thought.

Chadwick's argument with the Cartesian position and its consequences lay in the reduction and devaluation of the body, considered as no more than a mechanical object, and the separation of this body from the operation of thought. As she noted in her *Filofax*, she hoped to rend apart the Cartesian system:

> Flesh into revolution. Independence of the body relative to mind
> <u>Disease as love of two alien species for each other.</u>
> Independence of the clash, detached from the mind. Revolt of body against the mind. Cartesian system rent
> *Filofax*, dated (unusually) 9.2.87

Just as her response to Boullée's *Essai* was traced above in terms of its attempt to alter the grounds of authority through a new emphasis on looking, so Chadwick's response to Descartes can be considered through this same link. Just as Boullée sought to emphasise the empirical aspect of looking, so Descartes is well known for his insistence on the independence of thought and world. In terms of its impact on architecture, Claudia Brodsky Lacour has argued that Descartes' elimination of the senses from his process of theorisation has particular consequences due to the removal of the 'cheat' of nature as a basis for predication: 'architecture must know itself independent of objects in nature.'[8] This would have an impact on the rules of proportion that Boullée attempted to sideline, which could no longer have any referential basis in the world, and subsequently any theories of beauty which linked to nature or natural proportion would be equally without authority. Brodsky Lacour explores the contemporary impact of Descartes' work through the architectural theories of Claude Perrault (1613–88):

> Just as Descartes, in disassociating mathematical orders from fixed geometric forms, was able to institute proportional relations arbitrarily, and [...] to construct solutions to previously insoluble problems, so architects, according to Perrault, must establish the proportions they use, basing that 'arbitrary' activity on free imagination, acquired knowledge, and accident [...] they were founded in '*fantaisie*', the Cartesian term for the free drawing of order from the mind [...] Architecture, defined by Perrault, [...] would be a single activity in which drawing manifests thought and nothing else.[9]

A great deal of Chadwick's thought can be understood to contest this exclusive privilege given to thought. In this context, her *Revolt of body against the mind* can be followed by focusing on the particular role of looking: drawing in discussion from the previous chapter, her intention to leave the *Cartesian system rent* can be followed through an optical metaphor that was, for this system and also for the empirical considerations of the eye that informed Boullée's *Essai*, restricted to the cone of vision models. Working against the Cartesian system, she sought to put *Flesh into revolution*: despite the revolutionary tone, it must be stressed that her intention was not to crush thought, but rather to establish a different relationship between body, mind and world. If we recall her notion of *Fleshood*, the rebalancing aspect of her thinking comes through:

> But consciousness is an indissoluble synthesis of our thinking selves and our physical apparatus: our body and sensory systems. It is experienced not as something solid and real, but as passing through, as *motion*. Fleshood is more than mere object or image, more than assigned meaning. It is dynamic, in process, a variable exchange of relations. (*WD* 69)

Considered within the present discussion of authority, her *Independence of the body relative to mind* intends to prevent the body being subsumed or overlooked by the mind, to maintain the flesh as an indissoluble dimension in experience, one that cannot be simply 'assigned meaning' by an external authority. Flesh 'sees' differently than the eye, it inscribes various non-optical modes of seeing: taken thus, the importance of Chadwick's *anti-eye* emerges here and plays a role both within the dynamic process of judgement, but also guards against any one point of view wresting authority away from the others.

Beyond Chadwick's considerations of the detail of either Descartes' or Boullée's work, these contributed to her belief that all claims to authority were ultimately groundless. The impact of Descartes, read through Perrault's work, for instance, served ultimately to highlight the arbitrary designation of all authority: although it was the mythical authority of the ancients and the authority of nature that were explicitly criticised, the authority claimed for the power of human thought was equally arbitrary. As Alberto Pérez-Gómez has argued, Perrault's *Ordonnance* (1683), while very much a rationalising product of its time, is something of a fraud, as 'His mathematical calculations are ultimately immaterial since his conclusions are barely affected by them'.[10]

The kind of detached, rational thinking that has become almost a caricature of the Cartesian system can be considered to disembody the eye; while this sits easily enough with Descartes' *fantaisie*, it also describes the moment of Boullée's *force majeure* when the power of the (creative) mind takes on a quasi-divine role. Chadwick's anti-eye works to resist this opportunity for detachment. She did not set out to rescue the authority of nature, but to alter the general dynamic of claims to authority; while Boullée juggled with regularity and variety, *force majeure* always underwrote the authority of regularity. Without such a get-out clause, the theoretical implications of Boullée, belied by the overwhelming impact of his architectural propositions, encouraged imagination and exploration. It was in this possibility of not only instigating but also sustaining curiosity, and the dynamic interplay of multiple systems or bisociation, that the appeal of Boullée's *Essai* lay for Chadwick.

Without a source of authority detached from the dynamic relations of experience, the role of 'authority' alters. In Chadwick's thinking, authority can most clearly be considered as a tendency that should be directed towards opening up curiosity and ongoing investigation. A clear example of this different approach occurs in the marginal annotations to her copy of James Lovelock's *Gaia: A New Look at Life on Earth*. Chadwick was concerned that Lovelock simply reinstates the authority of nature without considering that all authority should be considered arbitrary. In the

Epilogue, her notes are in open disagreement with Lovelock's position, and she alters his claim that 'Intelligence is a property of living systems and is concerned with the ability to answer questions correctly' (*G* 146) by adding 'NO' in the margin at this point, and replacing answer with *'ask' questions correctly*.

Although much of this discussion has focused on Chadwick's interest in the early modern period, where the work of Boullée and Descartes framed her engagement with its approach to rationality and science, other ingredients helped to develop and expand her thinking regarding the ways in which questions could be asked rather than answered. Recall: *Science not only way of gaining access to truth of universe. Access nature of reality thro' non scientific means.* A related interest was intertwined with this material, concerning a number of enduring, non-scientific attempts to account for the *truth of the universe*.

biblical authority versus *the inverted eye*

In her notebook entries referring to *Wreaths to Pleasure*, a project series executed during 1992–3, Chadwick reflected on her own approach to 'gardening' and its ability to operate with an alternate analogy for nature to those underlying the systems just discussed. Rather than being manifest in a harmony based on visually derived geometric properties of nature (such as the golden section) Chadwick's interest was in more 'illogical' arrangements that she linked to the 'inverted eye':

> the inverted eye, seeing inwards, into self
> inner pathologies of mood + emotions [...]
> -Not ikenbana[11] [*sic*]
> formal rules of arrangement + composition
> →move from 'golden section' to more illogical dysfunctional proportions
> + arrangements
> harusphamancy–divination by entrails less contrived + 'balanced'
> 2003.19/E/11.5

Chadwick's rejection of Japanese flower art Ikebana, or 'The Way of the Flowers', reiterated her reservations about mathematical explanations of the visual (or aural) patterns of nature, particularly where these were taken to grant this particular version of nature authority over other things. Indeed the propensity of mathematical nature to predict behaviour, to provide answers, to underscore architecture or artistic composition, explains its enduring appeal as a source of authority. As she wrote here, her interest lay in *more illogical dysfunctional proportions + arrangements*, the aspects of 'nature' that were laundered during the establishment of a composite image that moved from the physical to the metaphysical. While this interest clearly echoes the *FAVOUR ASYMETRIC—anti-eye*, the phrase *the inverted eye, seeing inwards* stresses the point made at the end of the previous section, that the *anti-eye* was not so much anti-looking as looking differently.

It is perhaps worth emphasising that the *seeing inwards* was fundamentally distinct from the kind of 'looking inside' characteristic of the emergence of modern science. The new empirical science, coupled with the invention of instruments like the microscope, was beginning to provide indisputable proof that traditional authority was wrong. For Chadwick, the importance of *seeing inwards* lay less in replacing one version of authority with another, than in altering the role of authority in order to support curiosity and questioning.

In tandem with her careful attention to science, she actively pursued other *less contrived + 'balanced'* approaches to the world: informing her thinking on these approaches was an interest in various biblical metaphors that linked architecture and knowledge. Although these could not claim to represent *divination by entrails*, they provided a useful vehicle through which she was able to rehearse her own position. Moreover, these metaphors had played a significant role during the early modern period, when they had enjoyed a complex relationship with the emerging authority of modern science. Regarding the Garden of Paradise, the Ark, the Tower of Babel, the Temple of Solomon (Chadwick's notes reflect all of these, and several of her realised projects explicitly or implicitly refer to them), Jim Bennett and Scott Mandelbrote have surveyed the complex role these metaphors played during this period. They argue that during the sixteenth and seventeenth centuries, there was an assumption that Paradise could be regained, that a return to a state of grace could be achieved, and that the increased popularity and circulation of these metaphors inspired many early moderns to think of their tasks as being the rescue of 'human knowledge and understanding of the natural world from neglect and depravity [...] As metaphors, they summed up contemporary aspirations to understand and control the natural world, and as historical exemplars they testified to the possibility that such hopes might actually be realised.'[12]

The natural world here formed a sort of battleground within and across which the struggle for authority was played out; biblical authority clearly lost out to the new power of science, though not without various interesting twists that attempted either to reconcile the traditional with the new, or to enter some sort of power-sharing agreement. The story of the Ark clearly struck a chord with the emerging trends towards rigorous collection, sorting and classification that prefigured the grand Encyclopaedic projects of the eighteenth century. But as Bennett and Mandelbrote observe, the Old Testament provided more than just these exemplars; it was frequently taken to be a literal history rather than an allegory, such that it would fit more comfortably into this new climate of investigation and control of the natural world.

The Temple of Solomon, for example, was sought with a conviction that it had really existed, that archaeological or textual traces could be used towards its reconstruction. If found, it would arguably have provided the last word, the indisputable authority for all architecture, giving up its divine secrets for use by theoretical mathematics and practical, universal measurement, geometry, and order, as well as providing 'irrefutable legitimacy'[13] for its particular architectural style. It was argued that the significance of such universal measure extended beyond the built object itself, and that it underlay 'the proper regulation of society'.[14]

While these moves represented an attempt at accommodation between the burgeoning authority of science and the traditional authority of the Bible, Chadwick's interest in these examples ran in the opposite direction. Rather than providing scientific explanations or proof for biblical stories, she was interested to *Access nature of reality thro' non scientific means*. Her motivation was to counter the moralising thrust of the biblical, translated into a similar removed authority in the modern age. Whereas these examples were frequently paired up (for instance, the Tower was twinned with or complemented by the Temple) as negative and positive models of human behaviour, Chadwick's thinking reversed the overtones of such pairing. The Tower was traditionally taken as a warning against human pride, as a reminder of the appropriate limitations of knowledge and agency compared to the all-seeing god. This contrasted with the endeavours of Solomon, who through hard work, a profound knowledge of nature, collective effort and due humility, provided an appropriate metaphor for the role of authority (where science covertly replaced god) for the new attempts to understand and control the natural.

One of her earliest notes suggests the detached aerial view enjoyed by god or science links, albeit obliquely, the static harmony of proportional geometry to the Tower.

<u>Golden Section</u>: Proportions 3:8
Point infinity off centre
Mathematical arrangement→static harmony

Van der Weuden [*sic*] ⎫
- Eyck   ⎬ Flemish School perspective (aerial)
Limbourg Brothers: *Trés riches Heures*

Battered babel tower
2003.19/E/1.29

That the Tower might be *battered* (presumably by perhaps the best-known of all Babel painters, Pieter Brueghel the Elder) is important, as it prefigures Chadwick's own considerations of this example. Although the metaphor of the Tower generally focuses on the result of this building project, namely god's punishment for human folly, Chadwick's interest was in the Tower as an exercise of agency, the human ability to act, to change one's environment, to communicate and be heard. God's punishment can be considered as the removal of this 'excessive' agency from humans, who were separated, dispersed, and have their ability to communicate through language removed, a reinstatement or reinforcement of divine authority.

Chadwick's project *Of Mutability* involved her most explicit alterations of these biblical metaphors, particularly the Tower and the Garden. In the part of this installation her 'Tower: chamber of decay' (2003.19/E/7.68) was known as *Carcass*, and marked a deliberate reversal of these metaphors, one that stressed the importance her thinking granted to the continuum of nature and artefact, in contrast to the carefully policed separation that sustains authority. As she noted, her Tower or *Carcass* emphasised:

> the body as continuous with nature
> deliberate mixing of pure + impure
> gift of tongues
> speaking in tongues } glossolalia
> 2003.19/E/8.84–5

This mixing and continuum were a key aspect of the exercise of agency, the chance to overcome the inability of individuals to communicate following god's destruction of the Tower and the consequent babble of language. *Glossolalia* was her ambition, the return of agency to the individual, marked by the ability to overcome restrictions on universal language (and this could be both the single language prior to the 'folly' of Babel, but equally the 'philosophical language' that was developed as part of the move of early-modern science to categorise, to produce universal knowledge in the *Encyclopédie* and the eighteenth-century gathering of everything).

Chadwick's *Glossolalia* repeats the sentiment of *the inverted eye, seeing inwards* by stressing a different way of considering the environment, what Marina Warner refers to as the 'invisible profane' (*OM* 48). In their traditional role, the Garden, the Tower and so on were still metaphors that supported a notion that (divine) authority was able to provide answers. They are all concerned with lost knowledge, and the prospect for knowledge found but safely guarded by the powerful. Chadwick's thinking, manifest in her project *Of Mutability*, inverts these assumptions and suggests these metaphors can be opened up to broader ambiguity, where they provide profane questions not answers.

> <u>Tower</u>: chamber of decay "Ocean Stream"
> <u>Garden of Delights</u>—floor: fallen sky, elevations onto walls of grief
> <u>Spheres</u>: idealisation of touch, rarefied into celestial project forms. spiritualised caresse [*sic*]
> [...]
> Myth, allegory, religion→metamorphosed into personal allusion to senses fleetingly passing through the body
> 2003.19/E/7.68–7

This metamorphosis of traditional metaphors and their fleeting contact were both important in Chadwick's theoretical position and manifest in this project. The fallen sky challenged the traditional reading of the Fall from Grace associated with the Garden: as with aspects of the grotto discussed in the previous chapter, Chadwick sought to overcome the atemporality of such metaphoric or utopian examples. *Of Mutability* challenged the atemporal Paradise, Paradise Lost, neither did it operate on the promise of a Paradise to be regained, but posited Paradise now. In her own words, she encouraged experience free from guilt or shame:

> Pleasure and pain are simultaneous in the illusory frame of this place, free from the dimension of shame and guilt. Neither solace not promise, as Eden at the beginning and Jerusalem at the end, mark the polarities of time, for there can be no arrival here. The boundaries have dissolved, between self and other, the living and the corpse. This is the threshold of representation, not quite real, not exactly alive, but the conscious implicate depths of reflection. (*OM* 29)

This ambiguity in experience was supported by the environment Chadwick designed, where instead of these biblical metaphors remaining aloof, atemporal, they were inverted, became everyday. Philip Staley, who helped Chadwick produce the installation, commented on its deliberate ordinariness, the clear presence of everyday office technology in its making, and the two-dimensionality of its architectural references, all of which enjoyed a heightened contrast with the classical architectural surroundings of the Institute of Contemporary Arts (ICA) on The Mall in London where it was shown. Chadwick acknowledged that such an approach was a gamble: 'both less yet potentially more than its original, the real is resurrected and set adrift' (*OM* 29).

The reflecting pool at the centre of the *Garden of Delights* included an allegory of the body in pieces, fragmentary and able to sustain infinite juggling. Chadwick describes how this example reflects on how an environment might support 'a discontinuous flux, a passage of impossible states leaping into successive configurations. These are dynamic allegories for events to be' (*OM* 29). Despite the difficulties deploying the body as a metaphor in the context of visual art, her notes link this vehicle with a broader attempt to support the role of the *Inverted Eye*:

> still life as hymn to nature + life: alive
> > vivant nature morte
>
> [...]
> <u>Still life</u> as vehicle for conveying metaphor for event/emotion + esp. memories + subconscious feelings
> 2003.19/E/7.58

Chadwick had elsewhere indicated the importance she attached to metaphors that were able to complement the ambiguity she required of environmental experience. Moreover, it was the ability of a situation to support the traffic between metaphoric and actual readings that was important. In a passage on the metaphorical use of scientific theories, Koestler notes how 'the word "magnetism" was used in a broader, metaphorical sense; it had a profoundly appealing ambiguity as another Janus-faced agency which pertained both to the world of the spirit and of matter' (*SW* 508). The importance of this Janus, combining both spirit and matter, appealed to Chadwick because it reinforced her determination to work with the real, and by supplementing this with individual emotions or memories, to position it not as the end point of experience (which would be expected to tally with the answer expected by authority), but as the start, as a question that could support inquiry. Chadwick expanded on this view in a note in her *Filofax*:

> Metaphor: false front that belies the substantiality that created it. Artificial luxury [...] Postmodern culture as 'false front' not to deceive but to reveal. Fake luxury.

It is in this play between metaphor and its substantial support that Chadwick sought to operate. The clearer the difference between these, the greater guarantee that the metaphor-as-Janus can mediate between reality and imagination, that it can *reveal* rather than deceive, and that it can thus *set the real adrift* while also sustaining it.

In contrast to the various metaphors that traditionally linked body and building, even city, which have supported the production of architecture based on visual systems of proportion, or on anatomical function of parts or systems, Chadwick's interest in the potential of metaphor in *Postmodern culture* lay in how it could support, even be legible, in ordinary experience.

myth, artifice, naturalism

The relationship between *false front* and substantial ground, between metaphor and the reality to which it is directed, draws together many of the diverse and conflicting examples that Chadwick drew on in her considerations of authority. The importance of providing metaphor with a revelatory rather than a deceptive role is important in terms of her desire to encourage individual agency in the experience of the environment. Manfredo Tafuri makes a related point: "'Myth is against history,' Barthes tells us, and myths carry on their mystification by hiding the artificial (and the ideological artificiality) behind the mask of a fake "naturalism."'"[15]

Tafuri criticises the smokescreen of 'new myths' issued by a succession of avant-garde artistic and architectural movements, behind which the need to gain real understanding of the situation in which they were working could be ignored. Recalling Chadwick's assertion *that there can never be 'Nature'*, her interest in the various roles accorded to nature by both science and biblical authority can be understood to be an interest in their operation as *masks*, behind which her thinking sought the artificiality, the ideologies, or authority. In this sense, her interest in the push and pull between nature and humanity, particularly the eighteenth-century situation that has been discussed in the last two chapters, can be understood as an interest in this mask. Cries for a return to nature, either in Boullée's 'Oh, Nature! [...] we can do nothing without you!' (*AEA* 89 [85v]) or Rousseau's belief that human beings had fallen from a state of nature into history, belied the increasing power humans had gained over their environment.

> Rousseau: the further man separated from state nature, the further he is separated from his true essence. Noble 'savage':
> Rationality→ degeneracy. Poisoned culture a prison.
> 'Savage': internal, self-contained, lives within himself.
> Man of society dependent, lives on externals.
> Animals ≡ unity with nature. No concept of death.
> Animal as familial: prelogical, free of consciousness of history, exists in state of timelessness in balance with nature. Animal instinctively lives in present. Unhistorical consciousness—pure vital life
> 2003.19E/7.13

This sort of angst, directed against the poison of culture and degenerate rationality, effectively repeated in secular form the biblical metaphors discussed earlier by presenting the artificial, ideological beliefs of the time

as if they were 'natural'. Joseph Rykwert links Rousseau's ideas to the
popularity of the idea of the primitive hut, discussed in the previous
chapter, because of its fake naturalism, its atemporal origins: 'I might
perhaps point out that the origins to which Rousseau returned to find the
types on which constitutional thought was based assumed a "natural"
condition before history, which was "primitive" and "original" in the
notional rather than in the paleontological sense' (*AHP* 47–8).

Chadwick's position that there was only the 'relatively natural' implicates
these various veneers of consensus, where deals were struck between
nature, origin, science, Good Taste and so on, for the benefit of
contemporary, but apparently atemporal, authority. Her stated intention to
work *away from Newtonian object to state flux temp. fixings* (2003.19/E/8.139), to
FAVOUR ASYMETRIC–anti-eye, repeat her determination to sidestep the
mask of this particular conventional binary discourse, where, in the words
of Elizabeth Grosz, 'Nature, in cultural and architectural discourses, is
conceived either as a passive, inert, ahistorical burden—in architecture, the
burden of site specificity or the natural limit of materials—or else as a
romanticized refuge or haven from the cultural, a cultural invention for its
own recuperatively included "outside".'[16]

Chadwick's insistence on limiting questions to the *relatively natural* marked
an attempt to push considerations of 'Nature' beyond these passive or
romanticised positions where it can be comfortably overlooked. Indeed in
this sense, Nature took its place alongside several of the other 'relative'
questions just mentioned. Informed by her interest in Koestler's
bisociation, Chadwick's position theorised, and set out to realise in her own
work, a *total pattern* established between these relative, different and
conflicting claims. Its ambition was notable:

Oval Court: Rococo—revolution ○+□ – heaven + earth, spiritual +
material
2003.19/E/7.61

Although Boullée's *Essai* was itself something of a thinly veiled attack on
the rococo, Chadwick studied his attempt to address both the empirical and
rational as part of his theory of architecture. Nevertheless, the *Essai*'s
implication was that the refined aesthetic sensibility associated with Good
Taste favoured, or even relied upon, a distancing from the immediacy of
sensation. Indeed Montesquieu stressed the difference between people with
acute senses, and those with an aesthetic disposition: 'when we hear
someone sing or declaim, two equally involuntary [*méchaniques*] things occur:
first, we hear the sounds clearly; second, we are moved by the sounds; and,
typically, the one who hears better is the less moved.'[17] Instead of one
quickly giving way to, or being subservient to, the other, Chadwick stressed

the desire to maintain and combine knowledge and physical experience.

> Earthly Pleasures + future bliss?
> fascination for things opposite to be complementary [...]
> Not in opposition or conflict but imaginative, complementary [...]
> Temptation resolved in contemplation of physical beauty. Conflict between body + spirit/will—resolve nature of desire: physicality expressed tog.[ether] with knowledge. Twin awareness, finding own fullness in state of perpetual joy.
> Cranach: full/ripe eroticism yet touched with knowledge of condition/mortality. Pre-fall + post fall.
> 2003.19/E/7.68–7

As something of a motor to prevent the kind of removed sensibility typified by Montesquieu, the relatively natural would constantly prevent claims for authority being made either on its behalf or with reference to it. Elizabeth Grosz, amongst others, has posited nature as non-static or predictable, non-determinable, as an active force:

> a rich and productive openness [...] as a revelry in the random and the contingent, as a continuous opening up of the unexpected, as relations of dissonance, resonance, and consonance as much as relations of substance or identity [...] Nature is the resource for all bodies, whether microscopic, middle-sized, or macroscopic. Bodies are the debt that culture owes to nature, the matter, attributes, energies, the forces it must make and make over as its own [...] I want to view nature—that is to say, materiality in time, materiality whose only destination is futurity, openness, and endless ramification—as the undoing of the aspirations of art and culture (which come together in unique form as architecture) to stability, identity, progress.[18]

This suggestion that nature supports cultural life *and* undermines it was anticipated by Chadwick's discussion of her work *The Allegory of Misrule*. This piece operated, according to the artist, partly by raising a 'moral question for us to internalise and thus determine our personal allegiances' (*AM* np), a question posed by the enigma of Venus:

> enigma [...] personified by the central figure, presumed to be Venus. As she enters the world's stage triumphantly poised between Civilisation and Nature, how are we to respond? Is she Vanity or Folly incarnate, bearing blight and ruin in her wake, or does she promise delicious pleasures that demand a joyful welcome? (*AM* np)

This timeless concern when faced with the uncertainty of nature, nature as support and resistance to culture, had particular relevance for Chadwick's own time. As much as her research and thinking explored the role of nature as this was 'controlled' by the authority of eighteenth-century science, the issues this raised were reflected in, and extended by, contemporary conjunctions of science and philosophy. As Plotnitsky observes, the realisation 'that nature itself obeys this joint model [of complementarity] was a major discovery of quantum physics'.[19] Indeed, with this in mind, it is worth suggesting that the issues massing around the eighteenth-century 'hinge' can be extended through related aspects of Chadwick's thinking, to cover issues relating to our present epistemological challenge. She became increasingly interested in the idea of the event, linked to a more dynamic nature:

> An Understanding of the dynamic function of nature: the diptych~
> convergences of the alternate = a pulse, a rhythm
> 2003.19/E/8.33

Chadwick's thinking pursued this diptych, linked to work on complementarity and the impact of modern physics and biology, and the possibility that these might inform another, more current relationship for art and architecture. 'Viral architecture', Chadwick's own (metaphoric) response, reconsidered some of the central concerns set out in this chapter, but with a non-optical approach to the body, not mechanical and visible, but chemical and complementary.

7 'Viral architecture' and the rapprochement of art and science

Concurrently with the issues explored in the previous chapters, Chadwick developed alternate ideas regarding the relationship between nature and humans. While these ideas are manifest throughout her œuvre, it was in her realised project *Viral Landscapes* (1988–9) that this approach was clearly stated for the first time, and to which her subsequent thinking in this area referred. My intention here is not to explore *Viral Landscapes*, but to open up Chadwick's thinking in order to suggest how this might be more broadly relevant to architectural discussion, how it might correlate to a 'viral architecture'.

Viral Architecture considers the conjunction of people and nature, reiterating Chadwick's interest in, and the importance she attached to, the understanding of nature and our place 'within' it. Moreover, it reiterates her dissatisfaction both with received explanations of this understanding on their own terms, and the role these had played in predicating art and architecture amongst other things. As these have been discussed in the previous two chapters, they have remained more or less within a Newtonian, mechanical understanding, or they have deferred to an exterior, divine authority: viral architecture offered an alternate approach to both of these.

The underlying concerns, as well as the inherent awkwardness, that presaged this thinking were announced in her response to Erwin Schrödinger's book *What Is Life?* Chadwick highlighted a question that Schrödinger posed early on in this book: 'How can the events in space and time which take place within the spatial boundary of a living organism be accounted for by physics and chemistry?' (*WIL* 3). To Schrödinger's own accounting, Chadwick adds + *art* in the margin, to which in turn I would add '+ architecture'.

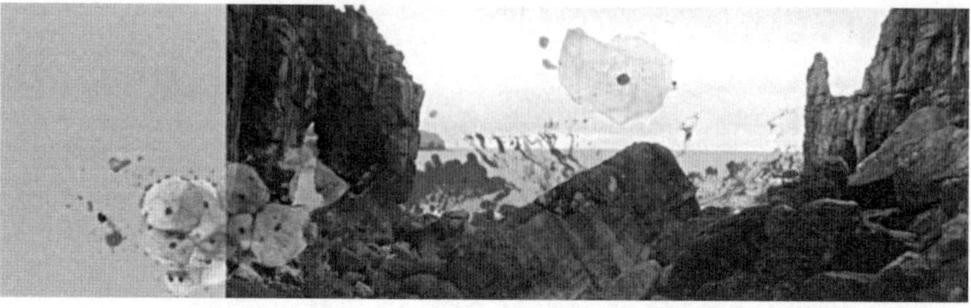

12 *Viral Landscapes*, 1988–9.

One of a series of five computer generated composite images combining photographs
of the Pembrokeshire coastal landscape with slides of her own cells.
(opposite) Installation Shot, MOMA Oxford, 1989.

Chadwick's interest in the events that *take place within* are clearly linked to
her observation and theorisation of the interface between self and world.
By this point, considerations of the interface had shifted away from the
Triplet associated with *Model Institution* and *Train of Thought*, becoming
relocated or reformulated away from the boundary of the physical body in
ways that reflected her growing conviction that the body was continuous
with nature:

the body as continuous with nature
deliberate mixing of pure + impure
2003.19/E/8.84

This deliberate mixing also ventured inwards, *within the spatial boundary of a
living organism*, and increasingly towards the cell. Although her interest in this
area was supported by an engagement with recent scientific research (and
included a residency at the King's College Hospital Assisted Conception
Unit in London during 1995), much of the research she encountered
appeared to occur within the same kind of organisational framework she
had criticised in the 'outward' organisation of nature.

In her copy of Andrew Scott's *Pirates of the Cell: The Story of Viruses from
Molecule to Microbe*, Chadwick highlighted the passage that follows. While
this might suggest that the provenance of her term Viral Landscape was
itself derived from Scott's 'viral architecture', his explicit classification of
viral architecture according to outward, geometric appearance is equally
noteworthy:

By looking at the structure of these four different types of virus you
should have gained a good overall impression of viral architecture,

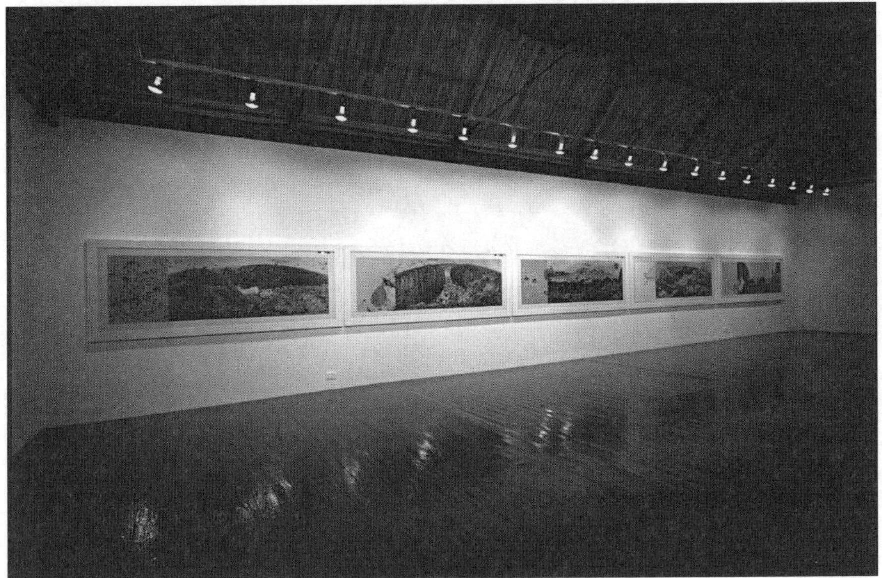

and the scope for variation within the same general plan. In addition to the helical and icosahedral viruses there are a few whose protein coats do not fit either of these designs. These are called 'complex' viruses, a name that refers more to the complex symmetry of the protein coat than to any great complexities of the viruses overall. <u>The division into helical, icosahedral and complex architectures</u> is one very broad means of classifying the viruses. (*PCSV* 40–1, Chadwick's emphasis)

A more self-conscious and interdisciplinary exploration of viral architecture put forward an argument that was similarly restricted by outward, geometric comparisons: A. S. Koch and T. Tarnai (incidentally, a virologist and an engineer respectively) in their article 'The Aesthetics of Viruses', published in *Leonardo*, the journal of the International Society for the Arts, Sciences and Technology, surveyed the potential for exchange between viral architecture and architecture understood more conventionally: 'In this paper,' they write in their abstract, 'structures produced by evolutionary processes are compared and contrasted with those designed by humans. It is noted that discoveries in geometry and architecture have had beneficial influence on research on viruses, and vice versa' (*AV* 161).

Chadwick took notes from both these sources, but she did not follow this line of investigation. Although they occurred at a different scale, these approaches can be understood to repeat what she took to be the mistakes of traditional, Newtonian science in that they remained too dependent upon visual, geometrical understanding. Her hunch anticipates more recent criticisms of molecular biology, directed both at the scientific community, and attempts to communicate the significance of this new science to a more general audience. John Marks has surveyed these developments and notes the 'Central Dogma' of molecular biology as the 'reductionist tendency [...] formulated from the mid-1950s onwards'.[1] Marks continues by suggesting that the influential work of François Jacob and Jacques Monod, who brought the advances of molecular biology to a general audience through books such as *The Logic of Living Systems: A History of Heredity*, and *Chance and Necessity: An Essay on the Natural Philosophy of Modern Biology* respectively (both originally published in French in 1970), did not just transmit the technical details of these important scientific developments, but that they also reinforced this largely reductionist and mechanistic view of the world that was typical of traditional science.[2]

Richard Doyle's analysis of this situation is significant in that it articulates Chadwick's implicit criticism of molecular biology's 'Central Dogma'. Doyle figures the work of Jacob and Monod as operating both literally and metaphorically around the boundary of the cell, when he argues that their work attempted to control 'what we might hazard to call the literal boundary between the inside of the organism and the outside, and the inside and outside of science'.[3] However pioneering early work in molecular biology was in terms of the increased insights it provided into the role and behaviour of cells, it still fell sway to the general tendency of the hard sciences, by believing that from these insights the evolution of the world could be explained. For example, one of the early, central paradigms was that the information contained in, and passed on by genes (DNA), often referred to as genetic coding or genetic blueprinting, was shielded from outside, environmental influences; that molecular biology had discovered something akin to the lowest common denominator of life, and that from this fundamental information the whole complex nature of the world could be extrapolated. At many levels of this interpretation, microscopic and macroscopic, literal and metaphorical, the boundary could only be traversed one way, information passed in one direction. In notes taken while reading Stephen Jay Gould's *The Flamingo's Smile*, Chadwick challenges this presupposition:

BOUNDARIES [...]
General question of boundaries in nature – definition of an individual as singular + autonomous
2 true + contradictory interpretations: paradox—the cell + the self are continua + not discrete objects with clear boundaries
2003.19/E/8.59

Her interest *within the spatial boundary of a living organism*, and in cells and viruses in particular, developed around this position that took cell and self as a *continuum*, where 'information' flows in both directions. Her exploration of cells in particular became more concerned with the processes of interaction, interdependency, and exchange across boundaries, and the alternate understandings these offered.

cellular biology: boundary, autonomy, scale

Chadwick's approach to the *cell* + *self* as *continua* is entirely concordant with her considerations of identity discussed earlier. According to her early formulation of this continuum, the cell figured in her thought as the highest limit of self-sufficiency and autonomy:

> Against closure as a principle ~ device of Western representation + selfhood. there is no self-sufficiency or autonomy beyond the cell itself [...] No limit to knowledge, information—exchange to be welcomed against curtain of mortality.
> 2003.19/E/8.10

In contrast to the articles she read based on the geometrical-visual analyses of cells and viruses, Chadwick's considerations were drawn by the cell's involvement in the transmission of information, where her thinking questioned the direction of information flow, along with her assignation of the limit of autonomy to the cell wall. (In a way, this mirrored the reductionism of early cellular biologists, which ceded to a more complex understanding of interaction during the 1980s.) These considerations of information exchange still had the human very much in mind, although they no longer granted a privileged position to the understanding of our place in the world. Approached at a cellular level, the *curtain of mortality* draws in a far wider range of potential exchange than more traditional anthropocentric models. From a different direction, it returns to Chadwick's assertion that nature *is really a 'moral' concept.*

With this in mind, her suggestion that there is *no limit to knowledge* needs to be taken carefully, as it could suggest that the traditional anthropocentric understanding that she criticised be replaced by an even more 'all seeing' model. Chadwick's take on the dynamics—and limits—of information flow, and their relation to cell boundary and identity, were developed in notes she made in her copies of Italo Calvino's books. In *Cosmi-Comics*, for instance, she repeats the importance attached to a pre-individual, pre-bounded continuum, and the interaction that occurs prior to the formation of object or individual, the importance located 'in that beyond which opens [...] in our true element which extends without shores, without boundaries'

(*CC* 153). Inside the back cover of *Time and the Hunter*, she draws infinity loops and jots down

> healing division, [...]
> trying to find out what the me is [...]
> V[iral]. Landscapes; perspective of self~ of cell~ of wave or land?'

The latter is particularly significant, as it marks a link between the insights of cellular biology and her more tentative engagement with quantum mechanics. This conjunction is made more explicit in notes to Pierre Teilhard de Chardin's *The Phenomenon of Man*: although his criticisms of the reductionist tendency to split matter up echoes examples from other sources already given, Chadwick's gloss to his text is given in explicitly quantum vocabulary. For example, while the resonance of de Chardin's claim that 'the more we split and pulverise matter artificially, the more insistently it proclaims its *fundamental unity*' (PM 45) is clear in the present context, more interesting is her qualification of de Chardin's section heading 'Unity' to which she added 'or Complementarity?' Moreover, inside the back cover, she wrote:

> relation of single to many to energy—system of interdependence
> queen to worker/cell to heart

These notions of *complementarity* and *interdependence* help to focus attention on the importance Chadwick granted to cellular biology around the implications it had on epistemology, on the ways in which our frameworks for understanding the world ought to change. Her interest in new biology, chemistry and physics lay in the ways in which they all offered to contest the previous framework associated with mechanical thinking that has dominated understanding since Newton. Moreover, these notions of *complementarity* and *interdependence* qualify our relationship with the unbounded continuum Chadwick drew attention to: the moment of observation, of involvement or engagement, represents a move from the boundless state to that of a contingent bounded one, a situation that is entirely concordant with Plotnitsky's interpretation of complementarity. Although Plotnitsky pursues his analysis through the lens of quantum physics, he does advocate the extension of his analysis to include both psychology and biology: 'Operating jointly or complementarily, the interpretive closures [...]—the closures of presence, difference, exteriority, alterity, continuity, rupture, finitude, infinity, and so forth—can be understood as a kind of "psychologically" or even "biologically" induced conglomerate of constraints, always differentiated in practice, that affect all our interpretive processes.'[4]

For Chadwick, the implications of such reconsiderations would resonate widely, linking her interest beyond the autonomy of the cell into broad socio-cultural questions:

> <u>Organic</u> Dynamic instability which is a product of <u>bio energies</u>, evolution, species, mutations [...]
> dialogue with Formlessness (see Bataille–formless)
>
> divide nature–culture— gap between people + natural world
> 2003.19/E/8.96

Although Plotnitsky gestures towards this resonance, it is helpful at this point to introduce the work of philosopher Gilbert Simondon, whose work *The Genesis of the Individual* (1964) not only anticipates Chadwick's own broad position (though there is no indication that she was aware of his work), but also operates with a similar conjunction of quantum and cellular processes. One of the most frequently cited contributions of Simondon's ideas is his examination of what he terms the pre-individuated state, which 'is something beyond a unity and an identity, something capable of being manifested as either a wave or a corpuscle, matter or energy'.[5] He goes on to emphasise:

> one could foresee how the two theories (of quanta and of wave mechanics), which had up to now remained impenetrable to each other, might finally converge. They could be envisaged as *two ways of expressing the preindividual state* by means of the various manifestations exhibited when it appears as a preindividual. Underlying the continuous and the discontinuous, it is the quantum and the metastable omplementarity (that which is beyond unity) that is the true preindividual.[6]

This resonates with the emphasis Chadwick gave to continua out of which the individual was defined, which for her involved '*2 true + contradictory interpretations: paradox—the cell + the self are continua + not discrete objects with clear boundaries*' (2003.19/E/8.59). Simondon's work helps to articulate the movement Chadwick sought between *cell + self*, and to extrapolate beyond this to relationships at a larger scale.[7] He stressed the importance of reading on the macroscopic level phenomena 'rooted in states of a system belonging to the microscopic domain'.[8] The balance between these two levels was important, and for him constituted a 'metastable system'. Moreover, the interaction between these two levels constituted 'the very boundary' of individuation, the key aspect of which was mediation:

form, matter and energy pre-exist in the system. Neither form nor matter are sufficient. The true principle of individuation is mediation, which generally presumes the existence of the original duality of the orders of magnitude and the initial absence of interactive communication between them, followed by a subsequent communication between orders of magnitude and stabilisation.[9]

Chadwick's thinking on the relationship *cell* + *self* similarly operated by keeping both micro and macro levels together, as Simondon's metastability demanded. Considering this preindividuated condition of continua between *cell* + *self*, which she too held to manifest both wave and particle characteristics, the difference between artifice and nature could be seen to be a contingent rather than essential separation, brought about by the transmission of energy or information. Considered thus, her earlier determination of the self-sufficiency or autonomy of the cell itself was increasingly called into question. Further study of the behaviour of cells, through their interaction with viruses, led to an acceptance that cells themselves were open to change, that their cell boundaries were in fact porous and able to receive as well as transmit information. Indeed this process—of viral infection—provided her with a metaphor that operated on various scales and processes, and led her to reconsider the relationships between artifice, humans and nature.

from cell to virus

From her appreciation of cellular biology, Chadwick's research into viruses caused her understanding of the cell to develop and figure metaphorically for an alternative, non-binary notion of subjectivity: beyond the autonomy of the cell wall, all other aspects of human life always already involved interaction with others. The cell was no longer considered as some sort of lowest common denominator, bearer of a primary, pure genetic coding. As she noted inside the back cover of her copy of Simon Watney's 1987 book *Policing Desire: Pornography, Aids and the Media*:

new metaphors for disease to $\equiv$ being/selfhood

issues of identification: with 'Other' as virus

Before the relationships that this metaphor was used to re-examine are discussed in detail, it is worth noting the basic mechanism at play in the exchange between cell and virus as Chadwick understood it. As she wrote in her *Filofax* around the same time:

Viral Landscapes
Virus attaches itself to cells, hijack their genetic mechanism—reproduce more viruses + destroy host cell by dissolving cell walls+ pouring out fresh viral material = 'lysis' is this process[10]
[...] The virus is amoral.
Process like a virus—breaking down coherence of image.
dissolving separateness of individual (component) images
Filofax, after March 1988

It was clear from her writings that she saw this metaphor as neither simply inevitable, nor worrisome (this was the era of the AIDS crisis), but positive. Stressing the amorality of the situation, she referred to 'Disease as love of two alien species for each other' (*Filofax*, 9.2.87), and furthermore considered this a relationship that could provide a '[l]esson in harmony to both virus + human' (2003.19/E/8.8). Regarding its political implications, this metaphor proved useful in indicating new frameworks for understanding identity, as well as alternate possibilities for art. Nevertheless, Chadwick was mindful of the potential resistance to such ideas, stemming as they did from *within the spatial boundary of a living organism*. During that particular decade, such fear was increasing within the general public consciousness. However, in taking viral disease seriously, Chadwick's motivation was not to replace one source of panic with another, an issue she highlighted in Arthur and Marilouise Kroker's essay 'Panic Sex in America', where they discuss a 'general anxiety about the silent infiltration of viral agents into the circulatory system' and ask whether this is brought about by a perception of 'an invasion which succeeds in displacing fear about the external situation into the inner subjective terrain of bodily fluids' (*BI* 13). As she stresses in the top margin at this point:

No suppression or exterminism implied—just exchange. No <u>'power'</u> <u>relations</u>.

This last point is particularly salient, for it raises the issue of the invisible assumptions regarding how received metaphors of illness are used to police the accepted roles of disciplines such as architecture. Elizabeth Grosz's discussion of this issue is worth citing at length:

There is much that is interesting in the tropes and metaphors of illness, invasion, contamination that abound in the medical literature beyond case studies. These metaphors are significant not just because they provide a rhetoric of medical intervention but also because medical discourses and practices are historically privileged in helping form and produce bodies and subjects. The way disease is conceptualised is both borrowed from and at the same time feeds into cultural and social life. Medicine is of course not the only body of discourse to make such social projections and introjections explicit. This is true of all the institutionally sanctioned disciplinary forces and discourses. Much the same could be said of the law. Or architecture.[11]

While the Newtonian-mechanical world-view did not contest the metaphorical role or status of the human body it had received from earlier systems it replaced, merely secularised the understanding and authority previously vested in god, Chadwick's interest in viral behaviour questioned the presumptions of the body-boundary as these continued to be upheld, and through this the various power structures still operating. In this capacity, her understanding of viruses bore on the assumed priority of human understanding, and the imposition of human designs, over nature. No longer should we figure as an active, controlling figure in a passive landscape. Instead, this relationship was refigured along the lines of the viral:

Culture
+ Human beings as Nature's Virus
We are viruses to the landscape
View of Sublime/poetic landscape = Romantic pre-scientific view of nature – idealised
reject this for <u>interpenetration</u> of living organisms + landscape

Viral Rococo

Are we nature's virus,
    nature's pollutant.
Filofax, after March 1988

Rather than considering ourselves 'masters' or 'stewards' of nature (target of Chadwick's acerbic final question here), her metaphor follows the developed logic of cellular biology, where the cell boundary is accepted as porous, and where contents from each side of this boundary always already infect the other. This runs contrary to the assertion and the framework underlying the accepted human dominance over, and separation from, nature, developed from the assertion of art as nature's ape. (Although it will be recalled that della Porta posited Nature as an active force or agency in his account of this relationship.) Chadwick expands on the dimensions of culture's viral process, emphasising its role as mediator of information.

Virus as chemical message: information i.e. as communication at micro
level. Art as ultimate viral process in symbolic level, abstract + self
conscious, rather than at macro level
Virus as mentation [*sic*]—lower term information + consciousness
Virus only active within a cell.
i.e. when actively <u>within</u> consciousness

Reproduction
develops as means adapting to changing circumstances within + without
Virus enters cell to be
Art must be perceived to be

Art is nature's virus
     called culture?
Filofax, after March 1988

This reiterates her warning against abstracted, idealised conceptions of
nature, and extends it to bear on conceptions of art that focus on the
object. She emphasised the role of consciousness, necessary for the viral
messages carried by art to take effect, an understanding that can be both
reinforced and qualified by introducing an observation made by Jane
Gallop, which Chadwick highlighted in her copy of Gallop's 1982 book
Feminism and Psychoanalysis: 'The "Freudian" Freud placed a premium on
"psychical reality" over actual "reality." Freud's contribution to man's
understanding of himself is a description of the human being in culture, not
of the natural animal, man. Distortion of Freud always seems to go in the
direction of some sort of biologism. Hence his descriptions of man's
inscription in culture are interpreted as prescriptions for normality based on
nature' (*FP* 3). While Chadwick was mindful of Gallop's warning, and
equally critical of any reductionist 'biologism', her developed interest in
cellular biology, as we have seen, contrasts with the clear distinction Gallop
drew between the cultural and the natural. On Chadwick's understanding,
psychical reality was both product and productive of actual reality, and
while she would have placed a premium on the former, and the socio-
cultural over the 'natural' world, her investigations into the potential role of
art were developed through a 'biological' analogy, a viral technique, one
that can be considered in terms of what could be called the host (the cell)
as much as the viral infection. The potential for, and the particular
dynamics of, interaction were developed around this understanding of the
mediation of information: important here was the complex nature of the
host, both for Chadwick's thinking on the viral analogy per se, and for the
necessary difference between viral technique as this might be relevant for
art, on one hand, and viral architecture on the other.

on viral technique: interaction and dissensus

Art is nature's virus. Art needs context and audience to survive, it does not belong to an ideal realm. It must be perceived to be … Chadwick makes these assertions several times. Notwithstanding the complexity of the host, simultaneously existing in different states and scales (like wave and particle), it is only upon interference from an observer that this interaction is fixed (or 'individuated'). While Chadwick's accounts of this general situation drew upon both quantum and cellular metaphors (the former, according to Plotnitsky, already including the latter), her continuing considerations of the virus and its position between art and nature help to position the particular role of the virus within her œuvre more broadly.

Virus = exist on borderline between living + nonliving matter.

Lesson in harmony to both virus + human: the between of nature

Nature + culture cannot be separated. Interaction between ecosystems
Process = act of deterritorialising to set in being other possibilities
Virus as dissident, cultivates dissensus as the possibility of change – open to evolution.
[…] dissensus […] composed of non hierarchical coming together on micro-macro scale that is non damaging, a relation of incompatible elements that is not seen as destructive
between landscape/arch
       body/non-biology
2003.19/E/8.8

The dissensual technique operated at this particular, complex boundary between cell and self, nature and culture, where it was charged not only with the transfer of information, but with the combination of unlike 'information' sets in ways that could bring about positive change. In this movement from the real to the metaphoric, Chadwick adds the nonliving matter that would not only include (inert) 'landscape', but would also extend to individual and collective memory, legislative rules and social mores, economic and cultural frameworks, all of which were factors in behaviour and experience. Where any one term fits is ambiguous: interaction is key. At this particular between, art (qua virus) is marked with the potential to disarticulate accepted relationships, to 'deterritorialise' the roles (of nature, of humans) that are taken for granted, and offers the possibility of change, rather than a repetition of the 'rules' of nature, as previous artistic and architectural techniques have sought to do at certain times in history.

Alongside the various ways Chadwick set out to challenge the authority of science or the divinities from within their own particular systems and hierarchies, this dissensual, viral technique aimed to contest authority through a different process. That said, the dimensions, the ingredients, of viral technique would differ according to whether it was directed at art or at architecture. While Chadwick only explicitly considered the former, it is interesting to pursue the questions raised by the latter. Both situations would share a common potential *lesson in harmony*, though the information set required for viral interaction would acknowledge the particularities of these two situations.

The important point concerns the question of how the virus can operate as dissident to the different ecosystems of art and architecture. Clearly, the environment or context within which art operates is different from that of architecture. In terms of viral technique, this has an impact particularly around Chadwick's advocacy of art having to be active within consciousness—*Art must be perceived to be*. To make a related claim for architecture is more difficult to substantiate, as agreement regarding the level of consciousness at which architecture ought to operate is contentious, ranging across a far wider spectrum between active and passive. While perhaps the most successful viruses are those that remain undetected and unknown, Chadwick's association of viral technique with dissensual operation implies that a viral architectural technique ought to operate at some level of active thought. Indeed, this raises the perennial issue regarding the relationship between architecture and building, and on the location of the 'art' or technique of architecture. Where, in this disputed nexus, should viral architecture operate? If viral technique can be considered as the introduction of another body of information into an existing ecology of mediation between humans and nature, this takes place within an ecology where architecture plays a role as both the physical situation of this mediation (*There is no such thing as Nature any more*), and the framework through which our understanding of the world takes place. Nevertheless, architecture appears already to be heavily naturalised in both these roles. Viral architecture, at the very least, must operate to set other possibilities into play by challenging this naturalisation.

Rather than turning away from Chadwick's expectations for art, a multidisciplinary approach, with art and architecture operating together, could pitch viral architecture operating within architecture against architecture. It could be the 'art' within technique, a strand of architecture that contrasts to building. Additional questions emerge across this ecology: for a start, who or what actually is the virus? Who constitutes or determines the information? Does viral technique work in the same role as other architectural techniques on offer, deployed by the architect during the process of design, and redeployed or referred to by architectural critics in the reception of these works? Or can it continue beyond the involvement of this extended profession?

In pursuit of these questions, it is helpful to introduce a more explicitly architectural example into the discussion. Ludwig Hilberseimer (1885–1967) was an architect and theorist whose work was explicitly influenced by and developed through reference to cellular biology; this aspect of Hilberseimer's thinking reached maturity during the 1920s. In contrast to Chadwick, he stuck with the cell, allowing a contrast to be drawn between cellular (in this extended sense) and viral architecture.

'viral' architecture versus 'cellular' architecture

Chadwick and Hilberseimer have certain concerns in common, beyond those aspects of their thinking that came with this cellular territory. In particular, both were explicitly against architecture considered or promoted as auratic object.

Hilberseimer was interested in cells, in cellular division and reproduction, and the theoretical and technical impact this understanding could have on architecture. In *Groszstadtarchitecktur* (1927), he wrote:

> The architecture of the metropolis depends essentially on the solution both of the elementary cell and the urban organism as a whole. The single room as the constituent element of the habitation will determine the form of the habitation, and since the habitations in turn form blocks, the room will become the decisive factor of urban configuration, which is architecture's true goal. Reciprocally, the planimetric structure of the city will have a substantial influence on the design of the habitation and the room.[12]

Architectural theorist K. Michael Hays, whose work has done much to raise contemporary interest in Hilberseimer, has demonstrated how Hilberseimer's position was to draw an analogy within modern building production, such that each building unit or cell should be identical to all others. As the quotation from Hilberseimer makes clear, he argued that this cellular similarity and repetition was not simply linear, working outward from the single cell, but that in fact it operated simultaneously at the level of the room and of the city, micro and macro.

Further similarity with Chadwick is raised through Hays' analysis of the flow of information within Hilberseimer's cellular system: 'The reproducible elements at the molecular level translate and relay information received from the global structure of the city, even as these same elements are, in turn, the prime constitutive units of that structure.'[13] However, the significant differences between Hilberseimer and Chadwick emerge at this point where the cell is held up metaphorically as the site of resistance to traditionally accepted meaning. For Hilberseimer, the close, reciprocal relationship between micro and macro announced the possibility of eliminating any kind of individuality, whether of form, content or interpretation. By following radically rationalised techniques of production, he hoped to eliminate difference from the production and experience of architecture at any level. Hays observes the way in which all particularity in the raw material of architecture or urbanism would be absorbed 'into the totalizing structure of the work itself, in which, in Hilberseimer's words, "the general case and the law are emphasized and made evident, while the exception is put aside, the nuance cancelled"'.[14]

In contrast, Chadwick was interested in cellular biology precisely because she saw in its process an opportunity to contest the dominance of the 'general case', to encourage the exception and to value the nuance. The different outcomes to this common interest must be prefaced with a reminder that Hilberseimer's considerations were based on the work of a discipline that was only emerging during those early years of the twentieth century, whereas Chadwick was in a position to draw upon the significant advances made particularly during the 1970s. Indeed, her metaphor drew not only on cellular but on viral understanding, combined with an appreciation of the observer's role drawn from quantum mechanics. With these extra ingredients, Chadwick's viral technique was charged not with the elimination of the gap between micro and macro as Hilberseimer's position sought, but with the acknowledgement of a more nuanced continuum between these scales that was both maintained as a gap and bridged at moments of individuation or encounter. Rather than the information coded in the cell acting as blueprint for the whole, at whatever scale, and whether operating in reality or metaphorically, Chadwick's insistence upon the dissident actions of the viral sought to disrupt this easy flow. Her motivation was to expand the potential for an individual's involvement with and response to a 'viral' work, whether artistic or by extension architectural, to include a wider variety of ingredients or dimensions to this experience. In contrast, the implications of Hilberseimer's formulation radically reduced the potential for the subject's encounter with architecture, as Hays spells out: 'the subject's conscious experience of interpretation (which used to correspond to its ability to contemplate, reason, and reflect) becomes little more than a process of witnessing the extension of a code, tracing the external network of socioeconomic and historical circumstances that determine and manipulate the subject'.[15]

Although Hays talks up the consequences of this passive tracing of rules and codes by suggesting an irreconcilable split within the modern notion of subjectivity—signalled in the *Posthumanist Subject* of his book title—this comes at the price of a crushing monotony in Hilberseimer's proposals. This split occurs precisely at the point where Chadwick sought continua, namely between cell and self, between individual experience and the world, however coded. Despite the radical changes that the cellular model reflected in terms of the relationship between artifice and nature, in terms of Chadwick's position it would usher in a new binary opposition: 'Seduction + Repulsion […] Who sees things like this?' (2003.19/E/11.28). Her ambition was to offer greater involvement, through engagement and viral manipulation of rules rather than the passive tracing of rules and codes that Hays observes in Hilberseimer. As she stressed in notes on *Viral Landscapes*, this ought to overcome binary differences, not return with a stronger version:

> Viral Landscapes
> Binary difference abolished ~ synchronous inter-existence, both inside/outside organism … Potential loss of identity as a very productive moment ∵ slippage of boundaries of self. Derelict corpse of body as spectacle abandoned. Edge of limits—letting go, desire for non being, welcoming other at most intimate.
>
> ecologies}
> anatomies} moving simultaneously inside + outside the organism.
> 2003.19/E/8.10

The importance of viral coding was that it offered Chadwick a way of considering resistance to the almost crushing inevitability of external coding networks consequent on cellular metaphors, illustrated by Hilberseimer's cellular position. While this cellular model acknowledges a radically new order of coding, the relationship it establishes between the human (qua individual identity) and nature-environment brings about a conjunction where the latter is if anything *more* removed and if not unknowable, then separate. Despite the new scientific knowledge that was used to develop this new metaphoric framework for understanding, it returns to the implications of earlier models of nature and the location of authority over understandings of our place in nature. Indeed Hilberseimer explicitly repeats a traditional positioning of creative authority outside the laws of nature: 'The creator […] is intuitive; free from law […] And all science and knowledge etc. cannot replace this naïve security of creation.'[16] While the subject of cellular architecture is reduced to witnessing the codes that condition their subjectivity, the creator is excused from obligations to those same codes. Both, in their own way, experience a freedom from laws that might be cause for naïve celebration, but more effectively than previously ensures their emasculation and the paucity of social process. Chadwick's viral response to this potential domination of cellular processes was to operate precisely within the laws. As earlier discussions of her *bissociative* technique stressed, she argued that creative process and agency could only be exercised within such limits. Freedom from laws was false freedom: viral technique, dissensual or bissociative technique, relied on creatively combining different laws, different codes, to produce variety. This combination was knowing, not naïve, and aimed to both demonstrate and pass on the possibilities of contesting existing codings through viral dissent, returning subjectivity and identity towards the individual.

With this in mind, it is interesting to observe that Hayes stresses the key role and status of epistemology within Hilberseimer's writings: 'a large part of what is at stake in his essays in an assessment of the status of our knowledge and a characterization of the distinction between artistic and scientific knowledge.'[17] Although this has a variety of implications for Hays, there is one particular strand of his investigation that is worth pursuing here. Hays develops this reading of Hilberseimer through the latter's interest in Nietzsche's *The Birth of Tragedy* and its reflections on art and science. 'The point is the Nietzschean one that both art and science are *together* illusory, that both are involved with the production of images of the world, "appearances" as Nietzsche calls them, and that know-how (*Können*) characteristic of science leads us into the worst kind of self-blinded illusion, an illusion that does not know itself to be one.'[18]

Around this point, it is interesting to reintroduce the images of the world that Boullée produced, and to compare them with Hilberseimer's illustrations and Chadwick's notion of composite images. Boullée's famous renderings were of unrealisable architectural projects that would nevertheless operate according to his theory of extended images or *tableaux*. As Helen Roseneau emphasises, '[Boullée's] philosophical interests were centred on the concept of analogy which to him illuminated the relationship between art and nature'.[19] Despite the gulf between the analogies drawn (on) by Boullée and Hilberseimer, the images of their respective worlds both characterise a situation where the subject is crushed by outside authority. Notwithstanding the difference between their neoclassical and modernist architectural vocabulary, the crushing monotony of Hilberseimer's proposals match the crushingly overbearing impact of Boullée's. While both explicitly work by analogy, transferring the latest scientific understanding of nature to underscore a world-view and set out its appropriate architectural setting, the latter fails in both cases to provide anything humane, perhaps because, as Hays warns, they did not realise they were only producing illusions, that the world continues to elude the grasp of both. In contrast to the certainty of these analogies, Chadwick considered her notion of composite images to operate as a FICTION.

> a series of composite images (not even a single instance as in a moment at which photograph is fixed ...) → Newtonian/Platonic view of reality as matter/mechanical model opened into quantum mechanics—open dynamic, inter-related fixing of occurrences as an 'image'
> i.e. FICTIONS
> 2003.19/E/6.147

Although this claim signals an important distinction between her work and the two architectural theorists just mentioned, as well as offering an oblique response to Neitzsche's criticism, there is clearly a danger that Chadwick's interest in science and nature could suffer the same fate as that of Boullée and Hilberseimer once it makes the leap to architecture. Following Roseneau on Boullée, it could comfortably be argued that Chadwick's theoretical interests were based on the concept of analogy which illuminated the relationship between art and nature, but as this chapter has made clear, this relationship was no longer based on *imitation* but on *viral interaction—Art is nature's virus called culture?* Viral interactions, while clearly more than 'fictions' in the medical world, operate analogically in the between of nature, to constantly call received frameworks into question. In contrast to Hilberseimer's analogy, which followed the logic of cellular coding towards the reproduction of the same thing, and the consequent outward homogenisation of architectural form and experience, viral interactions emerge from within the metastable system of 'nature'; they can be brought about by the combination of cells or codes already existing there to produce entirely new, dynamic and contingent experience.

Part Four: Theory and practice

8   Geometry, 'stereonomy' and surface

Chadwick's interest in and concerns regarding geometry are evident in her earliest notebooks, where she observed a paradoxical pull between static repose and dynamic asymmetry that can reside within geometrical proportioning systems:

> <u>Golden Section</u>: Proportions 3:8
> Point infinity off centre
> Mathematical arrangement→static harmony
> 2003.19/E/1.29

This announces a life-long preoccupation with mathematical harmony and its relationship to proportion, representation, truth, and so on. In particular, the *off centre* balance hinted at a certain paradox associated with geometrical systems, and proved rich ground for consideration. Chadwick's explorations in this area were motivated by a dissatisfaction with situations based on a presupposition not only that geometry underlies everything, but that it can be used to explain everything. Although questions regarding this conjunction run through the entire history of Western philosophy, Chadwick approached these from a slightly different tack. Nevertheless, central to her investigations was the role of both Euclidean plane geometry, and three-dimensional Platonic solids. Her early research examined the symbolic associations of certain shapes and geometries, such as those associated with Christianity.

> Symbolism of Shapes in χianity
> Circle; sphere; disc; ring:—
>   eternity, heaven, perfection
> octagon: 8 sided —intervening shape between circle + square Universe

pentagon: 5 wounds of Christ
square ≡s earth (opp[osite] of circle)
2003.19/E/5.66

Chadwick was a vocal opponent of any move to reduce the role of geometry from a fuller, holistic understanding towards a more mechanical, predictive situation. That said, she was clearly aware of, and uncomfortable with, situations where the consideration of geometry had itself taken on quasi-religious significance. She highlighted passages from Koestler's *The Sleepwalkers* where he discusses 'katharsis of the soul [...] achieved by contemplating the essence of all reality, the harmony of forms, the dance of numbers. "Pure science"—a strange expression that we still use—is thus both an intellectual delight and a way to spiritual release [...] "The function of geometry," says Plutarch of the Pythagoreans, "is to draw us away from the world of the senses and of corruption, to the world of the intellect and the eternal"' (*SW* 37). Chadwick writes here 'away from personal detail to immutable laws/forms'. She expands on her response to Koestler in notes made around the same time:

Geometry draws away from corruption of age adulthood to eternal. Purification + liberation. Science helps contemplation of eternal. Ecstasy of discovery
2003.19/E/5.102

This captures the ambivalent nature of her relationship with geometry; at once interested in the holistic underpinnings of early systems, critical of their increasing reduction in the hands of modern science, and nervous that the consideration of geometry generally leads away from the world. While it had offered both liberation and removal (that is to say, ecstasy or escapism), geometry had become increasingly secularised in the wake of Descartes and Newton, it had lost its mystery and link to such big questions. On the threshold of these developments, Koestler situates Johannes Kepler (1571–1630), whom he considers the last great geometer. Koestler tellingly entitles the chapter devoted to Kepler 'The "Cosmic Mystery"': In it, he explains how Kepler's first major publication, the *Mysterium Cosmographicum* ('The Cosmographic Mystery' 1596), develops through considering the relationship of the earth to the orbit of the other planets, and 'what affinities and sympathies exist between the various planets and the various solids, and so on—all this by *a priori* deductions derived straight from the Creator's secret thoughts, and supported by reasons so fantastic that one can hardly believe one is listening to one of the founders of modern science' (*SW* 256). These affinities were developed from Kepler's idea 'that the universe is built around certain symmetrical figures—triangle, square, pentagon, etc.—which form its invisible skeleton' (*SW* 249).

Chadwick marked this sentence in the margin, and it provides a key link to ideas in her realised work and thinking from this point forward. She was influenced by Koestler's enthusiasm for Kepler, particularly for the latter's capacity to combine rational pursuit with 'energies derived from an irrational obsession' (*SW* 267). Chadwick's own interest in the latent potential of geometry—in its links with each individual person rather than generalised as some universal law—was signalled in a note she added at the head of this page: 'metaphysical fancy/speculation of defining each geo. form for an age and inherent "sympathies" between shapes and person.'

A few pages later, she summarises her position, reiterating her disquiet about the wane of meaningful geometry while also clearly feeling concerned regarding the scope of the task that faced her.

> We now live in a perceptual world that shrinks from infinity + ellipses + struggles to maintain a geometric structure in society, surroundings + the pattern + reason in life.
> my work:—primitive relapse
> i.e. harmonics/idealised + symbolic model→departs from 'physical' + holistic view of interacting forces + fusions[?] of past/present/future in spiral of DNA to macro-organism + energy.
> quest from Geometry→physics no longer relevant to my project?
> (*SW* 340 marginal note)

In addition to these theoretical ruminations, Chadwick was around this time working on her first 'operatic' work, *Ego Geometria Sum* (literally, I am Geometry). While this work in itself has become one of her best-known pieces, it contained as many questions as it did answers, acting as an enduring point of reference in her ongoing consideration of these issues. (It also knowingly operated according to what could be described as a 'Keplerian' creative process, through the combination of both rational and irrational, conscious and unconscious aspects, which Koestler suggests 'often [leads] to a synthesis of much wider consequences, brought about by a fusion of the two previously unrelated frames of reference' (*SW* 341).) Koestler here is discussing Kepler's ability to move the insights of his work away from the inherent problems of theory, that is to say, to jump from 'bad' geometry to 'good' physics. More metaphorically, Chadwick was attempting the same thing, a leap from theory to experience that produced results beyond the sum of the parts, in order to revitalise geometry and open up other kinds of measure.

'primitive relapse': *i am geometry*, and other kinds of measure

Chadwick alludes to her project *Ego Geometria Sum* in the margins of *The Sleepwalkers*, noting its ingredients: 'my life + past:—with geometry and objects combined' (*SW* 341). She elaborated on this in *Imaginary Women*, a programme made for television by Gina Newson and Marina Warner and screened in the UK on Channel 4 during 1985, where she describes how *Ego Geometria Sum* was an attempt at examining her personal past in such a way as to give it some sort of order. It was a 'personal history in ten boxes', where 'flesh [was] converted into geometrical truth'. On a flier for *Ego Geometria Sum*, Chadwick rehearsed some of the questions that the project addressed:

EGO GEOMETRIA SUM
Suppose one's body—isolated in solitude—could be traced back through a succession of geometric solids, as rare and pure as crystalline structures, taking form from the pressure of recalled external forces [...]
... the incubator, laundry-box, font, pram, boat, shoe, wigwam, bed, piano, desk, horse, temple, door ...
... and if geometry is an expression of eternal and exact truths, inherent in the natural law of matter and thus manifestations of an absolute beauty, pre-destined, of divine origin ...
... then let this classical model of mathematical harmony be infused with a poetry of feeling and memory to sublimate the discord of past passion and desire in a recomposed neutrality of being.
2004.19/2 Postcard/flier for *Ego Geometria Sum* (printed on one side with the pram and the cube, with this text) HMI Box 81, 'Ego Geometria Sum'. A slightly shorted version is published in *Enfleshings*, p. 9.

On her account, traditional, classical geometry provides an insufficient or impoverished model for the world and our experience in it. Instead, *Ego Geometria Sum* began to explore how this might be expanded, where geometry might be 'found' to operate in the world, and how this affected architecture as both theory and creative process. The photographs used on the objects in the project were of her body posed awkwardly in order to fit the geometry of certain, selected objects from her childhood (*the incubator, laundry-box, font, pram* and so on), and reduced in size accordingly: she referred to these as 'absurd images', an attempt to get beyond classical conceptions of the body as an external referent for geometry, epitomised in the model of the Vitruvian man.

But this absurdity also indicates the more metaphorical role of geometries that parallel the socialisation process, such that 'the effects and constraining influences of socialisation [shift from] initial curvilinears to the progressive angularities of growing up. The abstract geometry embodies the principles of permanence—the tough fabric of matter being somehow more substantial than lived experience and more emphatic than simulacra' (*EF* 11). In this 'compression' the body and the self are forced to become more architectural; the self is constructed according to the rules imposed by society. *Ego Geometria Sum* attempted to contest this rigid geometry, and open a space around such geometrically determined objects where personal memory could resonate and new formulations be established. Chadwick would later refer to this project in terms that suggest she considered it something of a failure, simply repeating existing Newtonian geometries without being able to communicate the personal or subjective: 'EGS Newtonian = All system – no subj. A dictionary of geometries'. (2003.19/E/8.7) The source of her disappointment was set down more clearly in a note she made at the time of the work:

> Geometry: frame of reference as to Kepler + Pythagoras.
> Unable to wrench it forward, my work left behind in geometry: static model of pre-Newtonian Universe. No depiction of dynamic changes: concept of momentum/impetus denied
> 2003.19/E/5.105[1]

While clearly frustrated at what she perceived to be the limited success of this project in terms of communicating dynamic change, she was equally reluctant to equate dynamic change with overtly complex geometries or forms. Indeed, this project, and her other major operatic work *Of Mutability*, both operated through a strong acknowledgement of classical geometry in both their layout and forms. Her attempts at reconciling the static aspects of pre-Newtonian understanding with more dynamic Newtonian models was informed by her reading of Boullée's *Architecture: Essay on Art*. Although connections with Boullée's *Essai* have already been discussed in different contexts, here Chadwick follows Boullée's interest in stereometric forms, those which for Boullée were, in her words, 'selected from natural forms based on Platonic perfect solids ~ most perfect form. Reasoned appreciation [...] ruled by laws of nature' (2003.19/E/6.25).

Chadwick detected something of a paradox in Boullée's interest in stereometric forms: while his *Essai* argued for the perfection of the Platonic forms—and in particular the sphere, which in his estimation was the most perfect—his theory of volumes emphasised the principal values of regularity *and* variety. Indeed, he argued that the volumetric harmony associated with regular volumes is a product of both these qualities (*AEA* 86 [78v]), and he illustrates this general assertion with reference to the sphere—he defines this as an 'undefinable polyhedron' (*AEA* 86 [79r])—

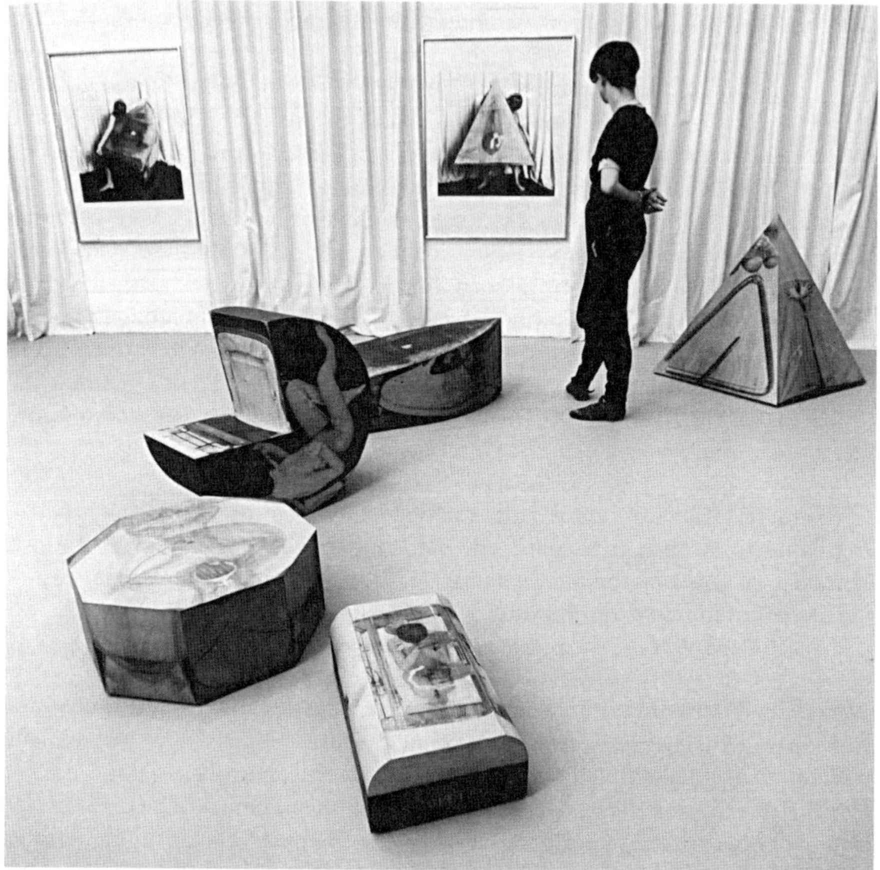

13 *Ego Geometria Sum*, 1983–5.

Installation shot of Chadwick standing in *Ego Geometria Sum* from the Riverside Studios, London, February 1985. On the floor are five of the ten geometric sculptures that make up the full piece, although in this show only six were included. (In the photograph, the *Incubator* representing birth is in the foreground, then the Font—three months, the Pram—ten months, the Boat—two years and the Wigwam—five years.)
On the wall in the background can be seen two of ten photographs in the series *The Labours* that she made in collaboration with Mark Pilkington showing her 'grappling' with each of the ten objects. *The Labours: Birth* is shown in detail opposite.

which enjoys a paradox produced by its possession of infinite variety and absolute symmetry. Chadwick was drawn to the potential, and the difficulties, of this combination:

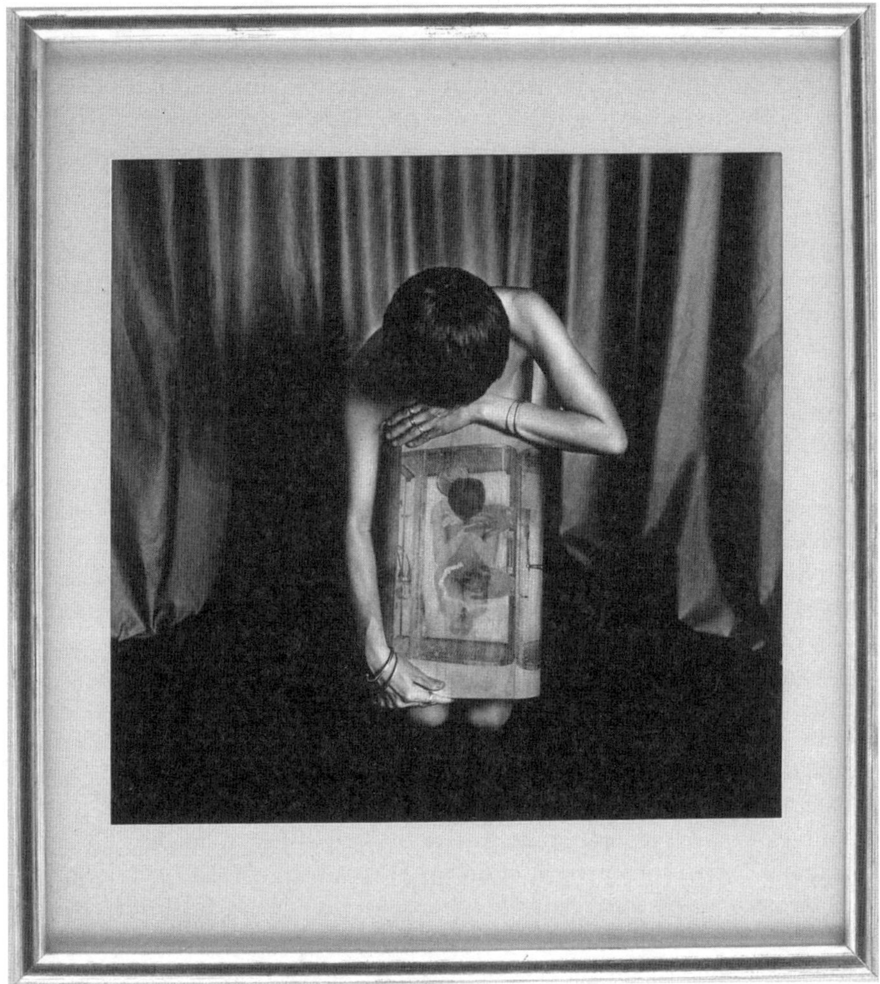

Architecture: Boullée : Sphere + Wall [...]
Stereometric order: symmetry →perfection
      + variety: pleasure/ stimulating
embraces soul – neoclassical—
      clarity/monumental symmetry,
perpetual, austere
          + <u>body: rococo</u>—transient,
      asymmetrical, picturesque, graceful, rich. [...]
Stereometric integration [of] opposites:
      Cenotaph for Newton
2003.19/E/7.61[2]

Although Boullée's *Essai* and his speculative architectural projects were an obvious challenge to the sensuous geometry and sensibility of the rococo, Chadwick felt that his claimed interest in variety and curiosity were far more likely to be sustained by rococo work than his own crushing neoclassical proposals. Within his theory, the variety inherent in stereometric forms was experienced through bodily movement; this attempted combination of universal geometry and personal experience was perhaps the aspect of Boullée that most appealed to Chadwick, and the aspect of his work that she felt offered to support her own attempts at *armonia*:

> stereometric forms → unity harmony
> Not in opposition or conflict but imaginative, complementary
> 2003.19/E/7.68

If her own move towards *armonia* was linked to the *imaginative, complementary* potential of a *stereometric integration [of] opposites*, it would find closer illustration in a project of Boullée's less well known than the *Cenotaph for Newton*. Although Chadwick would not have seen it in the version of Boullée's *Essai* that she read (Helen Rosenau's English edition), his *Temple à la Nature et à la Raison* would have perhaps provided a more pertinent link to this aspect of Chadwick's work, demonstrating what Jean-Pierre Mouilleseaux has described as the 'dialectic of chaos and architecture'. Mouilleseaux describes the project thus: 'The building contains at its centre a crater of rocks where a statue of Nature (or Artémise d'Éphèse) is placed, according to an iconographic programme closely following that for ephemeral decorations used in churches adapted to temples of Reason [...] This project unites the perfect sphere of the dome with the annular structure of a coliseum.'[3] Mouilleseaux's essay borrows its title 'Il faut concevoir pour effectuer'—*one must have an idea in order to act*—from the beginning of Boullée's *Essai*, where the latter criticises Vitruvius for being 'familiar only with the technical side of architecture' (*AEA* 88 [83r]). Vitruvius' 'flagrant error' was to define architecture as the art of building, mistaking 'the effect for the cause' (*AEA* 83 [73r]). Boullée clarifies his own position by suggesting that architecture is an act, a 'product' of the mind, and that 'the art of construction is merely an auxiliary art which, in our opinion, could appropriately be called the scientific side of architecture' (*AEA* 83 [73r]). While his critics could point out that he followed his own advice only too well, inasmuch as his projects did not seem to avail themselves of this auxiliary art at all, it is interesting in the present context to explore some of the broader issues this raises regarding geometry and its capacity to mediate between these two 'arts'.

For Boullée, the ideas required in order to act were to be derived from, but not attempt simply to copy, Nature. Stereometric forms were charged with the mediation of this complex relay; from the conjunction of *la Nature et la Raison*, the geometry of Platonic forms was deemed capable of communicating, through architecture, the universal truths that reason could find there. However, Chadwick's gloss on Boullée's *Essai* pointed to its limitations or blind spots that this relay set up: *embraces soul – neoclassical [...] + body: rococo.*

Analogous to her interest in attempting a recombination of soul and body was her interest in this awkward relationship between abstract geometry and the world, or universe, it was meant to describe. Although Boullée comfortably returned to the Platonic stereometric forms associated with classical geometry, the static universe to which they were originally associated had, by his time, been replaced with the modern, dynamic understanding ushered in by the work of people like Kepler and Newton. Notwithstanding their significance, it is important to reintroduce Descartes into the mix at this point. Although Chadwick frequently referred to Descartes in her notes, such asides were chiefly directed at the legacy of Cartesian philosophy that she identified as the split between soul and body. That said, Descartes' contribution to geometry was also significant, particularly around this relationship between soul and body, abstract and real. The difficulties encountered by classical thought of mediating between the real world and abstract mathematics were overcome, thanks to Descartes, through the application of geometry, the one crucial thing they can be taken to have in common. Claudia Brodsky Lacour, writing on Descartes, traces how classical geometry, number and algebra all experienced a lack of fit between their ideal realm and the real world. While this was explained by denigrating the changeable, dynamic world, taking it as a pale imitation of a prior, static metaphysical realm or quintessence, Brodsky Lacour argues that Descartes, in his work *A Discourse on Method* (or *Discours*), actually brought the ideal and the real into a far closer relationship than they had previously enjoyed.

'The method' of the *Discours* is also the *thinking together* of two kinds of mathematics, geometry and algebra, so that the language of abstract analysis provided by algebra could be used to refer to the corporeal world. This was Descartes' great innovation as a mathematician. It was also his limitation as a physicist, for Descartes' *Géométrie* creates a writing of bodies in mathematical terms to which the substantial properties of bodies do not conform.[4]

While the scope and detail of Brodsky Lacour's book are beyond the present discussion, the dual role of geometry, linked with Descartes' limitation and innovation, is relevant for Chadwick's position. Brodsky Lacour implies that although Descartes has become associated with rational, disembodied thought (the cogito), the Cartesian formulation of the cogito always exceeds attempts to explain it: practice—even here the practice of theorising—always outstrips theory. Geometry is the relay in this outstripping, where it acts as a messenger between two worlds.[5] Brodsky Lacour emphasises the point in terms that echo Chadwick's enduring interest in geometry: 'to the artificial, visible regularity of the written Descartes adds the fact of immediate, material unintelligibility. The order of method, he suggests, is like the order we produce when attempting to read script that is at once distinct and illegible, "writing disguised beneath unknown characters".'[6]

Although Descartes, and much geometry before and since, attempted to move through the illegible towards the distinct, even universal, Chadwick's desire to combine not only universal with personal, but also the legible with the illegible, made broader demands of geometry. Indeed, it is perhaps because of the complexity this brought to geometry's role (aside from the relative complexities of classical or modern geometries) that she never fully reconciles how geometry ought to operate in her work. These issues return us to an earlier consideration, Chadwick's identification with the Tarot figure of *Le Bateleur*.

In this context, Brodsky Lacour's keenness to emphasise Descartes' thinking-together of the artificial regularity and material unintelligibility chimes with the Paracelsian connotations of *Le Bateleur* as a relay between earth and heaven. Moreover, Chadwick's interest in *Le Bateleur* was in large part, and against all received readings of the Tarot, in his capacity to look the other way, the wrong way, to look beneath the exoteric form of things and find (maybe) a hidden order, and to return this understanding to the world. For her, geometry offered a similar capacity, an untapped, alternative way of measuring. At this point, it is interesting to force an analogy with another, more obscure, geometrical practice that was charged with the mediation between virtual and real, theory and practice: stereotomy.

stereotomy

Stereotomy as a word is unfortunately close to the stereonomy it offers to challenge, a difficulty we will just have to live with. Stereometric forms refer to measurable volumes, most commonly to the pure, Platonic, geometric solids. In contrast, stereotomy most frequently refers to a process or a procedure of cutting solids: it can be considered as either an art or science. While its architectural role—a specialised branch of stonemasonry—will be discussed here, as a term it is also found in medical dictionaries, something that Chadwick would have appreciated.

In his 1995 book *The Projective Cast: Architecture and Its Three Geometries*, Robin Evans devotes much of his fifth chapter, 'Drawn Stone', to the 'defunct technique' of stereotomy. The awkwardness regarding the usage of the word, and the procedure to which it referred, has evidently always been a characteristic: in his opening remarks, Evans notes how eighteenth-century theorists such as Baptiste de La Rue and A. F. Frézier used the word *stéréotomie* as much to refer to the general principles of abstract geometry as to the practice of cutting involved in stonemasonry.[7] Evans observes how stereotomy gathered several existing techniques of stonecutting, the basis of which was the *trait,* a special kind of assembly drawing. He argues that *traits* 'are not illustrations and yield little to the casual observer. They are orthographic projections, but they are not like other architectural drawings. They were required only in exceptional circumstances.'[8] Indeed, it is the exceptional, or perhaps the excessive, nature of stereotomy that appeals to Evans. He argues that stereotomy was:

> at the very edge of architecture. It was also at the edge of mathematical geometry, at the edge of technical drawing, of structural theory, of practical masonry, and military engineering. Within architecture, it is impossible to periodise for the same reason. It was on the edge of classicism and every other stylistic category—baroque, rococo, neoclassical, Gothic, and even modern [...] It flourished only where definitions blurred, where one thing began to slide off into others, where structural theory met technical drawing, where neoclassical blended with rococo, where mathematical geometry came into contact with architectural composition, and so on. This was what was remarkable about it: being peripheral to each, it was shared by all, like an unrecognised border joining many diverse regions.[9]

Although the broad sentiment of Evans' account would clearly have appealed to Chadwick, I am more interested here in exploring how the potential of stereotomy's peripheral condition can support conjecture regarding Chadwick's take on geometry. In particular, stereotomy's combination of theory and practice, mediated by complex geometry (both abstract and applied), offers to reopen, even reverse, the illegibility of the world that was 'overcome' by Descartes. As Evans notes, in the exceptional situations in which it was used, stereotomy permitted architecture to appear uncomfortable or incomprehensible, to defy rational, good order.[10]

This discomfort was brought about through a tension manifest in the architectural surface, where the interplay between theory and practice could be experienced. This surface tension stems from a remainder or excess available to experience. It contrasts with traditional expectations of architectural form, which were to be read superficially, as exoteric forms: everything required for full experience was to be 'written' on the outside using the classical language of architecture. Although stereotomy relied upon a quasi-Cartesian abstract geometry (and on a quasi-Newtonian physics), the rationality of this, when combined with the logic of proportioning geometry informing that classical language, produced discordant experience. Surface language was interrupted by constructional virtuosity; abstract geometry was interrupted by applied geometry. The latter's capacity not only to produce, but moreover to theorise or account for the unseen complexity of and behind a surface, leaves stereotomy unsynthesisable, incomprehensible.

Evans discusses a number of examples, ranging from the simple confusion over the relative importance of certain surfaces (the priority of Gothic ceiling vaulting, compared to that of classical walls or facades), to the awkward combinations of classical surface appearance—where an increasingly cosmetic structural 'logic' was legible through columns and pediments—with increasingly sophisticated virtuosity of Gothic structural and constructional techniques. (Boullée anticipated Evans' observations: his *Essai* argues for the superior appearance, the aesthetic, of classical architecture as a model, while acknowledging the importance of the Gothic developments in structure, and describing how Gothic structural techniques can be inscribed within classical compositions.) Evans delights in this confusion, and describes stereotomy as a middle ground between Gothic and classical: in this capacity, it mediated between illusion and reality, a balance that Chadwick's broader thinking suggested was particularly important to sustain. Writing notes in her *Filofax*, she raised this issue in terms of 'surface exchange':

> Defy the surface –exchange between actual + surface of simulation
> In flight from here + now of encounter—displacement from the real
> Hard edge geometric abstraction making a <u>cut</u> into space + revived utopia
> of sensation + desire

Although Chadwick suggests the importance of geometric abstraction lies in its movement outwards from the surface, *a cut into space*, the defiance of singular readings of actual surface can also move inwards, towards its construction. It is this inward movement that Evans analyses in the context of stereotomy, where the role of geometry in the production of drawings that allow the complex pieces of masonry to be cut is never sufficient to account for the encounter with the actual surface. Indeed, he argues that the trick of stereotomically determined masonry was to use more, while showing less, geometric regulation, and suggests that such surfaces were produced through the application of the stereometric forms of classical geometry, the very forms that had 'absconded' from the traditional surface of classical architecture to determine the substance of this new approach. The effect of this apparent erasure 'is largely dependent on a normative idea about what geometry looks like, but there was, in the more advanced examples of stereotomy, a careful removal of the evidence that would lead the mind back to that normative conception'.[11]

Chadwick's defiance of the surface operates in a related way: the *flight from here + now of encounter—displacement from the real* suggests a similar removal of evidence to that which Evans identified in the operation of stereotomy. Her hope was to open a gap for a wider range of encounters than those simply determined by legible geometry. In this sense, her position can be considered to contest the role played by geometrical 'cutting' in a Newtonian or classically understood universe, where it enjoyed a privileged position of explanation, either laid over (to make knowable) or under (to design) the universe respectively. Instead, her hope was that *surface exchange* would precipitate an alternate role for geometry, one that blocked any return route to geometrical certainty, and that opened instead towards *sensation + desire*.

Although Chadwick's awareness of geometrical systems ranged from classical, Cartesian to modern, her interest in surface exchange lay more in the way that the relationship between geometry and surface could be orchestrated, such that experience could continue to defy geometrical explanation irrespective of the system used. The *hard edge geometric abstraction* has connotations of the 'Deconstructive Architecture' emerging at the time Chadwick was working, and of which she was fully aware, though this should not be taken to suggest that she believed this to offer the best or only way forward. More recent developments in the design and production of architectural surfaces should be considered with similar caution. Chadwick's own realised work anticipated the complex, curvilinear forms now possible thanks to file-to-factory technology, which offers to relay instructions determined by geometrical systems far more complex than those associated with the 'common sense' Cartesian-Newtonian understanding and harnessed by advances in computational software used by designers, directly to computer-controlled machines that cut or form materials. However, her consideration of the *surface exchange* was precisely not to reduce it to shape, but to explore how the experience of surface might bring about an interplay between practice and theory where geometry does not fit fully on either side.

This can be clarified by returning to her criticism of Descartes. While acknowledging the magnitude of his impact bringing geometry closer to the observed world, Chadwick could not subscribe to his unswerving belief that this could decipher 'writing disguised beneath unknown characters'. She suggested instead a balance between writing and the unknowable, and here stereotomy provides a useful device through which the relationship between geometry, the 'cut' and a surface can be considered more broadly.

> a binding of difference
> The opposing order of language/ structure geometry
> + emotion—transience: image
> HMI Box 19 (*Lofos Nymphon* file) loose notes

Traditionally inscribing imaginary Platonic, stereometric forms while dealing with the reality of surface, the cutting that stereotomy referred to was also ambiguous, both imaginary and real, associated with the design and the production, mediated by the drawing or *trait*. While both were hidden from the end user (that's another story), the viewpoints involved were different in kind, combining the impossible, theoretical, architectural viewpoints with the embodied point of view of the mason.

Chadwick's interest lay in the ways that the relationships across a surface could mediate between reality and illusion (real and imaginary cutting), between writing and the unknowable. To push the stereotomic analogy onto her theoretical position, it would describe not the geometrical determination of a cut *per se*, but the imaginative, not prescriptive, role of geometry and cutting as this was mediated across the surface. Stereotomy can be taken here as an inside line, involving a cut beyond the quasi-Cartesian cut that provides the logic for orthographic drawing. It cannot be considered a 'section' in any conventional orthographic sense, but rather it relies on another more complex modality of 'cutting' and form than this, one that remains in two modes at once.

As Evans made explicit, stereotomy has never enjoyed anything more than an awkward, marginal role in architectural theory or practice. Even though it sets out to mediate between geometry and production, as with many other architectural theories, it has lent itself to a general turning inwards, towards an autonomy of form. Preston Scott Cohen, for example, whose recent work has resuscitated the themes of stereotomy within the complex geometrical software systems just noted, has argued that stereotomy was caught up in an architectural process necessarily at one remove from its material or finished product, and the projects his group produced were explicitly autonomous architectural objects.[12] Nevertheless, his claim raises a number of questions that can bear on the stereotomic analogy transformed through Chadwick's research. In particular, her theoretical position sought to think experience, material product and (architectural) process together, so that these work to sustain each other. More than this, the broader question of architecture's medium is raised at this point, as the awkward mediation carried out by stereotomy both links and separates mental and material contribution to both production and the experience of the 'object'. Disturbing the clear, Cartesian claim to flush out writing from beneath unknown characters, stereotomy, when read through Chadwick, re-evaluates where and what the architectural object might be: no longer tied exclusively to the prior design of the architect, *surface exchange* offers the architectural object as a site around which an individual's experience is deemed to include both the general and the personal.

Without repeating the many other issues that Chadwick believed would contribute to this combination, this raises interesting questions regarding the role of cutting and its relationship to geometry and materials. Indeed, stereotomy provides a parallel analogy for understanding the world: not only is it impossible to be removed from the process of establishing (contingent) meaning, the approach to encounter and enquiry is revised. Chadwick's 'cutting' is established as a way of measuring the world differently. She argued that the potential for abstract geometry to *make a cut into space* far exceeded the limited understanding that underlay architectural production. Marking the distinction between the Newtonian strength of buildings and her own position, she introduced her alternate way of measuring 'natural' forces:

> measur[ing] "natural" forces—not as anatomist (mechanical) cutting into the body as a solid, as a machine … but as new chemochanical gel–soft + viscous—an apparent stability … dynamic but not deterministic … consciousness/self as organic potential + dynamics of identity.
> HMI Box 19 (Lecture Notes) Preparatory Notes for Tate Gallery Liverpool 'Piss Flowers' Gallery Talk, *c*.1993

In contrast to Preston Scott Cohen's willingness to separate the process of steteotomy from the material product, Chadwick's non-mechanical cutting reflects her consideration of what it is that will be cut; *chemochanical gel*. While mechanical cutting can stand as both a metaphor and indeed an Enlightenment model for gaining ever greater, even more complete understanding of the world or universe, Chadwick's argument was that no matter how much one cuts, there will be significant amounts of other stuff that escape this process. Her response to Minkowski's notion of 'reverberation' (*retentir*) similarly warns against disentangling the various complex ingredients encountered in experience by cutting through them in a geometrical sense: where Minkowski suggests that reverberation appropriates everything it finds in its slice of the world, he emphasises that 'The word "slice" here must not be taken in its geometrical sense. It is not a matter of decomposing the world virtually or actually into sonorous balls' (in *PS* vii-xiv). Similarly, her idea of *chemochanical gel* offers to theorise the role of cutting in a different mode to this mechanical decomposition (in this it is clearly sympathetic to the earlier discussion of viral architecture), and through such theorisation offers a reflection on the links from theory to praxis that are mediated by geometry.

cutting, looking, and geometry

Minkowski's warning against geometrical slicing has further metaphoric resonance. Chadwick's enduring interest in geometry was sustained by its potential to aid our understanding of the world. Her return to *armonia* was not reducible to the geometric harmonies of the classical age; while classical geometry had traditionally been associated with permanence, more recent developments were now able to account for some dynamic change. In both these situations, though, Chadwick warned against mistaking the support that geometry can provide with knowledge itself.

The analogy of stereotomy helps to clarify this distinction, particularly through considerations of the relationship between abstract and applied geometries, and the experience of their products where the 'traces' or traits of such geometries are hidden from sight. As Chadwick's broader theoretical position emphasised, attention should be paid not to the particular form associated with any geometrical system—she did not ultimately privilege rococo over neoclassical forms, for example—but to re-directing this debate away from formalism and inward-looking analysis towards the role that geometry might play as part of a framework for understanding. There is, admittedly, something of the Louis Pasteur about this suggestion, in terms of the 'invisibility' or intangibility of modern geometries and their relationship to everyday experience. While Pasteur (1822–95) struggled to convince the medical professions, and thence the broader public, of the existence of germs, Chadwick experienced her own difficulty relating complex, modern geometries to everyday experience. Although these applied and theoretical geometries, increasingly harnessed by the exponential development of computational technology, can tell us more about the world, they remain beyond the grasp of most people. This sounds a warning to the architectural profession: as Chadwick would advise, their role lies not in the replacement of one formalised geometry with another, perhaps more incomprehensible, system, but with a reconsideration of the role that geometry might play in the production and experience of contingent understanding. A recurring motif in her notes, the combination of rococo and neoclassical, provides a salient warning for current architectural theory and practice by advocating the creative combination, not of these particular architectural styles or their underlying geometries, but of *both* the individual *and* universalising tendencies she took them to represent.[13] Her extended theoretical position demanded that beyond the inward stereotomic analysis of Evans, and the outward engagement that crops up in her own notes, any stereotomic analogy really needs to combine both these positions if geometry is to usefully retain its age-old liaison with architecture and form in some renovated way. Pulled inwards and outwards, both moves reiterate her exhortation to *defy surface.*

Returning these observations to read her interest in the figure of *Le Bateleur* with and through geometry, the awkward connections between stereometric forms and stereotomic process can be forced further. As Gettings observed, *Le Bateleur* was charged with seeing beyond exoteric form, but failed to do so. To maintain the distinction introduced in Chapter 1, Chadwick's own identification with the figure of The Juggler was such that these traditional criticisms of *Le Bateleur* were taken as precisely as the qualities she sought. Moreover, it was suggested there that The Juggler was not restricted to a singular identity, but in fact doubled as the creative persona of both architect and audience. This raises the overlooked and confusing issue of who looks and in what direction, so often left out of discussions of geometry.

Identifying not only Chadwick's complex take on the creative persona, but also available as a metaphor for her take on geometry and its relationship mediating between worldly experience and design, *Le Bateleur*'s defiance operates on the surface of his table, or perhaps what ought now to be referred to as across an interface between the physical and virtual. *Le Bateleur*'s defiance contests traditional views regarding his lack of access to geometry qua knowledge, assumed because he did not seek out the spiritual understanding legible to the initiated in the 'writing disguised beneath unknown characters' of the objects on his table.

However, Chadwick's thinking implicitly asks what happens if *Le Bateleur* outsmarts the system? Her position holds that *Le Bateleur* looks at the mundane world by choice, not by accident or through ignorance. He looks (down) at things rather than (up) at the privileged realm of ideas, but crucially, he looks down having already looked up. *Le Bateleur* may use geometry to cut through or produce illusion. Analogous to Evans' observation regarding stereotomy, we might say that *Le Bateleur* enjoys more geometry, though is quieter about it, than the traditional systems he contests.

This analogy is not quite so straightforward though, because *Le Bateleur*'s position as creative persona can be occupied by more than one person; as

Chadwick argued, the creative process carries on after the artist, or architect, has left the table, and the 'product' of their work was described earlier as 'multistable' to reflect this. So while *Le Bateleur* might enjoy more geometry, this 'more' points to how geometry is enjoyed in a more complex way than simply 'stable' two-dimensional orthographic section or three-dimensional static form. Looking 'up' and 'down', they pass on a combination of both the legibility *and* illegibility that geometry cuts through.

Although Evans had referred to this relationship, stressing the erasure of legible geometry, his concluding remarks to his chapter on stereotomy contain a terrific sting-in-the-tail regarding the whole technique. He suggests there that *stéréotomie* only solved the problems it raised for itself. 'Invariably presented by its advocates and practitioners as eminently useful for the resolution of pressing practical problems, it was nearly useless. The only problems it helped solve were those solicited by its availability as a technique. Other, less troublesome methods could always have been found.'[14] That is to say, he suggests that it was a technique of sheer virtuosity, through which other aspects of architectural debate were played out (such as the arguments over style between the classicists and the proponents of the Gothic).

But he doth protest too much.

Despite his closing remarks regarding stereotomy, Evans implies that although 'useless', it can provide a useful lesson for architecture, one that encourages it to go beyond the prosaic solution or 'less troublesome method', the quick fix, the easy, the known. For Chadwick similarly, architecture—indeed, life—must not be reduced to the easy option, the already-known, the convenient solution.

Stereotomy, however useless, moves away from the instrumental, utilitarian, causal programme for geometry. Its promise is not just more or less geometry, but is really directed somewhere else, offering both a means to ground formal considerations differently, and a different point of view, shared and contested. Geometry, in Chadwick's view, ought to aid a different kind of understanding, rather than remaining an architectural end in itself. The promise of The Juggler or quasi-stereotomer lies in the fact that they offer to deliver an understanding of the universe that exceeds the Newtonian. While The Juggler looks as much at stuff as ideas (and these both together), he oscillates, like the stereotomer, from practice to theory and (nearly) back again. Clearly not anti-intellectual, The Juggler accepts that theory never fully accounts for practice, and operate in this excessive domain.

9 The role of making

Chadwick's œuvre is run through with works that she clearly delighted in making. Her material selections were eclectic and frequently iconoclastic, her making techniques wide ranging yet accomplished, and the extant works themselves demonstrate a high quality of finish and resolution. Yet beyond the importance of this very direct work with stuff, her manipulation and enjoyment of materials and processes were caught up in a broader range of considerations or experimentations.

Close friends and collaborators have described Chadwick as an 'artificer',[1] a term which captures her activities both as a careful maker (fastidious in her construction of things), and also as a maker of messages, something of a trickster: a spinner of meaning and lies. In this capacity, her work with materials, and her investment in making, extended beyond the immediate materiality of the (art) object to less tangible material concerns. Writing in the *Journal of Philosophy and the Visual Arts*, she introduced some of the questions that she associated with this extension:

> The materiality of art is undeniably problematic. As commodity, it is enduringly finite and implicated in a network of economic structures. Art has an exchange value often irrespective of content. Is there a materiality of the object that is unpredictable and temporal, a pure physical exchange that might celebrate the discharge of energy that occurs in touch? A libidinal materialism that values the heat of our physicality as impulse to activity, a bestial reason to counter the ruptive forces of mind and money valued over body? (*WD* 73)

Chadwick's suggestion of an unpredictable materiality raises a number of questions concerning where making occurs, and by whom. The exchange she explored in the encounter between audience and object has echoes of the discussion of geometry in the previous chapter, where the excessive site of practice demonstrated a resistance to the dominance of theory. Here too, she invested the material encounter with an ability to exceed the traditional domination of material by form, playing out an age-old tension between idea and making.

This exploration of *libidinal materialism* was anticipated in her interest in the 'primary identification' she linked with '*Thing*' over 'object'. Recall:

> tulip/plum: too 'object' like—unnameable, formless blobs of primary identification
> construct 'Thing'
> (foot of *BS* 13)

Chadwick associated the *undeniable problem* of materiality with the object because of the links it had enjoyed with form; the value of making in both art and architecture had traditionally granted priority to the making of ideas over the formation of matter into material objects. In this arrangement, the artist's or architect's status rested with their role as form-giver: material was servant to form. Her interest in '*Thing*' developed in part from her determination to explore the possibilities of a materiality that could escape the attention of form, mind or money, and opened on to an alternate appreciation of the material encounter. Echoing other aspects of her theoretical position, this consideration led not to a simple reversal of the existing hierarchical relationship, but opened onto a different under-standing within which *materialism* could pass on the activities of making to an audience, underwritten by an ambiguity carried by a brute materiality continuing to escape the theorised version of good form.

materials out of place

Notwithstanding this claim, several of Chadwick's projects enacted a very direct reversal of hierarchies, brought about by a deliberate misuse of materials. These were not just a material low-blow, however, and can raise a number of questions. The *bestial reason* Chadwick mentioned in her *Withdrawal* essay she linked to the 'Reality of flesh, maps of 'temptations' (2003.19/E/7.67–8): she considered this reality could be acknowledged by an approach to making that employed the conventional role of materials out of place, combining 'Pre-fall + post fall' (2003.19/E/7.67–8). She elaborates on this potential in the context of some notes she made for her 1989 project *Nostalgie de la Boue* (figure 14):

> 'Nostalgie de la Boue': reverse brain/bowel
>   associations higher/lower ~ hierarchies
>   elevate lowly. Scalp descends [...]
> Arse Cartouche

Look at apes' arses
2003.19/E/8.56

The suggested *Arse Cartouche*, as with many other works that were actually realised in this extended series, enacted the broad *reversal brain/bowel* by working with 'lowly' object and materials—tongues, scrota, earthworms, and so on—but worked to inscribe these 'lowly' materials into the accepted forms of higher associations. Through her fastidious, careful handling of these 'disgusting' materials, hierarchies were not so much overthrown as raised as a question. Her claims for *Nostalgie de la Boue* should thus be taken with a pinch of salt: '*Nostalgie de la Boue* is a term for the yearning for a debased physical life without civilised refinements' (*WD* 73). As Georges Bataille (whose early writings she read extensively around this time) stressed, simple reversal would miss the point: instead, work should emphasise both transcendent and base materialism, manifest more broadly in Chadwick's works that juxtaposed higher/lower: brain and genitals, earthworm to brain, hair to pubes, and so on. As Marina Warner has written of Chadwick's work, it is through the inclusion of impurities thatit offers to bring about change:[2] impurities provide the grit that makes the pearl.

This juggling of material expectations carried out through the selection and making of this series of works chimes with certain aspects of Manfredo Tafuri's argument, put forward in *Theories and History of Architecture*, regarding the wane of the object in art, and the loss of its analogy to humanity. The connection is not clear, but is worth pursuing, as it can expand the understanding of Chadwick the artificer. Although she could not be considered to be coming to the rescue of the object in Tafuri's sense, her theoretical and practical positions towards the object—be it artistic or architectural—do work to maintain a contradiction within it. In this particular context, but within a wide-ranging discussion, Tafuri mentions in passing Piranesi as a critic who prophesies this dilemma: a related, but more extensive exploration in *Sphere and Labyrinth* develops the relevance of this link. There, Tafuri argues that Piranesi's work anticipated an important distinction between 'architecture' and everyday buildings. Piranesi is discussed as the 'wicked architect', putting into question the activities of thinking and writing, and particularly of thinking and describing an action, instead of committing it.[3] This applies not only to Piranesi's better-known drawings, such as the *Carceri d'invenzione* or *Vedute di Roma*, but also his realised work, questioning the relationship between design and architecture, between creative thought and creative act. That is to say, it calls into question the role of making in architecture. Discussing the Janus qualities of Piranesi's realised altar of San Basilio in Santa Maria del

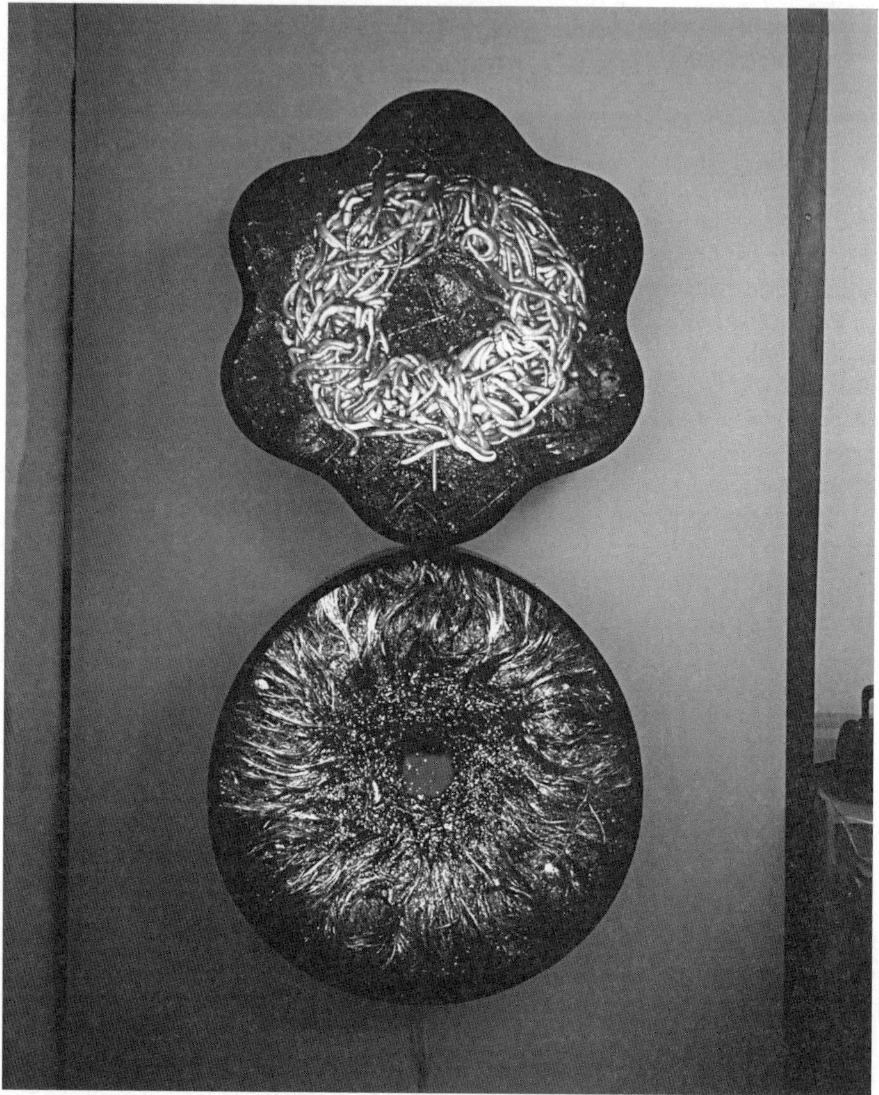

14 *Nostalgie de la Boue*, 1989.

Priorato, Rome (*c*.1765), Tafuri points to these two aspects of architecture, so frequently kept apart, here legible, writ large in this project:

> What is given as *evident*, as an immediate visual stimulus from a *common* point of view, reappears purified, rendered pure intellectual structure, on the reverse side, on the *hidden* side [...] What the two faces, *together*,

of the altar of San Basilio make brutally clear is the discovery of the *principle of contradiction*.[4]

It is the two faces of Chadwick's realised Siamese twin cartouche that bear out this observation. Rather than the simple reversal threatened with the *Arse Cartouche*, the realisation of this piece, and others in this series, deploys the principle of contradiction. Related to her material selection in *Nostalgie de la Boue*, based on the reversal or valorisation of 'disgusting' materials, Chadwick here works with similarly 'disgusting' human forms, with deformed fœtuses and other 'monsters'. Associated with this project, she took notes on William Hogarth's notion of the 'Line of Beauty'.

Line of beauty (Hogarth) brocades

Replicate Siamese twin to form frame around cartouche as hole, like decorative border

multiplication + singularity e.g. Cloning
2003.19/E/13.99

Hogarth's notion is particularly interesting here; he discusses the Line of Beauty in his book *The Analysis of Beauty*, in the context of the perception of a beautiful object. Objects that refuse to give themselves up to the intellect, that enjoy the *principle of contradiction* we might say, can be said to play to our 'love of pursuit, merely as pursuit [...] implanted in our natures, and design'd, no doubt, for necessary, and useful purposes'.[5] Hogarth goes on to define the intricacy upon which the beauty of such forms is based as 'that peculiarity in the lines, which compose it, that *leads the eye a wanton kind of chace* [...] *the beauty of a composed intricacy of form*'.[6]

Chadwick's attraction to the Line of Beauty can be understood for a variety of reasons: not only was the line, in Hogarth's *Analysis*, serpentine, echoing the rococo sensibilities that appealed so strongly to Chadwick, it was also independent of overall compositional geometries that traditionally underwrote the coherence of a picture. Moreover, Hogarth's explanation of the operation of the Line of Beauty steers a course between the eye and the mind's eye, an issue that can be run alongside much broader considerations of the relationship between making as idea and making as production.

piss, shit, snow, chocolate and flowers

Alongside this interest in Hogarth's *Analysis*, Chadwick clearly considered the disruptive contribution of matter itself. She explored a number of material situations where matter played something of a parallel role to the

Line of Beauty, thanks to its ability to behave independently from broad expectations that it remain subservient to an overall compositional or stable idea. Moreover, these considerations emphasise the importance she attached to the role of making, over and above the consequences of straight physical assembly. For her work, it was necessary that the role of making led through a certain legibility in an object to the ideas or connections that it could demonstrate. This interest was not focused on the mutability of materials per se, but concerned the impact this change could have on (material) experience, both for makers and audience. As she emphasised, her projects aimed beyond material manipulation as an end in itself:

> About change not death—sequence of changing forms alive, as universe
> cannot die but will ultimately reorder itself
> <u>not</u> about materiality but divinity, eternity
> celebration of life force + how it cannot be destroyed but only changes.
> 2003.19/E/5.123

Her acknowledgement of the extent of this independence of matter was manifest in a variety of ways. An enduring interest was how this potential exceeded materiality, and linked through matter to provide a window on the universe, to see the future. From her earliest notebooks, she recorded a wide variety of divination techniques predicated on the reading—and change—of matter. In a note that chimes in particular with the *principle of contradiction*, she explores divination by entrails:

> harusphamancy–divination by entrails less contrived + 'balanced'
> —marbling, dripping, resistance of materials to one another—oils + water
> "emulsions" as false balance—artificial mediums
> 2003.19/E/11.5[7]

Although projects such as *Nostalgie de la Boue* offer examples that literally deal in entrails and so on, the broader impact of her theoretical position can be felt on the framework within which objects might be considered. By pointing to an alternate conception of objects based on force and energy, rather than a more traditional material–form distinction, she implied that there was no real antagonism between her interest in chance and divination, on the one hand, and her fastidious control over her own projects on the other. To repeat her opening question:

> Is there a materiality of the object that is unpredictable and temporal,
> a pure physical exchange that might celebrate the discharge of energy
> that occurs in touch?

Chadwick's developing interest in these issues of unpredictability and energy was manifest in, or explored through, a number of vehicles. One that had particular resonance was her consideration of snow, where the *principle of contradiction* (form-idea v form-matter) was further complicated through her acknowledgement of the mechanisms of control that are exercised over the link between materials and knowledge. Although she took every opportunity to emphasise the independence of matter and form, she acknowledged the realpolitik demonstrated in the clear connection between control of materials and broader notions of authority:

> new realities—control–not always benevolent
> Vulnerability/threat
> Autobiog/emotional exp. caught in idealised forms
> formalist control of materials—modernist skills
> How use those ~ close + not open issues
> Stress power of ambivalence
> Pose problems
> Single sheet of paper, inserted in back of *Filofax*

For Chadwick, snow was an exemplary material through which some of these difficult questions and preconceptions could be explored. Writing of the Amalienburg Hall of Mirrors following her visit to that building, she made a strong link between its rococo interior and the melting snow she witnessed immediately outside.

> <u>Amalienburg</u>: Spiegelsaal: Room as art concept
> The dance, dizzy rhythms. "The world as idea"
> Rocaille as snow, melting spirit, allegory of spiritual love/thaw.
> 2003.19/E/7.61

Attracted to the similarity between the rococo Spiegelsaal and the snow, architectural conceit and nature, Chadwick noted the attempt of the architecture to cross over between the protean matter that served as model, and the denial of this inherent changeability by the architectural treatment of this model inside.

> Rococo cartouches for tactile + emotive curation
> ornaments of non existent protean substance = emotion
> a substance resembling both inorganic + flesh/skin
> wavers between them, as protean material desire
> *RO,* notes on inside back cover[8]

While the wavering combination of inorganic and flesh has already been mentioned, one of her own projects that explored this most directly was her work *Piss Flowers* (1991–2: figure 15). Inverting the relationship between melting snow and rococo Spiegelsaal, her *Piss Flowers* reworked and reordered the sequence, precipitating the melting of snow by pissing. Rather than a natural model preserved, petrified, even elevated, by architectural conceit, snow itself became a mould that contained, and contributed to the capture of, protean substance. In contrast to the high-brow connections traditionally struck up between architecture and the natural world or the body (rococo rocaille or bodily geometries), *Piss Flowers* was made through a different avenue of connection: snow's mutability brought about with human effluvia. As Chadwick described the process, 'Piss paintings in the snow ~ Pee flower ~ like cells' (2003.19/E/8.45). Pushing this piss-take, the *Piss Flower* objects were then cast using a very old lost-wax technique, a reference that Marina Warner referred to as a 'witty mockery, it mocks the sort of grandiloquent monumental statue made of bronze'.[9] Chadwick's likening of her piss paintings to cells ties her interest in making to her broader concerns and world-view. Writing in another notebook, she emphasised the link between traditional authority and stasis, and the contrasting denigration of contingency manifest in a general cultural association of changeability with women:

> Mutability ~ curse of Eve
> All things subject to change
> extend from χian [Christian] curse to new physics: theories relativity/probability.
> space/time continuum
> All is change ~ from moral to philosophical + amoral interpretation
> 2003.19/E/7.52–1

Her work must not be considered as a simple replacement of female for male. As discussed in detail already, her intention was to explore the potential of working with a different interpretation informed by new physics, where mutability was taken as an essential attribute of a system understood around force and energy, rather than form and matter. Another project that explored this shift was *Cacao* (1994), which again involved bodily effluvia as a central referent. Although the project itself nodded to shit rather than pissing, and thanks to its beautiful making and punning title joins the broad series of works already introduced in this chapter, the active principle of making and change legible in the objects of the *Piss Flowers* is actually played out in the bubbling fountain of *Cacao*. As Chadwick herself wrote of this link:

From the frozen liquidities of Piss Flowers → to "Cacao"
to morphologies of pure unbridled flow.
Gender as a leaky, dissipative + viscous sensibility.
form as a temporary stability in patterns of potentiality + flow, not fixed +
given.
Handwritten notes for a lecture 'Trophies to Ambivalence: to the value of a
doubtful status', Glarus—1.7.95. HMI Box 19

Beyond this difference between static and kinetic sculpture, Chadwick's reflections on *Cacao* situate all these works within her developing theoretical position. Referring to issues that are played on in *Cacao*, some draft lecture notes reiterate the importance of protean qualities of snow, while suggesting their broader role not just for the artist, the maker, but also for the epistemological situation within which they work:

Lecture for Tate? : "Warm Dark Matter"
Chocolate: "warm dark matter' ≡ state of body as fluid not fixed form
energies
moves + arouses ∴ obscene − the fecal + the delicious; a bodily fluid −
mobile − unstable
viscosity − unlike water, thick brown plasma − lascivious slow movement
excess/greed "effluvia" stuff (of body) + vapours from decaying matter
flowing out [...]
Representations through the Body : physical energy topologies
the temporal + transitional state
instability
Relationship all
sculpture to the body
Tactility/ activity

away from Newtonian object to state flux temp. fixings
2003.19/E/8.139

Although these issues have been discussed already, in the context of Chadwick's consideration of making these notes reflect how her alternate material understandings might have an impact on the genesis of form, with all the baggage that carries with it. Maintaining the potential link between architecture, identity and the body, Chadwick's thinking nonetheless challenges the authority and validity of the traditional formats of this architecture–body analogy. With the body linked more to matter and effluvia, *Representations through the Body* shuttle between (architectural) objects and bodies via materiality and material change rather than geometry,

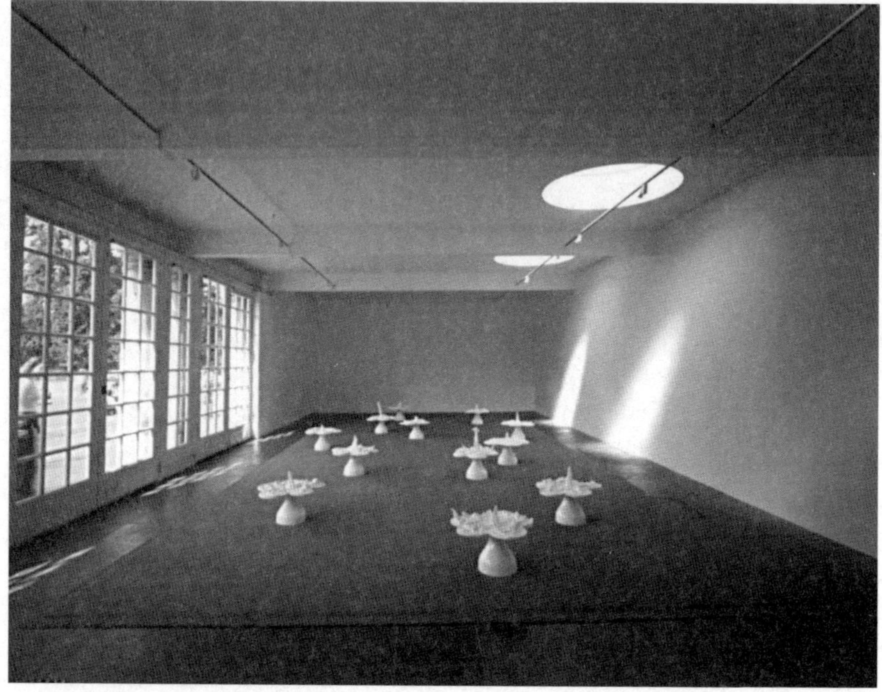

15 *Piss Flowers*, 1991–2.

A group of twelve sculptures developed as part of her residency at the Banff Arts Centre in Alberta, Canada (1991–2) made with David Notarius by forming, and then pissing into, mounds of snow and then casting the resulting cavities. Here, an installation shot from the Serpentine Gallery in London, 1994, and (opposite) a detail of one piece from the series.

disrupting conventional artistic, humanistic conceptions of material dependence on form, and opening instead onto a relationship based on an acceptance of the *state of flux with only temporary fixings.*

'new theories genesis of forms'

This attention to effluvia was part and parcel of Chadwick's take on the continua of nature. Something of a Siamese twin, those aspects of her work emerged together with these considerations of the medium of potential material and cultural equivalences between bodies and other objects. While such considerations can be understood to emphasise matter rather than ideas, she pursued the consequences of this understanding on the broader conception of making, or the 'genesis of forms' as she puts it in a note regarding *Wreaths to Pleasure* (1992–3):

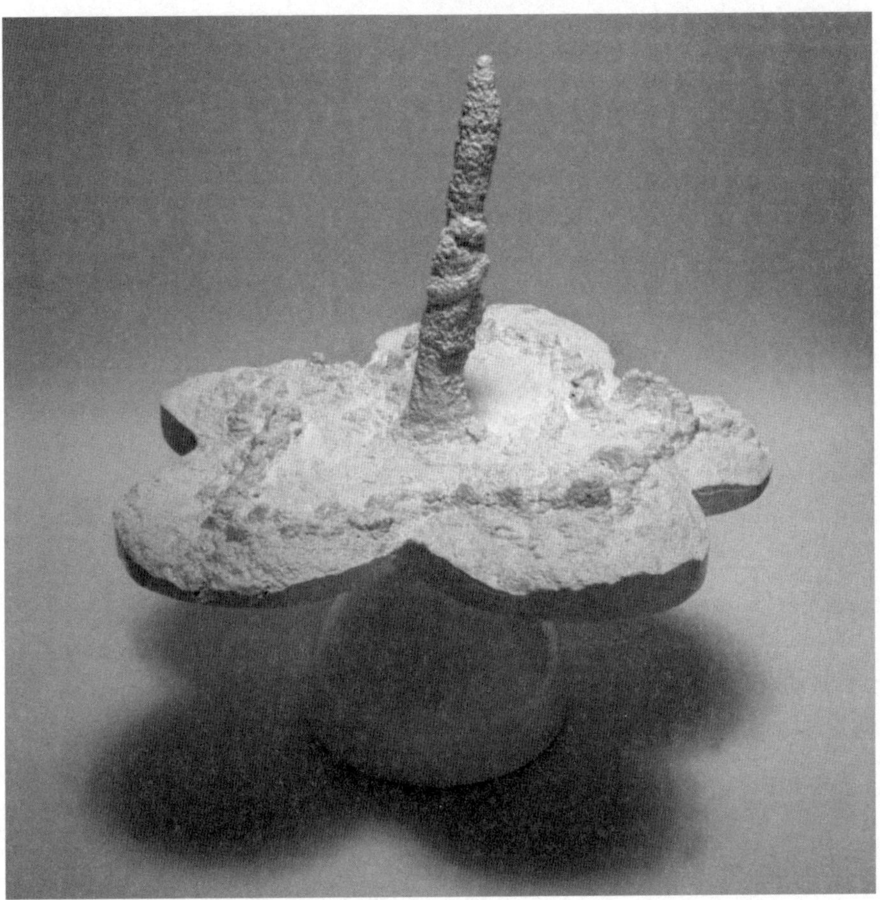

<u>Wreaths</u> an accord between flesh + flower not nature as other but bodily
equivalent, highly 'cultured.'
'Abstract' way reading them as temporal + transitional forms or states of
matter than more trad. symbolic $\equiv$
New theories genesis of forms; topologies.
see 3 texts from Journal of Philosophy.
2003.19/E/8.100

It is most likely that this reference is to an edition of the
Architecture.Space.Painting: Journal of Philosophy and the Visual Arts (1992), in
which her own essay 'Withdrawal: Object, Sign, Commodity' appeared.
This volume also included essays by Catherine Ingraham, 'Architecture,
Lament and Power', and Christine Battersby's 'Hermaphrodites of Art and
Vampires of Practice: Architectural Theory and Feminist Theory'. In the

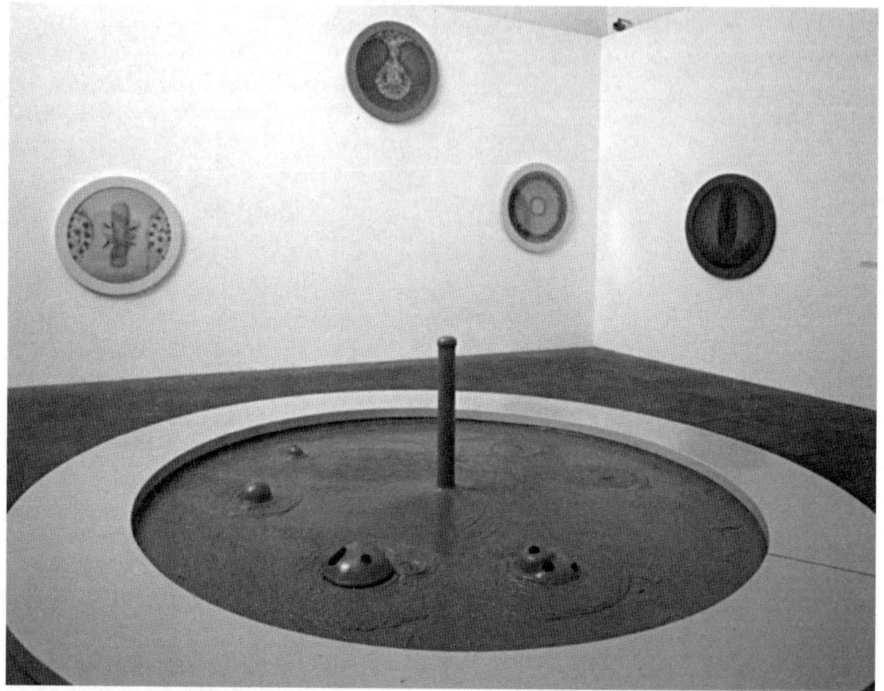

16 *Cacao*, 1994.

A fountain of bubbling chocolate. In the background of this installation shot, again from the Serpentine Gallery in London, 1994, can be seen some of the *Wreaths to Pleasure*.

context of Chadwick's interest in *new theories genesis of forms; topologies*, it is the latter that is most relevant. Battersby discusses distinctions between the creative act and the (natural) reproductive act, noting that the former traditionally assumes mental labour comes first, and then follows the physical labour, usually with the artist's own body being put to work in the service of the idea. Within a wide-ranging exploration, Battersby notes how female characteristics such as instinct, imagination, sexual appetite, and so on, which were roundly disparaged by the Enlightenment world-view with its demands for predictability and measure, and for the dominance of form over matter, were adopted by male artists to account for their genius. Battersby cautiously refers to the notion of the androgyne to signal this move, while emphasising the limits imposed: 'Genius was theorised as being *like a woman*, but *not a woman* […] the terms "androgyne" and "hermaphrodite" were employed in gender-discriminatory ways' (*JPVA*, 29, 31, original emphasis).

The sleight of hand and hypocrisy of this move aside, Chadwick would have been interested in the acknowledgement that it signalled regarding the conception of making, namely that expectations of the static good form of the world had to be put to one side while 'making' occurred. For Chadwick, this ought not to be merely a momentary switch, nor should it only be acceptable for male 'genius' artists. As her own interest in the hermaphrodite Herculine Barbin reinforced, no one should be considered as a having a simple, single sex. Chadwick attempted to produce work where the role of making fell sway to this hermaphroditic conception, by not simply exceeding or suspending the good form of traditional artistic or architectural production, but proceeding instead in a way that was informed by and part of a continuum understood in terms of the energetic relationships described by the vocabulary of modern physics. As she noted of *Meat Lamps*:

<u>ML</u> Not one or two but one and two
continua of moment of twinning
fission and fusion
2003.19/E/8.13

The role of the maker was not to stand above or outside the stuff of the world and give it shape based on some overarching, organising idea, but to operate within a world understood according to the continuous transference of energy, where hermaphroditic characteristics were essential not only to the maker, but also for audience or user, and the stuff of the world.

Battersby's essay includes over 20 *Propositions* that sketch out potential links between these broad observations regarding hermaphrodites, and architectural design in particular: while none of these furnish much detail, Chadwick would clearly have been sympathetic with Battersby's intentions. Their respective trajectories of thinking pass most closely in Battersby's *Proposition 18*, which advocates the adoption of other models of thinking time within our experience of the built environment, where time is not figured as spatialised (linear, discrete, measurable) but 'structured via symbolic resonances with the user's life' (*JPVA*, 32). The centrality of resonance—or 'reverberation' (*retentir*) to recall Minkowski's term—for Chadwick's conception of the (human) body was discussed earlier. In the present context, the essential energetic resonance of particles offered an alternate conception of making based around the manipulation of force rather than the imposition of form upon matter. This informed the complex considerations of light, as both metaphor and an ingredient in the making and the experience of her work. Given the long and complex history of the use of light as a metaphor, with its clear address to the traditional hierarchy of form and matter (where 'pure' light contrasted with base materials), and to knowledge and power (where 'light' was linked to valorised 'knowledge' and authority), Chadwick's interest in resonance marked an attempt to reconsider these roles alongside the more slippery aspects of doubling and mirroring. Denying the traditional categorical separation between light and matter, she sought a reconfiguration influenced by her quantum understanding:

> Meat: as a mirror (for living) for being alive
> flesh mirror
> $l=m(eat)c^2$
> Life as negative entropy
> The brain + the bowel [...]
> enfleshings→social→ontological→biological mirror
> 2003.19/E/8.25[10]

Through her making with meat and effluvia, Chadwick hoped to address these major issues. Reflecting on the development of her work from '①Autobiographical projects' that explored her own selfhood and identity, she noted the increasing abstraction of her projects, which she linked to her interest 'no longer just [in] my body—more universal'. In this context, she introduced the notion of her alternate technique, positioned with respect to a complex relationship between image and object:

> ② "Meat mirrors" called 'Meat Lamps' Portraits for being alive
> ③ Light – 'metaphor for living' ~ alive ~ 'on' Animates image.
> [...]
> ⑤ Technique also "between" Object/image: i.e. body—status of being
> Objects—a kind of libidinal materialism
> 2003.19/E/8.55 This page titled 'Conference. Japan ("A Subjective View")'

While this mention of libidinal materialism returns us to the questions set out in the opening quotation of this chapter, her interest in *the discharge of energy* and *bestial reason* stated there can now be explored more thoroughly through her consideration of technique. Historically, the notion of technique has played an important role in the mediation of ideas into realised form. Although Chadwick's development of an alternate theoretical position, based around a libidinal materialism and addressing the issues raised above, did not lead to an explicit reformulation of technique, the implications for technique can be rehearsed by considering various experiments in unmediated production. These speculative outings suggest a potential to shift technique from its place within the traditional hylomorphic understanding of the relationship between form, matter and making, to a consideration of the maker as a conductor of energy.

unmediated production

Chadwick explored a number of questions raised by projects that included aspects of unmediated production. Although her take on this varied, as did the media she linked to it, notes written in the context of her project *Of Mutability* introduce some of the most significant issues associated with her thinking on this issue more broadly. *Of Mutability* shares something of the re-evaluation of base materials and the subversion of traditional values noted above. She described the inversion of heaven and earth deployed by the project's *Oval Court* room, the clean execution of which was in turn contrasted to the stinking *Carcass* (or *Tower: chamber of decay*) in the next room. Within the *Oval Court*, she used ordinary materials and techniques such as raised office service flooring and photocopies, rather than those usually associated with high artistic production. The photocopier in particular was a device she reflected herself through, and reflected upon:

> Machine
> Naturalism – crude truth to life of machine-made image to propose illusory nature love
> Automatic image
> Photocopy: pure surface – totally 'superficial' no depth, surface illusion
> World of pure surface of things – imaginary depth, infinite space feeling + pleasure
> Fathomless
> Combine natural with fantastic
> Epic still life [...]
> Concrete realism + fantasy combined.
> 2003.19/E/7.55

Although Chadwick's interest here in the *automatic image* produced by the photocopier needs some qualification, given the careful collaging these subsequently enjoyed, the *totally 'superficial' surface illusion* she believed the automatic image of the photocopier provided marks a locus of her reconsideration of the relationship between making, object and image. In contrast to traditional considerations of artistic technique, which were charged with the production of form-as-object in accordance with a prior form-as-idea, Chadwick's musings here state her interest in the possible easing of this strict connection.[11]

Her adoption of ordinary, office-based materials and reproduction techniques, and the associated exploration of the machine-made image, mark one strand of her attempts to bring about such an easement. Marina Warner has discussed the unmediated production through Chadwick's direct application to the photocopier in terms of its role as an 'echo chamber', where original authorial voice and echo are—unusually—indivisible, where the images produced are not imitations but direct copies, literally off the mirror of the copier. With the closure of this gap, and the *crude truth to life* it brings, Chadwick sought to open a space for a broader 'truth' to operate, based around the *principle of contradiction* introduced above, the combination of both idea and reality.

Through her collaging fragments of pure surface, Chadwick the artificer plays on the truth of the photocopy, undermining the *concrete realism* inherent in each fragment through the juxtaposition of other truths and the obvious display of its making. She made notes regarding the 'truth' of the photocopy in the margins of Alberto Veca's book on *vanitas* where he discusses the *Kunstkammer*. The parallel with her work—and *Of Mutability* in particular—is clear, as the *Kunstkammer* is described as 'a jumbled collection of precious things, [...] objects both artificial and natural, exotic and domestic' (*VST* 172). Veca notes how, in the *vanitas* tradition, the actuality of these objects would be appreciated while their ultimate decay was also considered; paintings in this genre would be admired for both their communication of the march of time and the verisimilitude of the real objects represented. 'Even though the two universes are antithetical [...] they seem to be able to coexist' (*VST* 174).

The antithetical universes of *concrete realism + fantasy* played out between the pure surface of things caught by the photocopier and the compositional fantasy of Chadwick's composite images coexist within the same flat raised-floor plane in this part of *Of Mutability*. However, in other notes, she explored how such composite images might be addressed to assumptions regarding the relationship between surface and form.

> Veiling of image over form as in EGS [*Ego Geometria Sum*] freed from 'terrestrial' prison—liberates as a series of composite images (not even a single instance as in a moment at which photograph is fixed ...) →
> Newtonian/Platonic view of reality as matter/mechanical model opened into quantum mechanics—open dynamic, inter-related fixing of occurrences as an 'image'
> i.e. FICTIONS
> 2003.19/E/6.147

While aspects of these notes have already been discussed in connection with Koestler's bisociative act, they also open onto the present consideration around the particular impact that bisociation could bring to the making and experience of objects, and the role of images in both these moments. Acknowledging the *total superficiality* of the *automatic image* or *pure surface* of the photocopy, what Chadwick calls 'image' here is more complex, thanks to its involvement not only with more of the same (and the contradiction played out in the collage), but with objects. Its potential as a composite is not simply to reiterate the *principle of contradiction* played out between stasis and dynamism, ideal and mundane, it also offers to veil form.

These particularly awkward considerations of Chadwick, exploring the relationships between the making of an image and the making of an object, can be if not clarified, at least extended through her relevant notes on Bachelard. For Chadwick, the interesting aspects of Bachelard included the radical novelty he assigned to the poetic image, and its ability to be trans-subjective. He observes the necessary 'split' in rational thinking when confronted with a new poetic image, and asks 'how can an image, at times very unusual, appear to be a concentration of the entire psyche?' (*PS* xiv). Chadwick underlines all this, and adds above 'image' the word 'object'. Bachelard suggests that the poetic act involves a 'sudden image'. While Chadwick's interest in the possibility of the unmediated production of an *automatic image* must not be confused with this, her thinking on this issue was clearly stimulated by it. Rather than conflating image and object, her explorations addressed how these might work artistically to sustain the poetic image and open onto a broader experience where the more *open dynamic, inter-related fixing of occurrences as an 'image' i.e. FICTIONS* might occur.

Addressed initially to the human (and frequently to her own) body, Chadwick noted her attempt to use multiple images in ways that retained or regained control of her own territory.

> <u>Representation Body</u> (Sue Arrowsmith – Egg of Night)
> Multiple images, refuse to hide traces or decide upon definitive line.
> Acknowledges own uncertainties
> Refuse to impose archetype upon herself
> Mapping out own territory – claiming her own body
> Act of re-possession.
> 2003.19/E/7.53

The ambition that multiple images could work against the establishment of an archetypal form (or the definitive line, to recall her considerations of Hogarth's Line of Beauty) was developed through projects that explored bodily representation. In the television programme *Imaginary Women*, Susan Hiller, one of the other guests around Marina Warner's table, talks about her own multiple-image self-portraits produced in photo-booths. Hillier's discussion anticipates several of the important issues that Chadwick's interest in unmediated production addressed. Hiller stresses how working in the photo-booths produced 'conventional' poses, despite, or precisely because, there was no photographer present, and she goes on to discuss how such fragments approximate a serial, episodic result that is more or less similar to the experience of images in dreams. The relevance of this for Hiller is that it questions the ideology of 'wholeness', the presumed unity of being, central to the Western tradition, and also offers to disrupt conventional artistic humanistic conceptions of material dependence on form. Although Chadwick's use of the photocopier cannot be directly aligned with Hiller's photo-booth productions, they clearly share some common ground in this area.

In contrast to the ideology of wholeness, Chadwick's own account expressed a desire that multiple images would combine to usher in an alternate conception: '→chance combinations around [the body] that lend interpretation become <u>active</u> field around it. Not still + arrested at moment but sequences leaving path/traces behind' (2003.19/E/7.52). She goes on to describe how this would mark a shift 'From single to multiple Static to Dynamic. Symbol→event. Energy not matter. Away from static physicality/sensuality to dynamic'. Likening her photocopied automatic images to *electrons!* she proposed reconsidering the relationship between *Image/object →Energy Field Actions*.

Now while her own work on *Energy Field Actions* was focused around the representation and reclamation of the body, this work has a certain resonance for architecture, although this relationship is not without difficulty. This quantum metaphor, while contesting the *Newtonian/Platonic view of reality as matter/mechanical model*, is difficult to accept, given the weight of traditional architecture–body metaphors and assumptions. Jane Gallop has noted the similar difficulty of accepting the (female) body as metaphor, due to the ease or convention of reading this literally. Notwithstanding Gallop's warning, there are examples of artistic production such as those of Chadwick or Hiller, or other nude (and more particularly female nude) self-portraits, that have addressed this situation directly, reclaiming authorial voice and selfhood. The situation for architectural production is very different; rather than granting *more* authority or autonomy to the architect, the potential *Energy Field Actions* of architectural production ought to be developed to the benefit of the audience or users.

It is important to acknowledge the difference between Chadwick's theoretical demands placed on multiple images, and existing architectural accounts that address the role of fragmented images within an approach to architectural experience. Although some accounts of architectural experience discuss the importance of fragmented images, these usually occur within theories of design or technique that assume fragments will be synthesised, and a complete picture of the whole architectural object will be established over time. One example already discussed would be Boullée's recommendation of the 'extended image' [*image étendues*] (*AEA* 89–90) where such images, part of the experience of 'variety', are anchored by, and return to, 'symmetry' and wholeness. Unlike such neoclassical or picturesque theories, where an initial ambiguity between image and object is clarified as image(s) are reconciled with form over time, Chadwick's address is to a different and more enduring complexity, where to each object, multiple images remain beyond synthesis, leaving room for *FICTIONS*. In this sense, hers are more like Piranesian compositions, where fragments resist a final 'true' account.

Exploring the potential of her quantum *Energy Field Actions* metaphor as this might be applied to the relationship between experience and the *totally superficial* image, she emphasised the need for the continuous addition of energy:

> The surface is always there, but only with the giving of light can it be seen
> *Filofax*, after 5 March 1988

Chadwick makes several similar notes: although these related to the experience of the spectator with respect to her own projects, they are also useful in extending her thinking beyond this arena towards that of the architectural user. Consider the following:

> Viewer as spectator, engaged in <u>poetic space of identification</u>.
> Between proj./screen move in to scrutinise surface ~~material~~ + image, move back to construe the ~~image~~ object: between these 2 processes we are held in place, witnessing event where light meets matter.
> Filofax after 9 February 1987, before 4 December 1987

Just as her interest in the composite image involves an awkward balance where image veils form, so this account involves two processes whose compatibility is not certain. Her notes in Bachelard's *Poetics of Space* suggest a similarly ambiguous relationship between poetic image and poetic object. The priority traditionally given to light is checked by the role of matter. As a metaphor for Chadwick, the projection of light on a surface opens an event of interpretation, rather than closes it down or models it on a coincidence of surface image and form. The importance of this was to contest the previous authority of form-idea; only once this was done could a potential series of composite images be 'liberated', as she emphasised in some preparatory lecture notes:

> overlay <u>image</u> onto another surface
> Image as light–frail/unsubstantial–alters authority of material substance

<u>light</u> as particle + a wave.

Filofax, 'Lecture/talk Camerawork', 5 March 1988

These suggestions in part were developed as part of her broader challenge to traditional assumptions regarding the role of technique, such that the relationship between making and thinking is not simply reversed, but the world view within which this could operate comfortably is questioned. In some ways, this returns us to Chadwick's early acknowledgement around the time she turned away from *architectural sculpture*, that *buildings stronger than people,—more enduring, more real than lives led*. Against the physical surface, whether of buildings or the screens of her later work, *LIGHT as subjectivity* was *halted, arrested*. The role of composite images was charged with clearing a *poetic space of identification*, where this ambiguity of image and object, or form and matter, could be enjoyed. While she noted this potential for composite images to evade traditional formal conceptions of experience, effectively driving a wedge between form and matter as this hylomorphic relationship was traditionally conceived, this came with a number of questions that here need to be pursued towards their architectural relevance, rather than maintained within the context of Chadwick's own œuvre.

To make this transition, it is to the role of the *Machine* that we can turn. Beyond the photocopier's role in the production of particular projects, her considerations open onto the impact of this and other reproduction techniques upon the relationships between the artist, the viewer and the particular media concerned. Around this nexus, it is helpful to return to Tafuri's analysis in *Theories and History of Architecture*. Tafuri cites the 'exceptional importance' of Walter Benjamin's well-known essay on the work of art in the age of its mechanical reproducibility in helping towards an understanding of this tendency. The relevance of Tafuri's and Benjamin's work here lies in their respective considerations of an artist's ability to work 'free from the equipment'. While equipment itself can clearly vary, the important issue concerns the extent to which new equipment, new technologies, are regarded. Tafuri borrows from Benjamin's analysis to categorise a number of approaches that remain too excited by new technologies to adapt to their radical potential; these, held in awe, are not (yet) free of the equipment.[12] In contrast, those who are able to go behind the presence of new equipment, to understand it sufficiently that they can invent new laws for its application, are free from it. The importance of the latter, for Tafuri at least, is that they are able to recognise, and value, a new nature of technological reality. Although Tafuri's analysis is fairly polarised, Chadwick positioned her work to deliberately span across the range of approaches he notes. Whereas Tafuri and Benjamin can be considered to be interested in determining which media are more meaningful for modern life, Chadwick's questions—while sharing similar ingredients—can be taken to be directed less at specific media or machines, and more at the epistemological structures through which experience, however mediated, might be understood.

Rather than being 'free of equipment', Chadwick combined mediated and unmediated production in an attempt to explicitly position her work in a 'zone between 2':

> evades 2D painting/3D sculpture
>   Image/object
> occupies zone between 2
> (reflects metaphysical uncertainty ~~of commodity~~ caught between image + reality.
> * Act of synthesis to evoke separation, merging 2D world of image with 3D world object—
> Flatness ptc. + depth photog. illusion
> counterpoint + polarity as own reversal of ptg→object/screen
> image→surface
> *Filofax*, after December 1987, before March 1988

Rather than deploying media that are perhaps 'most meaningful for modern life', this deliberate mixing of techniques and media set out to alter the dimensions usually relied upon to frame experience. Neither two- nor three-dimensional, *between 2* addresses the issues associated with libidinal materialism introduced at the beginning of this chapter. *Bestial reason* copes with this ambiguity; the associated uncertainty as Chadwick's work attempted to hold open a space between image and object permits its operation.

There are a couple of instances in Chadwick's notes where she associates these intentions with the possibilities of working with the newly emerging promise of computers. For her, this promise lay in the analogy she perceived between the computer's sphere of operation and the role of art.

> With digital scanning + image manipulation—like genetic engineering of the visual world/field
>
> The virus is amoral.
>
> Process like a virus—breaking down coherence of image.
> dissolving separateness of individual (component) images
> *Filofax*, after March 88

Working at the computer, and despite her naïve excitement at the prospect of this new technology (remember this was 1988, when computer interfaces for CAD and image manipulation software were particularly unfriendly—one entire notebook is kept just decoding the interface instructions), Chadwick identified the computer's ability to operate in precisely the field beyond individual coherence that traditionally predicated architectural and artistic production.

Despite the great development in computing, both in sheer computational power and in the intuitiveness or user-friendliness of software interfaces, Chadwick's interest in the potential contribution of the digital world identifies its deeper promise, one that remains pertinent despite the speed of change in this area. It must be said, her view of the computer was very affirmative: it was with the computer that she identified a promise concerning an approach to making that could echo something of the continua she saw in the world. The potential for the computer to provide an alternate interface between creative self and world was linked, in her mind, to the ways in which computer technology was mounting a challenge to the traditional role of the image in the production, mediation and experience of the world, and to the understanding of technique as this traditionally pertained to the relationship between image-making and object-making.

> Fusion on digital level of computer technology, which is the language of conversion from one kind [of] information into another. Fluid state.
> Comp. as an interface for this mixing + translation of sea into self
> *Filofax*, after March 1988

For Chadwick, the opportunity she read in the potential of the computer *as an interface for this mixing + translation*, its offer to open up connections between things usually kept apart, was related not simply to the impact this could have on the practical consequences of the computer's role in making, but to the more thoroughgoing impact that this new interface would have on the epistemological and theoretical framework within which the role of making was considered and through which our experience of the world was channelled.

Unable to anticipate the magnitude of the impact of computers in contemporary society, much of the promise she read has failed to materialise at this deeper level. This is not to suggest that no change has taken place here; in fact, there has been such an enormous shift in the economy of mediation that Chadwick's interest in this area must be picked over carefully. The computer has affected so many facets of life that we might believe we have become *free of this equipment*; ease of use and the omnipresence of computer-generated stuff serve to reinforce rather than challenge the epistemological status quo.

In her own practice, Chadwick only gained partial freedom from this equipment; along with other media or techniques that she learned in order to realise particular projects, her work with computers was difficult. At this time, computer interfaces did not provide a transparent medium that could allow unmediated production. Working with them was indeed *like genetic engineering,* in contrast to the ease with which we might splash around with software such as Photoshop™ today.

Although this contrasts to the unmediated production she claimed for her work with the photocopier, the subsequent collaging and combination of these *totally superficial* images to produce *composite images* set out to introduce a delay or diversion in the traditional unobstructed relay between form and image. Her computer-generated work for *Viral Landscapes* produced a different kind of composite image, but the technique she used to produce this involved a similar delay or obstacle. While there are contingent explanations for this, it is important to pause at precisely this point in order to consider the ways in which her thought could continue to bear on the current processes of making, and particularly how it might qualify the use of computers (and other *equipment*) with respect to the making of stuff, whether art or architectural objects, and also how this implicates, supports or contests the making of knowledge.

For Chadwick, the appeal of computer technology is easy enough to understand; both as *equipment* and by analogy, it offered a chance to combine material and ideas, respectively, across the *fluid states* of the world that so interested her, allowing her to work primarily through and address force and energy rather than form and matter. The digital offered access to the world of flows, of energy, circumventing the old world of hylomorphism. Nevertheless, neither through the unmediated production of the photocopier, nor through the 'virtual' digital fusions of the computer was her work set free from material considerations, despite the suggestions of her writings. These various working techniques were developed as so many ways of addressing libidinal materiality, they were not an attempt to produce work with *no* materiality. Their main target was the coherent, whole image, and the acceptance of total coherence that underwrote this, irrespective of medium.

While it would be true to say that she—like everyone else at this time using computers for draughting, designing or imaging—was struggling to work with new equipment, Chadwick's enthusiasm for this technique cannot be fast forwarded through the intervening years to suggest that the digital level of computer techniques can offer up the composite images she sought, at least not with the richness and complexity involved in her thinking. Their real promise and attraction were their contingent ability to act *like a virus* on the coherence of individual images. Her struggle was not simply with the interface, but with the complex relay it was caught up in. But now, thanks to the relative transparency of software interfaces, the simple equivalence between different modes and scales of information, the ease of *conversion from one kind [of] information into another*, there is no inherent grit to make the pearl.

This is not only relevant to the more obvious file-to-factory technologies now available to architects and designers, which have their own impact upon architecture's relationship to processes of making epitomised in the material-less objects of rapid-prototyping, but also in the context of other, non-architectural, ways of making. As a less visible parallel to these imaging technologies, complementary programmes such as the National Building Specification (NBS) signal the attendant and increasing pressures to adopt normative solutions to making, where the material appreciation, knowledge and expertise of the maker is removed to a remote, third party document concerned primarily with cost and risk management. In many ways the absolute opposite of *libidinal materiality*, the NBS stands as the next and final step in the logical sequence where images have been deployed, both practically and conceptually, to play a controlling role over matter. The NBS approach to material specification and treatment represents an attitude of mind, a systematic and over-rationalised economy of materiality that marks the end-game of hylomorphism. Moreover, the implicit consequences of such an approach include the removal of agency from those involved in the making of the objects (in the case of the NBS, these objects are buildings, but the situation is more widespread), and the strange re-apportioning of responsibility, on legal and financial grounds, through the whole system.

It is precisely at this point that Chadwick's intention to break down the coherence and the underlying logic of the 'coherent image' must be understood. Her interest in the *Composite Image*, although operating in her examples of realised work through image manipulation, was not addressed primarily to, nor does it stop with, images: instead, she believed it offered a way through to an image's modality, where the assumptions regarding the evenness and operation of images could be called into question.

In terms of the last example, the promise she associated with computer technology lay in the potential mixing of information that was usually held apart. Rather than this technology epitomising an *unmediated production*—and the difficulties of Chadwick's phrase some into stark relief at this point— she encountered an operation where she was able to make connections between kinds and scales of information that were difficult or impossible to realise elsewhere. The computer's attraction lay in this bypass of hylomorphic conceptions of making, rather than in the 'virtual' making with which it has become associated. In the broader context of her œuvre, and considering Chadwick-the-artificer, this marks one of a number of instances where she would adopt new techniques of making, where she would 'skill up' and learn new trades in order to explore or realise particular pieces. As artificer, these new tricks were frequently deployed according the 'rules' (or rule-breaking) of her bisociative approach.

But across all of these bisociative approaches to making, Chadwick knowingly sought to combine stuff that was usually kept apart. Although this is obvious across most of her œuvre, there is a particular danger that her enthusiasm for the bisociative potential of computer technology be read as an invitation to work without a concomitant material understanding, in its most extreme version to work in an entirely virtual world. In this situation, work with computers becomes a two-dimensional collaging exercise, catalogue shopping for effects or exercising the false authority vested in the designer through the NBS illusion of democracy and agency.

Instead of these approaches, Chadwick's thinking must be understood as a demand, a challenge, to explore and expand computer-based approaches to and techniques for making beyond either the increasingly instrumental application of normative systems, or the solipsistic escape into a virtual zone. This challenge is most interesting when the asymmetry between the literal and metaphorical role of images, and between their reception by the eye and by the mind's eye, is considered. Her address to these (for example, literally making metaphors of meat and light, flesh and knowledge, mind and body and so on) was directed towards their roles within both technique and experience. The broader point concerns the gap that such exercises knowingly opened up between the 'good' application of technique, and the subversion or misapplication of that technique.

Whereas 'good' technique (traditionally conceived as the obedient application of practical knowledge) lay implicitly at the service of a controlling idea linked directly to the 'good' image, Chadwick's unmediated production invited theory and practice to enter different relationships. Holding apart image and surface allowed an alternate space where a different process of making could operate, a bisociative process where rules could be misapplied, techniques misdirected, materials mishandled. Thinking about this alternate space in the context of Chadwick's interest in computer technology provides only the latest opportunity to consider the long relationship between technique as theory and as practice, but an opportunity that nonetheless offers to return energy to matter and experience rather than establish a framework of doing and seeing that is based on the longstanding axes of form and matter.

Chadwick's interest in the veiling of image over form is relevant, in different directions, to both art and architecture: it was her intention that this would muddy the assumed links between idea and reality, form and matter. Her *Composite Images* were about contesting the authority and control exercised over making and experiencing work, although for these two disciplines the problem lies in different structures. Chadwick's thinking held the image as the (or part of the) interface for experience. Within her own realised work, the image was an overt conceit, an articulate assemblage that combined various conventions of thinking and making with the intention of energising the event of experiencing and thinking about the pieces. Even the primitive, unmediated productions of the photocopier were subsequently collaged into assemblages that belied the automatism of Chadwick's claim for the individual images. For architecture, unmediated production proves a more awkward relay, though historically it has been opened on to territory similar to Chadwick's artistic target. Architecture could experiment with unmediated images to reveal the processes of its own making, and offer to maintain these open, beyond its control. This calls upon an alternate notion of making that is addressed not only to the object but to the various idea-images that are involved in the object's production, and to the idea-images that are produced during peoples' experience, their remaking, of that architecture. This alternate notion has the composite image acting as conduit for the ongoing transmission of energy rather than as an overarching, controlling idea. It does not reduce architecture to idea by ignoring or eliminating its materiality, but in fact encourages a greater material understanding and experimentation by operating within different ecologies of knowledge that maintain it open as a question.

Conclusion

For Chadwick, the promise of creative imagination was that it might open up what had previously been closed down. The 'civilisation' it threatened was hollow, thin, based on the *tissue of received information* that constructs and maintains our identity, but a tissue that was itself based on an increasingly narrow, deterministic world-view.

Chadwick did not advocate the replacement of this tissue with another. Instead, she argued that imagination and creativity, far from being a threat, could broaden the appreciation of what civilisation could be. While she warned against an unhealthy obsession with theory, she recognised the importance of contesting those theories that maintain the 'tissue'. Recalling her analogy of the OXO cube, she sought to dish up a richer experience:

> let the [work] use theory but only as an OXO cube to the dinner, let stronger meats carry the appetites
>
> 2003.19/E/6.145

Her entire œuvre was directed at exploring the effects that a direct, material encounter could bring. While she warned against trying to generate this with excessively theoretical ingredients, she also found a certain reassurance that this encounter revealed the site of practice itself to be excessive, to exceed full theoretical accountability. Far from being anti-intellectual, her own approach to knowledge was to understand how it played a part in the received tissue that maintains our subjugation, identity or position in the world, in order to suggest ways in which it might be torn through to reach other knowledges and understandings, other experience that lay beyond 'civilised' accounting.

If 'civilisation' is maintained through the 'correct' application of accepted, sanctioned knowledge, then for artists and makers the corollary would be in an approach based on applied understanding or *techné*. For Chadwick, there ought to be something more: although she never used the term, it is useful here to introduce another kind of knowing-making designated by the Greek word *métis*. *Métis* shares much with *techné*, as a way of accounting for knowledge that embraces both mental *and* manual aspects, language *and* material, knowing *and* doing. Crucially, though, it calls on a range of activities that exceed the accepted domain of *techné*, and operates by continual shape-shifting, guile and trickery. *Métis* carries a twisting sense of movement, multiplicity and ambiguity that contrasts with the linear application of *techné* and the stable good form that the latter was charged with producing.

The 'dangers' of imagination and creativity are acknowledged by *métis*, which pushes making beyond the considerations of (good) craft or 'truth to materials', embraces the potential and power of the object, and opens experience to a territory beyond knowing. The issues of geometry, discussed at length earlier, can be returned to here in order to provide but one example.

As a method and a metaphor, geometrical understanding can have either a withering or expanding effect on the possibilities of our understanding of stuff in the world. Even with Platonic geometries or their development in the Newtonian-Cartesian age, Chadwick found reason to be enthralled and repulsed at the same time, for they provided a framework so far-reaching, so universal in ambition, that it became difficult to take up a position outside this frame. With an interest in Boullée and Hogarth, neoclassical and rococo, Chadwick explored behind the surface of objects (or spaces) set up and understood in this way. Probing behind the surface, stereotomy—although a potentially redundant practice even when it was first developed, and potentially still taking architecture ever more into its inward-looking, formal applied-geometrical labyrinth—provided a metaphor for being in several (inoccupiable) places at once.

Stereotomy gives a possible way into *métis* considerations that are at once theoretical and practical, growing out of the 'needs' of practice as *techné*. Stereotomy was discussed as an *excessive* theory, a geometry that remains illegible behind the surface (the 'tissue'), an exercise of formal, geometrical virtuosity, of self-effacing craftsmanship, producing an illusionistic structure or object that can return a work's role carrying meaning within accepted frameworks. For Chadwick though, such conflict between systems of understanding, making and experience—between *métis* and *techné*—ought to be played out in full view. The creative process ought to take place on the working surface, for the reasons discussed around *The Juggler's Table*.

Indeed, The Juggler, *Le Bateleur*, can be understood to employ a good deal of *métis* in their work, which involves imagination, cunning and looking the wrong way. As an 'artificer', juggling both *métis* and *techné*, Chadwick's identification with *Le Bateleur* can be understood to have strong similarities with different mythical figure, Hephaistos. As Cheryl De Ciantis describes him,

> Hephaistos is the one Greek god who possesses both techné and métis [...] One of his titles in Greek is *amphigueeis*. This is an ambiguous term, which can be translated in two ways, either 'crippled' or 'ambidextrous'. Hephaistos, the god of technology, is both. The deformed, circular march of the god with crippled feet is an emblem of his métis, or mental ambidexterity. It is the source of his magical creative ability. Hephaistos symbolizes both the practical, technical skills and knowledge we rely on as well as the elliptical, ambiguous and ungovernable nature of creativity. Hephaistos presents to us an image of a highly functional and yet creative way of behaving that is not only familiar, but one that has been and continues to be discounted and rejected.[1]

Mentally ambidexterous, left-brain and right-brain, rational and irrational, thinker and doer, Chadwick brings the figure of Hephaistos back to contemporary concerns. As De Ciantis and others have argued, to step back to this old myth can provide lessons for the complex material and social tasks in our 'information' age.

Notes

Preface

1   Helen Chadwick, Lecture notes entitled "'Trophies to Ambivalence: to the value of a doubtful status" Glarus—1.7.95' held in the Helen Chadwick Collection, Henry Moore Institute, Leeds (hereafter HMI), archival Box 19.

2   Helen Chadwick, notebook, HMI archive accession no. 2003.19/E/6, p. 145. This referencing convention is explained in more detail in the section on the *Integration of Sources* (pp.xv–xviii), and references from this point forward will be given in the main text.

Integration of sources

1   Although the HMI holds almost all the Helen Chadwick Estate, there is a small collection of papers and images in the Drawings Collection at the Victoria and Albert Museum (V&A) in London. The V&A holds Chadwick's *Of Mutability*, and to complement this piece they have documents relevant to this project.

Introduction

1   In lecture notes from which this article developed, Chadwick stressed the importance of both identity and collapse: 'a possibility for beginning to look at <u>identity</u> and the conditions where it <u>collapses</u>'. The text as it is produced in *JPVA* is based on a lecture Chadwick gave at the Symposium for Photography in Graz (October 1990), also printed in *Camera Austria* #37, pp. 4–10 (with different illustrations), and also clearly used as a base for other lectures given until 1995.

2   Chadwick asserts this many times. Here is just one example: 'A container can effect how we feel+think. If shape of instruments effects the musical note, so the shape of a space/thing must effect ourselves if part of us is exposed to/contained by it … Energy of body influenced by shape+containing structures, & vice versa … The geometrical space in which activity occurred modifies the person. result: physical → mental' 2003.19/E/5: 98–9.

3   It is possible to account for these changes by following biographical or contemporary contextualising approaches. These would point to the straightforward maturation of her artistic language (*Model Institution* was produced shortly after Chadwick finished her MA at Chelsea); or to the ways in which the changes in her work from a punky social realism to sort of New Romanticism reflected broader changes in the cultural scene following the emergence and development of Thatcherism; or to the shared strengthening of theoretical influences among the artistic community during the 1980s. While mindful of the relevance of this context, to follow this exclusively is to launder

the promise of her *œuvre*. While the projects themselves clearly differed, her motivation and the artistic method she adopted were more consistent, resulting in an invigorating artistic approach. It could be said that Chadwick's work moved away from directly addressing the person in space, reflecting the changes taking place as her understanding of identity formation and politics.

Chapter 1

1 Chadwick is here roughly paraphrasing Gettings *BT* 17–18.

2 *Hand Signals* was a group show that began at the Icon Gallery, Birmingham in 1985, and later toured.

3 And compare '*Artist not citizen of society—bound to explore beyond its parameters outside structure of society if necessary. Artist has "No social responsibility."*' *Filofax* c.1987 (previous page '9.2.87').

4 Charles Zika, 'Images of Circe and Discourses of Witchcraft, 1480–1580', in *zeitenblicke* 1 (2002), no. 1, §10. Emphasis added.

5 Allen G. Debus, *Paracelsus and the Medical Revolution of the Renaissance: A 500th Anniversary Celebration*, exhibition catalogue, US National Library of Medicine, Bethesda, Maryland, 1993. (The exhibition was held at three sites in 1993 and 1994: The National Library of Medicine, Bethesda; Hahnemann University, Philadelphia; and Washington University, St. Louis: http://www.nlm.nih.gov/exhibition/paracelsus/paracelsus_1.htm reproduces the text of the exhibition brochure, with slight editorial changes to the order of materials appropriate to the online version.)

6 Allen G. Debus and Robert P. Multhauf, *Alchemy and Chemistry in the Seventeenth Century*, Los Angeles: William Andrews Clark Memorial Library, University of California, 1966, pp. 6–12.

7 Debus, *Paracelsus and the Medical Revolution*, np.

8 This valorisation of card zero, *The Fool* or *Le Mat*, as the foundation or beginning of all creation, action and knowledge is also offered according to a layer of Tarot symbolism derived from ancient Hebrew cosmology.

9 Debus, *Paracelsus and the Medical Revolution*, np.

10 Chadwick notes almost identically in the margin to her copy of Koestler's *The Sleepwalkers*; 'here my work departs: left behind in geometry:—static model of pre Newtonian universe, no depiction of dynamic of change' (*SW* 341).

Chapter 2

1 'The creative act itself is for the scientist, as for the artist, a leap into the dark, where both are equally dependent on their fallible intuitions [...] Intellectual illumination and emotional catharsis are complementary aspects of an indivisible process' (*GM* 227).

2 In addition to this note, Chadwick highlighted and underlined the adjacent passage: 'Out of this combination [of iconoclasm towards the old and naïve credulity to new concepts] results that crucial capacity of perceiving a familiar object, situation, problem, or collection of data, in a sudden new light or new context [...] The discoverer perceives relational patterns of functional analogies where nobody saw them before' (*SW* 529).

3 Manfredo Tafuri, *Theories and History of Architecture* (1968), tr. Giorgio Verrecchia, Granada, London, 1980, p. 56.

4 Here, Chadwick writes 'installation' in the margin; similarly on p. 548, she adds 'Installation: a concrete model of the abstract space/time.'

5 Tafuri, *Theories and History of Architecture*, p. 205.

Chapter 3

1   Barker writes 'The proliferation in the dramatic, philosophical and political texts of the period of corporeal images which have become dead metaphors for us—by a structured forgetting rather than by innocent historical wastage—are the indices of a social order in which the body has a central and irreducible place [...] The glorious cruelties of the Jacobean theatre thus articulate a mode of corporeality which is structural to its world' (*TPB* 23).

2   Ritta and Christina were one of the most famous pairs of conjoined twins, born in Sardinia in 1829, and brought to Paris for public exhibition. They had two heads, two chests with four arms attached, but a common lower torso and single lower extremities. Their emotions, affections, and appetites were different: contemporary accounts suggest a stark contrast between Ritta, on the right, who was weak and melancholy, and Christina, who was happy and energetic. They lived barely nine months. Their skeleton is allegedly still held in the collection of the Museum of Natural History in Paris.

3   Georges Bataille, 'The Deviations of Nature' (1930), in *Visions of Excess: Selected Writings, 1927–1939*, translated, edited and introduced by Allan Stoekl, University of Minnesota Press, Minneapolis, 1985, p. 55.

4   Chadwick writes 'Liquid World' in the margin at this point: the relevance of 'Liquid World' is clearly a corollary to her conception of body as site through which many forces run.

5   Kunsthaus Glarus, Switzerland, a gallery where Chadwick showed work on more than one occasion.

6   Elizabeth Grosz, *Architecture from the Outside: Essays on Virtual and Real Space,* MIT Press (Writing Architecture Series), Cambridge, MA, 2001, p. 28.

7   Ibid. p. 22, 23. While working her way towards the Deleuzian concept of the body just mentioned, she is at this point explicitly critical of the misconceptions around the 'choice' that such a concept might bring, which she blames squarely on queer-theorists' misreading of Judith Butler's notion of *performativity*.

8   At the foot of that page, Chadwick writes:
> tulip/plum: too 'object' like—unnameable, formless blobs of primary identification construct 'Thing'

9   As well as citing Freud's contribution, she emphasises the importance of Heidegger's work, particularly *What Is a Thing?*

10   Discussing Perrault's *Ordonnance* (1673, 1684) as something of a motif for these broad changes in world-view, Pérez-Gómez argues that while this work was very much a (rationalising) product of its time, it is actually something of a fraud, as the mathematical calculations are little more than a smoke screen. 'In Claude Perrault's theory, architectural proportion lost for the first time, in an explicit way, its character as a transcendental link between microcosm and macrocosm.' Alberto Pérez-Gómez, *Architecture and the Crisis of Modern Science* (1980), MIT Press, Cambridge, MA, 1983, p. 32. Elsewhere, in his 'Introduction' to Perrault's *Ordonnance for the Five Kinds of Columns After the Method of the Ancients*, tr. Indra Kagis McEwen, The Getty Centre Publications Programs, Santa Monica, CA, 1993, Pérez-Gómez makes a strong case for the relevance of (re-)considering such work from the dawn of the modern era in our current circumstances, which is effectively what Chadwick does.

11   Louise Pelletier, *Architecture in Words: Theatre, Language and the Sensuous Space of Architecture*, Routledge, London & NY, 2006, p. 2, original emphasis. In particular, she explores Nicolas Le Camus de Mézières' *The Genius of Architecture: Or, the Analogy of That Art with Our Sensations* [*Le génie de l'architecture, ou l'analogie de cet art avec nos sensations*, Paris, B. Morin, 1780; Minkoff Reprint Geneva, 1972], tr. D. Britt, Robert Middleton (Introduction), The Getty Centre, Santa Monica, 1992.

12   Elizabeth Grosz, *Architecture from the Outside*, p. 167.

13 Walter Schwarz, 'Quantum thinking by a quantum person', *Guardian*, 'Personal' section, no date on cutting, *c.*1990, p. 39.

14 In addition to *A New Science of Life*, Chadwick had a copy of Sheldrake's *The Rebirth of Nature: The Greening of Science and God*, Century, London, 1990, which is inscribed 'For Helen/ All best wishes/ Rupert/ On the occasion of our dialogue at Kettle's Yard June 5th 1991.'

15 Arkady Plotnitsky, *Complementarity: Anti-Epistemology after Bohr and Derrida*, Duke University Press, Durham, NC, and London, 1994, pp. 32, 33. The General Economy was a common interest of both Chadwick and Plotnitsky, which both link explicitly to the work of Georges Bataille mentioned above, albeit in passing, around the necessary divergence of each individual from the common measure.

Chapter 4

1 Capra is citing John Wheeler, in J. Mehra (ed.) *The Physicist's Conception of Nature*, D. Reidel, Dordrecht, Holland, 1973, p. 24. (For more on the 'participatory universe' see John Wheeler, *Quantum Theory and Measurement*, Princeton University Press, 1983, esp. pp. 184–94.)

2 Niels Bohr, *Philosophical Writings of Neils Bohr*, Ox Bow Press, Woodbridge, CT, 1987, I: 11–12, 54, cited in Plotnitsky, *Complementarity*, p. 102.

3 Plotnitsky, *Complementarity*, p. 103.

4 Bohr, *Philosophical Writings*, II: 25. For him, these referred to the traditional paradigms of science, including but not limited to Newtonianism, rather than the everyday in the sense of that which is prior to or removed from any specialist discourse.

5 Tafuri, *Theories and History of Architecture*, p. 28.

6 Manfredo Tafuri, *The Sphere and the Labyrinth: Avant-Gardes and Architecture from Piranesi to the 1970s* (1980), tr. Pellegrino d'Acierno and Robert Connolly, MIT Press, Cambridge, MA, 1987, p. 36.

7 Ibid, p. 38, original emphasis.

8 The potential for such a linkage is evident in the recent work of Don Ihde, who has drawn on multistability to refer to 'our' ability to perceive stable views of an environment in different modes, much like the work on visual illusion just noted, but he has extended the conceptual range of multistability to involve ingredients not just from beyond the visual, but also from beyond the physical, through his emerging philosophies of cyberspace.

9 Helen Rosenau, 'Boullée and Universal Architecture', in Helen Rosenau (ed.), *Boullée and Visionary Architecture*, London, Academy, 1976, p. 28.

10 Much as Chadwick draws on work in the sciences—here in particular, biology—there have been a number of attempts to link scientific discussions of dissensus with politics and philosophy or ethics. Margret Grebowicz's article provides a good review of the various directions these links have taken, before advocating a particular kind of link that is sympathetic to Chadwick's position and drawn out of Donna Haraway's work. Just as multistable behaviour discussed above must remain radically open, so Grebowicz advocates a dissensual model that demonstrates multistability both within its framework of encounter and in the outcome of such encounter, both of which avoid universalising tendencies:

> In contrast to the "consensual critique"-model of science as democratically-oriented, critical interaction which benefits everyone, Haraway proposes a "dissensual critique"-model, starting from the assumption that contest and polemic are irreducible and epistemically valuable, and indicating that dissent *qua* dissent does real work in the production of knowledge. For Haraway, dissent functions as an end in itself, not as a means to greater clarity and community. Unlike Longino's call for pluralism, for endlessly many knowledges, Haraway is

interested in the differences between knowledges as politically and epistemically valuable.

Margret Grebowicz, 'Consensus, Dissensus, and Democracy: What Is at Stake in Feminist Science Studies?' *Philosophy of Science* 72 (December 2005), p. 998.Grebowicz is referring to Donna Haraway's work 'from the late seventies', and cites in the bibliography Donna Haraway, 'Animal Sociology and the Body Politic, Part II: The Past Is the Contested Zone', in Evelyn Fox Keller and Helen E. Longino (eds.), *Feminism and Science*, Oxford University Press, 1996, pp. 57–72 (originally published in *Signs: Journal of Women in Culture and Society*, 4 (1978), pp. 21–60.

11   Grebowicz, 'Consensus, Dissensus, and Democracy', pp. 989–1000.

Chapter 5

1   Giovanni Battista della Porta (1527–1628), *Natural Magick* (1558), Derek J. Price (ed.) facsimile of the English edition (1658), Basic Books, New York, 1957. Della Porta's work is cited and discussed in Carolyn Merchant, *The Death of Nature: Women, Ecology, and the Scientific Revolution* (1980), Harper, San Francisco, 1990, Ch. 4, 'The World as Organism', Chadwick references 'Carolyn Merchant 1981 "The Death of Nature," Havard, Wildewood House Publishers' in her *Filofax* (the next dated page is 4.12.87), though it is not clear whether she read it.

2   Merchant, *The Death of Nature*, pp. 108–9.

3   As Louise Pelletier has observed, the increasing rationality of the Enlightenment, associated with an architectural tendency towards rigid neoclassical style, found release in a variety of outlets that sanctioned creative play, typified, she suggests, by Louis-Sébastien Mercier's advocacy to 'Follow your spirit … it knows more than the rules'. Pelletier, *Architecture in Words*, p. 110. She is citing Louis-Sébastien Merceir, *Du theatre, ou nouvelle essai sur l'art dramatique* (1758).

4   Tafuri, *Theories and History of Architecture*, p. 124.

5   Ibid., p. 82

6   Ibid., p. 32, original emphasis.

7   Victor Burgin, 'Geometry and Abjection', in *AA Files*, 15 (Summer 1987), p. 35: see also Victor Burgin, 'Perverse Space' in Beatriz Colomina (ed.), *Sexuality and Space*, Princeton University Press, 1992, pp. 218–240, which covers similar ground to 'Geometry and Abjection'.

8   John Dixon Hunt, *The Figure in the Landscape: Poetry, Painting and Gardening during the Eighteenth Century*, Johns Hopkins University Press, Baltimore and London, 1976, p. 67.

9   'It's dizzy', she later wrote in her catalogue essay, 'like a kind of dance, and there's no sense of function at all. It's a place that began as a dream […] All the architect's resources went into manufacturing a dream reality […] It's not about power but about pleasure' (*OM* 43).

Chapter 6

1   Montesquieu's article on 'Taste' *goût* was published as 'Fragment sur le goût', in *Encyclopédie ou Dictionnaire raisonné des sciences, des arts et des métiers*, Vol. VII, 1757, pp. 761b–767b. (The passage cited here, p. 764.)

2   William Ray, 'Talking About Art: The French Royal Academy Salons and the Formation of the Discursive Citizen', *Eighteenth-Century Studies* 37 (2004), p. 528.

3   Downing A. Thomas, 'Negotiating Taste in Montesquieu', in *Eighteenth-Century Studies* 39.1 (2005), p. 78.

4   Ibid., p. 77.

5   Boullée cites his reference as *Essai philosophique concernant l'entendement humain, où l'on montre quelle est l'etendue de nos connaissances certaines, et la manière dont nous y parvenons. Traduit de l'anglois de Mr. Locke, par Pierre Coste, sur la quatriéme edition, revûë, corrigée, & augmentée par*

l'auteur (translated by Pierre Coste, from Locke's fourth edition, revised, corrected and expanded by the author), Henri Schelte, Amsterdam, 1700.

6   Georges Bataille, 'The Deviations of Nature', in *Visions of Excess*. All quotes here from p. 55. Bataille's essay is named after Regnault's 'The Deviations of Nature' (1775), which Bataille describes as a 'luxurious album of engraved and coloured illustrations': p. 53.

7   As if to reinforce the relevance of Bataille's essay, Boullée goes on to use the analogy of the human face, and to mention the 'hideous' appearance of contorted face in contrast to the symmetry of the beautiful.

8   Claudia Brodsky Lacour, *Lines of Thought: Discourse, Architectonics, and the Origin of Modern Philosophy*, Duke University Press, Durham, NC, and London, 1996, p. 118.

9   Ibid., p. 121, 120, 132.

10   Alberto Pérez-Gómez, *Architecture and the Crisis of Modern Science* (1980), MIT Press, Cambridge MA, 1983, p. 30. This assertion is reinforced shortly afterwards: 'In Claude Perrault's theory, architectural proportion lost for the first time, in an explicit way, its character as a transcendental link between microcosm and macrocosm.' Ibid., p. 32.

11   Ikebana is the Japanese art of flower arrangement that emerged in the late fifteenth-century. In contrast to a typical Western approach to flower arrangement, which relies on full stems of flowers, Japanese Ikebana composition is based on the line of twigs and leaves, and is considered to symbolise heaven, earth, and man, and relates back to the early role played by flower arrangements in Buddhism.

12   Jim Bennett and Scott Mandelbrote (eds), *The Garden, the Ark, the Tower, the Temple: Biblical Metaphors of Knowledge in Early Modern Europe*, Museum of the History of Science in association with the Bodleian Library, Oxford, 1998, pp. 8, 10.

13   Ibid., p. 9.

14   Ibid., p. 9.

15   Tafuri, *Theories and History of Architecture,* p. 7. He is referring to Roland Barthes, *Mythologies*, Éditions du Seuil, Paris, 1957. English edition *Mythologies*, selected and translated from the French by Annette Lavers, Jonathan Cape, London 1972.

16   Grosz, *Architecture from the Outside*, p. 97.

17   Montesquieu, *Oeuvres complètes*, Caillois (ed.) II:48. cited in Downing A. Thomas, 'Negotiating Taste in Montesquieu', pp. 75–6. 'Lorsque nous entendons chanter ou déclamer, il se fait deux choses également mécaniques: l'une, que nous entendons clairement les sons; l'autre, que nous sommes émus par ces sons; et il arrive tous les jours que, de deux personnes, celle qui entend mieux est la moins émue.' Thomas goes on to argue that 'radicalized, this abstraction from use and from sensation would become the basis for claims to autonomy, disinterestedness, and self-referentiality as aesthetic discourse developed into the nineteenth century.'

18   Grosz, *Architecture from the Outside*, pp. 98–9, 100.

19   Plotnitsky, *Complementarity*, p. 30.

Chapter 7

1   John Marks, 'Molecular Biology in the Work of Deleuze and Guattari', *Paragraph* 29:2 (2006), p. 85. He suggests that this 'is expressed most explicitly in the so-called "Central Dogma" of molecular biology, originally formulated by Francis Crick. The Central Dogma is based around the scientific claim that the flow of genetic information goes in one direction from DNA to RNA to protein.'

2   Ibid., p. 89. Marks refers to Jacques Monod, *Chance and Necessity: An Essay on the Natural Philosophy of Modern Biology*, tr. Austryn Wainhouse, Collins, London, 1972; and François Jacob, *The Logic of Living Systems: A History of Heredity*, tr. Betty E. Spillman, Allen Lane, London, 1974.

3 Richard Doyle, *On Beyond Living: Rhetorical Transformations in the Life Sciences*, Stanford University Press, Palo Alto, CA, 1997, p. 66.

4 Plotnitsky, *Complementarity*, p. 240.

5 Gilbert Simondon, 'The Genesis of the Individual', tr. Mark Cohen and Sanford Kwinter, in Jonathan Crary and Sanford Kwinter (eds) *Incorporations*, Zone Books, New York, 1992, p. 302. This article formed the introduction to *L'individu et sa genèse physico-biologique (l'individuation à la lumière des notions de forme et d'information)*, Paris, 1964 (PUF, second edition, J. Millon, coll. Krisis, 1995).

6 Simondon, 'The Genesis of the Individual', p. 304.

7 Moreover, his work provides a good example of moving between the insights of hard science and their broader applicability to the humanities; his own analysis develops from an understanding of crystal formation, but he observes that as this is applied to 'the domain of living things, the same notion [...] can be employed to characterise individuation' (ibid., p. 304.) but without the quantum-like, abrupt changes of state as individuation is effected. Instead, he refers to a 'theatre of individuation', ibid., p. 305.

8 Ibid., p. 304.

9 Ibid., p. 304.

10 Lysis (from *lyein*, to separate) refers to the death of a cell by breaking of the cellular membrane, often by viral or osmotic mechanisms that compromise its integrity.

11 Grosz, *Architecture from the Outside*, p. 29. An alternative example of the accommodation of disease, the removal of its threat, is provided in the conclusion of A. S. Koch and T. Tarnai's article, 'The Aesthetics of Viruses' *Leonardo* 21.2 (1988), pp. 161–6. In their case, the thread of viral disease is dissipated through its aestheticisation, a solution that would have appalled Chadwick: 'The viron's ability to initiate infection by releasing the genetic (mis)information is in fact due to the imperfection (quasi-perfection) of its structure [...] in this particular aspect, viruses, the notorious invisible agents of disease (or often of disaster) in humans, animals, plants and microbes, seem to have made (at least partial) amends for their "sins" by inspiring architects and geometers to decorate the human environment with attractive, modern and friendly constructions' (p. 166).

12 Ludwig Hilberseimer, *Groszstadtarchitecktur*, Stuttgart, Verlag Julius Hoffman, 1927, pp. 98–100, cited in K. Michael Hays, *Modernism and the Posthumanist Subject: the Architecture of Hannes Meyer and Ludwig Hilberseimer*, MIT Press, Cambridge, MA, 1992, p. 173. Translator not credited.

13 K. Michael Hays, 'Inscribing the Subject of Modernism: the Posthumanist Theory of Ludwig Hilberseimer', in John Whiteman, Jeffrey Kipnis and Richard Burdett (eds), *Strategies in Architectural Thinking*, MIT Press, Cambridge MA, 1992, p. 119.

14 Ibid., p. 121. The same discussion is repeated, more or less, in *Modernism and the Posthumanist Subject*, p. 173.

15 Hays, 'Inscribing the Subject of Modernism', p. 121. Again repeated, more or less, in *Modernism and the Posthumanist Subject*, p. 177. Hays later concedes that Hilberseimer 'understands Riegl's concept of *Kunstwollen* as a complex and mediated relationship between subject and object, a "creative struggle" between artistic will and material conditions'. *Modernism and the Posthumanist Subject*, p. 208.

16 Ludwig Hilberseimer, 'Schöpfung und Entwicklung,' [*c*.1922] MS, Hilberseimer Archives, Art Institute of Chicago, p. 11, cited in Hays, 'Inscribing the Subject of Modernism', p. 122. Translator not credited.

17 Hays, *Modernism and the Posthumanist Subject*, p. 205.

18 Hays, 'Inscribing the Subject of Modernism', p. 122.

19 Helen Rosenau, 'Etienne-Louis Boullée 1728–1799', in Rosenau (ed.), *Boullée and Visionary Architecture*, p. 10.

Chapter 8

1   The bones of this note were first set out in the margins of *The Sleepwalkers*: 'although the functions of gravity and inertia are reversed in the Keplerian cosmos, his intuition that there are *two antagonistic forces* acting on the planets, guided him in the right direction. A single force, as previously assumed [...] could never produce oval orbits and periodic changes of speed' (*SW* 341). Here, Chadwick notes 'here my work departs: left behind in geometry:— static model of pre Newtonian universe, no depiction of dynamic of change.'

2   Repeats more or less verbatim notes from an earlier notebook 2003.19/E/6.20, 23, 24 and 27: there, she was making notes on Boullée's *Essai*.

3   Jean-Pierre Mouilleseaux, '"Il faut concevoir pour effectuer": architecture et project dans l'œuvre d'Étienne-Louis Boullée', in *Les Architectes de la Liberté. 1789–1799*, École national supérieure des Beaux-Arts, Paris, 1989, p. 17. *Temple à la Nature et à la Raison*, now held by the, Gabinetto di Stampe e Disegni, Uffizi Museum, Florence. My translation.

4   Brodsky Lacour, *Lines of Thought*, p. 44 (original emphasis). The works referred to here are René Descartes, *A Discourse on the Method of Rightly Conducting the Reason, and Searching for Truth in the Sciences* (*Discours de la méthode pour bien conduire sa raison, et chercher la verité dans les sciences*) 1637, and *Geometry* (*La Géométrie*), first published the same year.

5   I am borrowing this phrase from Robin Evans, whose work will be introduced and discussed in more detail below.

6   Brodsky Lacour, *Lines of Thought,* p. 139. She also demonstrates that Descartes held up the architect's line (drawn in isolation and alone) as exemplary of the non-discursive formation of method, although this in turn can only be relevant, only come alive, through discursive method; '*in order to become method, drawing must be made available as discourse*' p. 92. Original emphasis.

7   Robin Evans, *The Projective Cast: Architecture and its Three Geometries*, MIT Press, Cambridge, MA and London, 1995, note 1 to p. 197. He is referring to Baptiste de La Rue, *Traité de la coupe de pierres* (Paris, 1728) pp. 167–83; and A. F. Frézier, *La Théorie et la practique de la coupe des pierres*, 3 vols (Strasbourg, 1737–9).

8   Ibid., p. 179.

9   Ibid., pp. 179–80.

10   See, for example, his discussion of how stereotomy allowed architecture to 'defy gravity'. ibid., p. 180.

11   Ibid., p. 195.

12   See for example Preston Scott Cohen, 'Stereotomic Permutations', *Architectural Design* (Spring 1996); or his *Contested Symmetries and Other Predicaments in Architecture*, Laurence King Publishing, London, 2001.

13   Peter Davidson and Don Bates make a very similar point in their editorial to *Architecture After Geometry*. In *After Geometry (3)* they stress that their interest is not about the annihilation of geometry, but architecture's possible role in developing further, new geometrical techniques and tactics:

> It is [...] a critical speculation [of the effects on architectural production] on the incorporation and expansion of new techniques and tactics for architectonic ordering and organisation. The permeability of these new techniques and tactics both to include and involve conventional geometries while at the same time fostering their replacement and substitution is in pursuit of their instrumental role.

Peter Davidson and Donald L. Bates (eds), *Architecture After Geometry*, Architectural Design Profile no. 127, Academy Editions, London, 1997, Editorial, p. 7.

14   Evans, *The Projective Cast*, p. 239.

Chapter 9

1 Phillip Stanley and Marina Warner, in separate interviews with the author (on 29 February and 9 June 2008 respectively), both used this term and discussed Chadwick in this way at length. Similarly, Andrew Benjamin referred to Chadwick's control over the ingredients of composition, colour and texture as 'knowingly classical' (interviewed 28 January 2008).

2 In this context, Marina Warner cites Primo Levi's 'in praise of purity' from *The Periodic Table*, tr. Raymond Rosenthal, Schocken Books, New York, 1984, p. 33 (see *GD* 42).

3 The term 'wicked architect' is borrowed from Pierre Klossowksi, *Sade mon prochain: Le philosophe scélérat* (1947), Paris, Seuil, 1970, in Tafuri, *The Sphere and the Labyrinth*, p. 47. (English translation *Sade my Neighbour*, tr. Alphonso Lingis, Northwestern University Press, Evanston, IL, 1991.)

4 Tafuri, *The Sphere and the Labyrinth*, p. 49.

5 William Hogarth, *The Analysis of Beauty* (1753), Ronald Paulson (ed.), Yale University Press, New Haven and London, 1997, p. 33.

6 Ibid., pp. 33–4.

7 For a much longer list of divination techniques, see 2003/E/1.14.

8 The main text approaches 'protean substance' as 'a characteristic feature of mannerist and baroque ornament' (*RO* 27).

9 Marina Warner, interviewed by the author, 9 June 2008, Kentish Town, London.

10 Annotations in her copy of Erwin Schrödinger's *What Is Life? Mind and Matter* make explicit her connection between his notion of negative entropy and her own *Enfleshings* series, undertaken contemporaneously with the *Meat Abstracts* (1989).

11 In an extraordinarily detailed interview with Mark Haworth-Booth, Chadwick discussed how she began making 'photocopies from life' to approach a representation of the body that was 'much more leaky and fluid' than those produced using traditional artistic media. This recording, which runs for about four hours, was made as part of the Oral History of British Photography project, run by the British Sound Archive and is available at the British Library.

12 As an interesting aside given the discussion in Chapter 1, Tafuri likens the futurists to the artist-magician, but accuses them of stopping short of the logic of their approach: 'faced by this *new universe of artificial "things"*, used as basic material for their artistic work, they still behave with a mentality anchored to the principle of *mimesis*.' *Theories and History of Architecture*, p. 32.

Conclusion

1 Cheryl De Ciantis. 'Gods and Myths in the Information Age', *Agir* 20–21: La société de l'information (December 2004), pp. 7–8.

Bibliography

sources for the present work

Bataille, Georges, *Visions of Excess: Selected Writings, 1927–1939*, translated, edited and introduced by Allan Stoekl, University of Minnesota Press, Minneapolis, 1985.

Bennett, Jim and Scott Mandelbrote (eds), *The Garden, the Ark, the Tower, the Temple: Biblical Metaphors of Knowledge in Early Modern Europe*, Museum of the History of Science in association with the Bodleian Library, Oxford, 1998.

Brodsky Lacour, Claudia, *Lines of Thought: Discourse, Architectonics, and the Origin of Modern Philosophy*, Duke University Press, Durham, NC, and London, 1996.

Burgin, Victor, 'Geometry & Abjection', *AA Files*, 15 (Summer 1987), pp. 35–41.

Debus, Allen G., *Paracelsus and the Medical Revolution of the Renaissance: A 500th Anniversary Celebration*, exhibition catalogue, US National Library of Medicine, Bethesda, Maryland, 1993.

Debus, Allen G. & Robert P. Multhauf, *Alchemy and Chemistry in the Seventeenth Century*, William Andrews Clark Memorial Library, University of California, Los Angeles, 1966.

De Ciantis, Cheryl, 'Gods and Myths in the Information Age', *Agir* 20–21: La société de l'information, December 2004, offprint paginated pp. 1–11.

Dixon Hunt, John, *The Figure in the Landscape: Poetry, Painting and Gardening During the Eighteenth Century*, Johns Hopkins University Press, Baltimore and London, 1976.

Doyle, Richard, *On Beyond Living: Rhetorical Transformations in the Life Sciences*, Stanford University Press, Palo Alto, CA, 1997.

Evans, Robin, *The Projective Cast: Architecture and its Three Geometries*, MIT Press, Cambridge, MA, 1995.

Grebowicz, Margret, 'Consensus, Dissensus, and Democracy: What Is at Stake in Feminist Science Studies?' *Philosophy of Science*, 72 (December 2005), pp. 989–1000.

Grosz, Elizabeth, *Architecture from the Outside: Essays on Virtual and Real Space*, MIT Press (Writing Architecture Series), Cambridge, MA, 2001.

Hayes, K. Michael, 'Inscribing the Subject of Modernism: the Posthumanist Theory of Ludwig Hilberseimer', in John Whiteman, Jeffrey Kipnis and Richard

Burdett (eds), *Strategies in Architectural Thinking*, MIT Press, Cambridge, MA, 1992, pp. 114–129.

———*Modernism and the Posthumanist Subject: the Architecture of Hannes Meyer and Ludwig Hilberseimer*, MIT Press, Cambridge, MA, 1992.

Hogarth, William, *The Analysis of Beauty* [1753] Edited and with an introduction and notes by Ronald Paulson, Yale University Press, New Haven and London, 1997.

Marks, John, 'Molecular Biology in the Work of Deleuze and Guattari', *Paragraph*, 29.2 (2006), pp. 81–97.

Merchant, Carolyn, *The Death of Nature: Women, Ecology, and the Scientific Revolution* (1980), Harper San Francisco, 1990.

Pelletier, Louise, *Architecture in Words: Theatre, Language and the Sensuous Space of Architecture*, Routledge, London and New York, 2006.

Pérez-Gómez, Alberto, *Architecture and the Crisis of Modern Science* [1980], MIT Press, Cambridge, MA, 1983.

Plotnitsky, Arkady, *Complementarity: Anti-Epistemology after Bohr and Derrida*, Duke University Press, Durham, NC and London, 1994.

Simondon, Gilbert, 'The Genesis of the Individual', trs Mark Cohen and Sanford Kwinter, in Jonathan Crary and Sanford Kwinter (eds) *Incorporations*, Zone Books, New York, 1992, pp. 297–319.

Tafuri, Manfredo, *Theories and History of Architecture* (1968), tr. Giorgio Verrecchia, Granada, London, 1980.

———*The Sphere and the Labyrinth: Avant-Gardes and Architecture from Piranesi to the 1970s* (1980), trs Pellegrino d'Acierno and Robert Connolly, MIT Press, Cambridge, MA, 1987.

Thomas, Downing A., 'Negotiating Taste in Montesquieu', in *Eighteenth-Century Studies*, 39.1 (2005), pp. 71–90.

Wheeler, John, *Quantum Theory and Measurement*, Princeton University Press, 1983.

Zika, Charles, 'Reuchlin's *De Verbo Mirifico* and the Magic Debate of the Late Fifteenth-Century', *Journal of the Warburg and Courtauld Institutes* 39 (1976), pp. 104–138.

Zohar, Danah (in collaboration with I. N. Marshall), *The Quantum Self: A Revolutionary View of Human Nature and Consciousness Rooted in the New Physics*, Bloomsbury, London, 1990.

general sources on Helen Chadwick

Benjamin, Andrew and Helen Chadwick, *Doubles, Helen Chadwick and Danny Leriche*, Les Cahiers des Regards, Galerie d'Art Contemporain du Centre Saint-Vincent, Herblay, 1991. Benjamin's essay is entitled 'Reconnecting the Body: Chadwick and Descartes'.

Chadwick, Helen, *Enfleshings*, Secker & Warburg, London, 1989.

Chambers, Gloria (ed.), *Stilled Lives: Helen Chadwick*, exhibition catalogue, Portfolio Gallery, Edinburgh, 1996.

Sladen, Mark (ed.), *Helen Chadwick*, exhibition catalogue, Hatje Cantz Publishers and the Barbican Art Gallery, Ostfildern-Ruit, 2004.